Teen Spaces

The Step-by-Step Library Makeover

Second Edition

Kimberly Bolan

American Library Association

Chicago   2009

Kimberly Bolan is a library consultant based in Indianapolis, Indiana. Over th' past twenty years, Ms. Bolan has worked in and with public and school libraries of all sizes. Her work has focused on facilities planning and design, strategic planning, teen and youth services, technology services, and customer service and marketing. Bolan earned her MLS at Syracuse University's School of Information Studies. She presents at numerous state and national conferences, is the author of *Technology Made Simple* (with Robert Cullin) and numerous journal articles, and was named a 2004 Mover and Shaker by *Library Journal.*

The paper used in this publication meets the minimum requirements of American National Standard for Information Sciences—Permanence of Paper for Printed Library Materials, ANSI Z39.48-1992. ∞

Library of Congress Cataloging-in-Publication Data

Bolan, Kimberly.
   Teen spaces : the step-by-step library makeover / Kimberly Bolan. — 2nd ed.
p.   cm.
   Includes bibliographical references and index.
   ISBN 978-0-8389-0969-0 (alk. paper)
   1. Libraries—Space utilization. 2. Young adults' libraries—Planning. 3. Library decoration. I. Title.
   Z679.55.T36 2009
   022'.31626—dc22   2008026621

The cover image depicts a space designed by Kimberly Bolan of Kimberly Bolan and Associates, DEMCO Library Interiors (DLI), and the teens of East Brunswick, New Jersey. Photo courtesy of DEMCO Library Interiors.

ISBN-13: 978-0-8389-0969-0

Printed in the United States of America

13   12   11   10   09   5   4   3   2   1

Contents

Additional material can be found on the book's companion website at www.ala.org/editions/extras/Bolan09690.

Preface

When I first began researching and designing library spaces for teenagers in 1995, I discovered the concept was nearly nonexistent. Even when I was writing the first edition of *Teen Spaces* in 2002, it was a challenge to find libraries that were actively engaged in services for their teen customers. At the time, teen space was a rarity. Just six years after the publication of the first edition, teen space is no longer the exception; it is gradually becoming the rule. This transformation in space planning and design for the thirteen- to eighteen-year-old is prevalent in public libraries and is growing in middle and high schools. Creating efficient, innovative, and inspirational spaces for teenage customers is a result of staff and administrators moving away from a traditional approach to library design and services, looking for a means to draw in this underserved customer base and increase future library supporters. Creating welcoming environments for teens in libraries has become an essential part of providing excellence in teen service. It appears that libraries are taking this to heart, as 61 percent of all library building projects in 2006 included a teen space.[1]

While most libraries and schools recognize the importance of teen services and space design, there are still a number of organizations that continue to struggle with planning and implementing twenty-first-century library facilities for teenagers. Others have made the first steps but are struggling with what to do next or how to improve on what's been done. Success is derived from basic principles such as successful, properly understood marketing; active and ongoing teen involvement and input; thorough analysis and well-thought-out planning; strong long-term promotion; and excellent, forward-thinking practices related to teen service and customer service. It's about being open-minded and collaborative.

The second edition of *Teen Spaces: The Step-by-Step Library Makeover* is a handbook for public and school libraries that shows how to successfully develop inviting, comfortable, user-centered environments to attract and engage their teenage users. It also illustrates how these environments are essential in transforming the role and image of libraries and encouraging positive use for recreational and educational activities.

WHO NEEDS THIS BOOK?

This book is a how-to manual for anyone in a public or school library who serves teenagers, including frontline staff, teen librarians, school media specialists, and youth and teen services supervisors. This book is also appropriate for administrators, board members, and library supporters such as Friends of the Library and parent-teacher groups who are interested in better understanding twenty-first-century library facilities design and ser vice to teenagers. Whether you are building a new library, renovating an existing facility, or working on a facility revamp, *Teen Spaces* provides key success factors and best prac- tices for developing dedicated, attractive, safe, motivating, teen-oriented space. Both the process and the end result provide a way for public and school libraries to acknowl- edge teen customers and their needs and to build a sense of teen belonging, community involvement, and library appreciation.

USING THE MATERIALS IN THIS BOOK SUCCESSFULLY

The second edition of *Teen Spaces* is intended to help libraries develop effective, dynamic spaces for teenage customers. In order to accomplish these goals, this book focuses on teen space as it relates to

impact

marketing and research

teen involvement and adult-youth collaborations

assessment

planning

implementation

promotion

policy and practice

evaluation

This framework is universal for facilities planning in the twenty-first century. Once it is understood, it can be applied to any project.

In order to make the ideas in this book more concrete, information and best prac- tices from public and school libraries worldwide are included. A number of templates, worksheets, professional resources, and model library information can be found in the appendixes. A supplemental web page that includes photographs of teen spaces from around the world and downloadable worksheets can be found at www.ala.org/editions/ extras/Bolan09690.

THE AUTHOR'S VISION

I have worked with teenagers in libraries for more than eighteen years and have over thirteen years' experience in library facilities planning and design. I've worked in school, academic, and public libraries and acquired both frontline and management-level experience.

I feel strongly that libraries of all shapes, sizes, and budgets need to more actively engage their teen customers in facilities design, providing an excellent opportunity for libraries to connect with their customers, in the short and long term. Strong facilities planning, design, and implementation are major elements in ensuring the future of libraries. I am certain that through proper facilities education, committed and ongoing collaborations, well-thought-out planning, and open-minded administrators and communities, public and school libraries can move strongly into the future. Instead of becoming irrelevant places of the past, libraries will become increasingly important and significant to teenagers in their youth and into adulthood.

NOTE

1. Bette-Lee Fox, "Library Buildings 2006: Betwixt and Be Teen," *Library Journal* 131, no. 19 (December 15, 2006), www.libraryjournal.com/article/CA6396445.html.

Acknowledgments

As with the first edition, the second edition of *Teen Spaces* was a true collaboration between me and many talented adults and teenagers. My thanks and appreciation go out to all those who gave their time, ideas, and support. You inspired me to write a second edition, and I know you will surely inspire thousands around the world.

To my research assistants Christine Ayar and Beth Overhauser and to my mother Linda Bolan, for their dedication and constant effort in gathering information and contacting model libraries.

To my husband and partner Rob Cullin, whose love, continuous encouragement, tireless support, and dedication to libraries made it possible for me to write this book while working full-time and planning a wedding.

To Laura Isenstein and Jim Alsip for sharing their knowledge and advice and, most important, for their friendship.

To the dedicated, forward-thinking architects, designers, and vendors out there who are not only open to new ideas and concepts but also shared their ideas and collaborated with me, especially Rolf Erikson, Jack Hedge and Design Group, Jane Dedering and Hammel, Green and Abrahamson (HGA), Marc Ciccarelli of Studio Techne, and Janet Nelson and the staff of DEMCO Library Interiors.

Special thanks to all the gifted public and school library staff who contributed photos, ideas, and success stories, and to all the teens who provided valuable input and information.

Chapter 1 | **Understanding Teens and Their Space**

The first rule in design—before any plans are drawn up or any furniture is purchased—is to make sure you understand the customer. In the world of professional design (and in the world of twenty-first-century libraries), successful projects and service are inherently the result of having a firm grasp on customer needs and wants. Responsive and successful design of space for teenagers comes from understanding the group you are serving. Learning to recognize teen behavior and needs, likes and dislikes, is essential in understanding what is necessary and appropriate for the ideal young adult area.

WHO ARE TEENS?

Based on 2006 data, there are approximately 25,616,753 people ages thirteen to eighteen in the United States, which is 8.5 percent of its overall population. Trends indicate there will be an estimated 26 million teens in 2010, 28 million in 2020, and over 30 million by 2030.[1] That's a considerable group and a clear indication that there is a population out there in need of attention, the services libraries offer, and a space designated just for them. So who are these teens and how can you, as the librarian and teen space facilitator, determine their needs and wants?

In simplest terms, teens are defined by their age. Social age is the level of social and mental development as compared to chronological age, which is the number of years a person has lived. It is possible that a teenager could have a social age that does not correspond to his or her chronological age. For example, a thirteen-year-old might be in sixth grade, or a sixth-grader could have the social age of a fourteen-year-old.

Peter Zollo, author of *Getting Wiser to Teens: More Insights into Marketing and Advertising to Teenagers,* defines teenagers as those twelve- to nineteen-years-old. Zollo also addresses the fact that the teen population is rising faster than that of adults.[2] The uniqueness of this group's size, as well as its diversity by gender, ethnicity, household income, geography, attitudes, and lifestyles, most definitely make it a challenging group to target. Ann Curry and Ursula Schwaiger summed it up best in their article on planning library spaces for teenagers:

> Teenagers have never been easy to understand. They straddle both childhood and adulthood, their minds and bodies filled with a restless energy as they hurtle through developmental milestones at an amazing rate, yet each speed is uniquely personal. They are filled with an amazing power, yet are often crippled by anxiety and self-doubt.[3]

Present-day teens fall into a broader group that is variously labeled Millennials, Generation Y, the Net Generation (or Net Gen), Internet Generation (or iGen), echo-boomers, the Gaming Generation, or the Digital Generation. They are defined as being techno-savvy, multitasking, self-confident, realistic, optimistic, connected, goal-oriented, service-oriented, and collaborative. They will not conform and often ask "why?" Although we have yet to know and define the next generation of teens, they too will have their own values, personalities, and ideas.

Most adults, including the World War II generation, Baby Boomers, and Generation Xers, would agree that being a teenager was one of the most difficult times of their lives, filled with a whirlwind of vastly differing experiences and emotions. A large part of providing quality service to teens and effectively working with them means understanding youth development. Youth development is multidimensional and includes meeting youth needs and building youth competencies to help them become successful adults. Instead of viewing teenagers as problems, it means viewing them as resources, building on their strengths and capabilities to develop within their own community. Youth development programs seek to build competencies, skills, and healthy attitudes and behaviors, with a focus on seven developmental needs of adolescents:

physical activity

competence and achievement

self-definition

creative expression

positive social interactions with peers and adults

structure and clear limits

meaningful participation[4]

These needs can be fully met in a well-planned, full-service teen library. For instance, to achieve self-definition, teens need and want a space of their own; one that is away from adults and young children. *Libraries can do this.* In conjunction with physical activity, teens need spaces and furniture that help them relax and move and stretch their growing bodies. *Libraries can do this.* Teens need the opportunity to participate in projects that allow them to be imaginative and creatively express their feelings and interests. *Libraries can do this.* Teenagers want and need a place where they can hang out with their friends and also experience positive interactions with adults. *Libraries can do this.* Teens want their contributions recognized and want to receive praise for their ideas and hard work. *Libraries can do this.* Finally, they need structure and clear limits. *Libraries can do this, too.* By building the ideal teen space and actively involving teens in the entire process, you are acting as their advocate, working to create a place with the potential for fulfilling all of their needs.

The Search Institute has spent years researching teenagers and their developmental needs. One of its key findings is that the more assets adolescents have, the less likely they are to participate in dangerous behaviors and the *more* likely they are to engage in positive activities. The Search Institute has identified forty building blocks of healthy development for young people, called developmental assets, that will help youth to succeed in school and to grow up physically healthy, caring, and responsible. (See figure 1.1.)[5] The forty assets are divided into external assets and internal assets and then separated into eight categories. Look at the list of assets carefully, and determine which ones can be applied to your design project. Pay close attention to assets such as community values youth, youth as resources, planning and decision making, and interpersonal competence.

Figure 1.1 Forty Developmental Assets

Category	Asset Name and Definition
Support	1. Family support—Family life provides high levels of love and support.
	2. Positive family communication—Young person and her or his parent(s) communicate positively, and young person is willing to seek advice and counsel from parent(s).
	3. Other adult relationships—Young person receives support from three or more nonparent adults.
	4. Caring neighborhood—Young person experiences caring neighbors.
	5. Caring school climate—School provides a caring, encouraging environment.
	6. Parent involvement in schooling—Parent(s) are actively involved in helping young person succeed in school.
Empowerment	7. Community values youth—Young person perceives that adults in the community value youth.
	8. Youth as resources—Young people are given useful roles in the community.
	9. Service to others—Young person serves in the community one hour or more per week.
	10. Safety—Young person feels safe at home, school, and in the neighborhood.
Boundaries and Expectations	11. Family boundaries—Family has clear rules and consequences and monitors the young person's whereabouts.
	12. School boundaries—School provides clear rules and consequences.
	13. Neighborhood boundaries—Neighbors take responsibility for monitoring young people's behavior.
	14. Adult role models—Parent(s) and other adults model positive, responsible behavior.
	15. Positive peer influence—Young person's best friends model responsible behavior.
	16. High expectations—Both parent(s) and teachers encourage the young person to do well.
Constructive Use of Time	17. Creative activities—Young person spends three or more hours per week in lessons or practice in music, theater, or other arts.
	18. Youth programs—Young person spends three or more hours per week in sports, clubs, or organizations at school and/or in community organizations.
	19. Religious community—Young person spends one hour or more per week in activities in a religious institution.
	20. Time at home—Young person is out with friends "with nothing special to do" two or more nights per week.

(cont.)

Figure 1.1 Forty Development Assets (cont.)

Category	Asset Name and Definition
Commitment of Learning	21. Achievement motivation—Young person is motivated to do well in school.
	22. School engagement—Young person is actively engaged in learning.
	23. Homework—Young person reports doing at least one hour of homework every school day.
	24. Bonding to school—Young person cares about her or his school.
	25. Reading for pleasure—Young person reads for pleasure three or more hours per week.
Positive Values	26. Caring—Young person places high value on helping other people.
	27. Equality and social justice—Young person places high value on promoting equality and reducing hunger and poverty.
	28. Integrity—Young person acts on convictions and stands up for her or his beliefs.
	29. Honesty—Young person "tells the truth even when it is not easy."
	30. Responsibility—Young person accepts and takes personal responsibility.
	31. Restraint—Young person believes it is important not to be sexually active or to use alcohol or other drugs.
Social Competencies	32. Planning and decision making—Young person knows how to plan ahead and make choices.
	33. Interpersonal competence—Young person has empathy, sensitivity, and friendship skills.
	34. Cultural competence—Young person has knowledge of and comfort with people of different cultural/racial/ethnic backgrounds.
	35. Resistance skills—Young person can resist negative peer pressure and dangerous situations.
	36. Peaceful conflict resolution—Young person seeks to resolve conflict nonviolently.
Positive Identity	37. Personal power—Young person feels he or she has control over "things that happen to me."
	38. Self-esteem—Young person reports having a high self-esteem.
	39. Sense of purpose—Young person reports that "my life has a purpose."
	40. Positive view of personal future—Young person is optimistic about her or his personal future.

How could these be incorporated into your overall plan? For example, look at the internal asset, social competencies and ask, "What are the implications related to this, the project, and teens?"

Most teen space projects should strive to encourage teens to work with others and to listen to other teen and adult opinions. Such projects should also strive to teach teens how to plan and make choices. All of these are reflected in assets 32 (Planning and Decision Making), 33 (Interpersonal Competence), and 36 (Peaceful Conflict Resolution). Taking this approach will shine a new light on your plans. What may have started as a project with the potential to increase library business could also quickly develop into something even more worthwhile for adolescents and their development.

At first glance, it might appear that creating a successful space for such a diverse group with so many needs is easier said than done. However, it's not as difficult as it seems. The key is gaining an understanding of them. The rewards for doing so successfully are well worth the effort.

Keep in mind that none of this has to be accomplished overnight or single-handedly. In fact, the libraries that have the most success are the ones that take their time, plan carefully, and work with their teen customers from start to finish.

UNDERSTANDING TEEN WANTS AND NEEDS

The first step in developing a successful teen space is marketing to and understanding your teen customers. Begin figuring out what teens are all about by considering their pastimes, friends, and personal preferences. Ask yourself a few fundamental questions:

Who are the teens you're serving—both library users and nonusers?

What activities (both educational and recreational) do teens primarily do?

Where do they prefer to hang out and why?

What is genuinely important to them?

Envision what it was like for you as a teen. Then think about what it's like being a teen today. What are your perceptions and assumptions? Validate your thoughts, and find out how things realistically compare by browsing through some of the resources found in appendix C.

After reflecting on these questions, begin considering how to apply the answers to the design plan. For example, if hanging out with friends is what is important to teens, how could this information be incorporated into the design of your library's teen area? If it's conclusive that the mall and sporting events are high on their list of where they prefer to hang out, how could you best apply that information? Keep in mind that the thought process behind the answers is equally as important as the answers themselves, because making the effort to try to think like a teenager gives an adult important insight into a teen's world and allows for a better end result.

MARKETING 101

Marketing is more than promoting and merchandising your library and its collection and services; it is a process. Marketing is about *understanding* your market (i.e., your teen customers, both users and nonusers) and bringing your products (i.e., your library, teen space, collection, and services) to your customers. In simplest terms it is a three-step process:

1. Identify your teen customers and target groups.

2. Identify your products.

3. Connect your teen customers to the products.

Often libraries and schools make the mistake of designing facilities without a complete or accurate understanding of their market. Knowing your customer is the foundation of good marketing and today's library *must* be customer-focused, which means first identifying all needs of your customers and potential customers. Marketing makes it all work. Just take a look at successful companies that cater to teens such as Apple, Gap, and Pepsi. Businesses such as these are marketing experts, and libraries can learn a lot from them when it comes to marketing, advertising, and retailing. Businesses with successful marketing targeted to teens know exactly how to tie in a teenager's wants with their companies' products. Therefore, don't waste time reinventing the wheel. Make some observations, do a little research, and borrow some ideas or practices. For example, Apple realizes that adults and teens want to apply personality to their technology, so the company developed products that express their customers' personalities (e.g., multicolored computer and iPod options).

Begin the first stage of marketing by conducting market research, making general observations, and informally talking to teens. Chapter 2 discusses how to get additional direct teen feedback and input through focus groups, committee work, brainstorming sessions, and surveys. All of the data and information you obtain from knowing your customers, combined with the information you get from studying your competition (i.e., bookstores), will help you gain a full understanding of the big picture and move forward more effectively with your space plan.

As you proceed, develop a marketing plan by using the marketing mix, or the four Ps of marketing:

Product—what you are selling

Price—cost in time and money to the library as well as the price to the customer (see chapter 3)

Place—location (physical and virtual) of where you provide and promote your product (see chapter 2)

Promotion—the P that everyone knows; this includes advertising, sponsorships, public relations, viral marketing, and more (see chapter 5)

By looking at your product (in this case, your teen space and related products and services) with the right combination of the four Ps, you can improve your results and marketing effectiveness. A marketing plan can also be a well-received addition to your final space plan as outlined in chapter 3.

See figure 1.2 for a marketing strategy grid. You will need to use details in the other chapters to help you fill in your grid.

Figure 1.2   Marketing Strategy

Product	Pricing
What do you have that teens need?	What is the cost in time and money?
What could you offer to attract teens to the library?	What is the "price" to customer?
	How can you get the most bang for your buck?
For example:	How should you evaluate (e.g., ROI—Return on Investment)?
Teen space	
Related services and products	
Placement	**Promotion**
Where is the most effective location to *provide* and *promote* your product?	How can you attract teens to your space and services?
	How do you inform them about the space and products and services you have?
Key: Think in terms of physical space (within the library and outside the library) as well as virtual space.	Find your "power" networkers and stakeholders—then outreach, outreach, outreach!

Market Research

To really *know* teenagers you need to find out what they're saying about their likes, dislikes, wants, and needs. You can find this information through market research, which commonly involves gathering primary and secondary data. The majority of the information will be of the secondary variety, already compiled and organized for you. Primary data involves carrying out your own research through written, online, telephone, and in-person surveys or conducting focus groups, observing teens, and having one-on-one conversations. Throughout the market research process, keep in mind that when it comes to talking to teens, the key lies in direct, open communication—really hearing what they have to say and sincerely making an effort to relate to them. More information on marketing-related concepts can be found in chapters 2 and 6.

Observation

Another excellent way to gather information is to observe teens. Familiarize yourself with their environments. For example, where do they like to hang out? Possible answers include their bedroom, friends' houses, the mall, bookstores, and coffee shops. Spend a Saturday afternoon or evening after school at the local mall or coffee shop. How do they use these spaces? What seems to be appealing to them? In addition to observing teens in other environments, closely examine how they use your library. Where are the most popular gathering places and why? Do they struggle using the library? If so, what are the issues? Which services are they using? Which don't they use? Are there any environmental factors that seem to influence their behavior and use of the library?

Careful observation of the things, places, and people that teens surround themselves with reveals a great deal about their personality, likes, and dislikes. For instance, if you notice that the majority of teens carry around snacks, cell phones, and MP3 players in their backpacks, this tells you that food, communication, and music are important to this age group. How can you use this information to develop an effective space for young adults? Knowing this, it would be wise for your library to

> provide provisions in library policy for snacking and drinking in the library
>
> create spaces that allow both quiet and conversational areas
>
> consider cell phone use policies, potentially integrating cell phone etiquette into the mix
>
> focus on music collections (CD and downloadable) as well as music-related books and magazines
>
> feature listening stations and/or a stereo into the teen area
>
> consider circulating MP3 players (in-house or externally)

The main point is to make a few observations and to see the correlation between teen surroundings and how they can influence the design of an area designated for teens.

Direct Feedback

If you *really* want to find out more about teens and their preferences, talk to them. If you ask, teens will be more than willing to answer your questions. Talk to them one on one, conduct surveys, form teen committees and advisory councils, and hold focus groups. (For more details on these practices, refer to chapter 2.) Getting teen input is critical to the entire design process. Teenagers are the ones who can honestly (and be prepared for complete truthfulness) tell you the impression your library is making—or not making—on them.

In fact, much of the information presented in this book was gathered directly from teens. During a series of focus groups held in communities across the United States between October 2006 and January 2008, teens were asked what they would like to see in libraries. The top fifteen common responses were

1. More space for teens
2. A separate, distinct teen area
3. Comfortable furniture
4. Warm, welcoming environment
5. More technology such as computers, TVs, listening stations, sound domes, gaming equipment
6. Teen-only computers
7. Areas for talking and socializing as well as quiet study
8. More natural light and better, "cooler" artificial light
9. More up-to-date materials such as graphic novels, music, DVDs, popular books, magazines, and video games
10. Good signs that look nice and make it easy to find things
11. Color (no white walls)
12. Food and drink options such as vending machines or a library café

13. Better advertising of services and programs

14. Cleaner, better organized library

15. Helpful staff and good customer service[6]

Over 75 percent of online survey respondents said having a space just for teens that is comfortable and welcoming, where they could hang out, would make them want to use the library more. Other top responses to increase teen library use included having a café (68 percent), bringing in more technologies such as listening stations, TVs, etc. (58 percent), adding music and DVDs (56 percent), adding more books (55 percent), and adding more computers (51 percent).

How can these insights help develop your library's teen space plan? Service plan?

How does their input and ideas influence your ideas and goals?

Being able to compile all your research, observations, and feedback and objectively look at it and incorporate it is the most important (and often overlooked) step in facilities and space planning projects.

WHY TEEN SPACE?

As the number of teenagers increases and as more school and public libraries look to understand their teenage customers and reevaluate their priorities and services, an unprecedented number will move away from traditional approaches of library service to a new approach of creating more efficient, innovative, appealing, and teen-inspired libraries. Such a reevaluation of priorities is supported by the fact that kids are not only using the library, they are visiting frequently; 78 percent of children ages eight to eighteen have library cards.[7]

The Council for Educational Facilities Planners and supporting research have proven that there is an integral relationship between the quality of educational facilities and the level of student achievement. Facilities impact the learning, development, and behavior of the user.[8] Three-quarters of Americans believe it is a high priority for local public libraries to offer a safe place where teenagers can study and congregate.[9] Equally relevant is the Harris Poll response to the question, "I would use my local public library more often if . . ." Twenty-six percent of the respondents replied, "If there was a space just for teens."

One example of why teen space works is verbYL, a stand-alone storefront youth space for young people ages thirteen to twenty-five, located in the main street of Yeppoon in Central Queensland, Australia. The space, developed with input from local young people, opened in 2005. It was developed in part because it is the only youth center in the area. Debra Burn, library manager at Rockhampton (Australia) Regional Council, developed the concept and continues to oversee the library operations. She says, "Critical success factors for verbYL include the equal partnership between the library council's youth services and library services; the development of a distinctive brand for the service; and the engagement of young people in the design and ongoing operation of the service." VerbYL was recognized in the national awards for local government 2006 as the winner, youth engagement category; and by the Queensland Public Librarians Association for innovative service provision to the community in 2006.[10]

At the Oprah Winfrey Leadership Academy for Girls (South Africa), teams of educators, architects, interior designers, artists, and others created what Oprah Winfrey calls "an atmosphere of possibility." "If you are surrounded by beauty, it inspires beauty in you," she says, adding, "Quality is a magnet for quality . . . It's been said that quality is never an accident—rather, it's the result of high intention, sincere effort, intelligent direction, and skillful execution." The school's library has a relaxed feel, with comfortable seating near the windows and around the fireplace; some pillows are covered with mud cloth from the Democratic Republic of the Congo. "Educational places don't have to be serious; they need to be inspiring," says Michelle Sakayan of Chicago-based Nagle Hartray Architects, who was one of many responsible for the campus's architectural work.[11]

When the school board at the Academy of Irving ISD Library (Texas) asked why a physical library was even necessary at their high tech specialty school, since students get all their information from the Internet, library director Caroline Kienzle gave a compelling presentation about the importance of the library for instruction as well as a place for community. "Our goal from the beginning was to develop a warm, inviting place that students felt comfortable visiting, whether to work on a project, browse for books, do homework, or just hang out during lunch," said Kienzle's colleague, librarian Gloria Willingham.[12] Creating appealing teen environments is a way to meet the needs of an important (and traditionally forgotten) group of library customers. It is a way to expand a library's customer base now and in the future, by appealing to both users and nonusers, creating a wider variety of customers from diverse social groups, backgrounds, and interests.

WHY TEEN SPACE?

- Build positive, safe environments for studying, socializing, and leisure activities
- Support teenagers and encourage teen belonging, community involvement, and library appreciation
- Expand your customer base by appealing to users and nonusers; traditional and nontraditional customers
- Effectively market your library, and draw teens into your library space, leading them to other services
- Increase current and future library supporters

WHAT IS TEEN SPACE?

After you have a general understanding of your teen customers and why teen space is important, it is essential that you understand what teen space is. Library teen space refers to both public library space as well as school libraries, and it can also refer to academic facilities. Teenagers say that a good teen area, no matter where it is located, must be welcoming, fun, exciting, clearly defined, attractive, and informal. Its contents must be up to date, functional, easy to find, durable, and eye-catching. At its best, a teen area in a public library should be its own separate space and the heart of teen activity. Similarly, a school library should be dynamic, inviting, and the hub of its school.

Public libraries constantly struggle with how to define teen space and its users. In school environments, it's generally more cut-and-dried—a middle school library serves middle school students, whether that is sixth through eighth grade or seventh through eighth, and so on. In public library environments, making this distinction becomes a bit more complicated. Does a teen area serve preteens or is it solely intended for those who are true teenagers? In an ideal world, based on developmental and chronological age, public libraries would have separate, designated, youth space for preschoolers, school-age children, middle school students, and high school students. In larger facilities, there may be an opportunity for this; in small and medium-sized facilities, this is not always the case. Teen space and the topics addressed in this book are geared toward the thirteen-through eighteen-year-old customer.

The definition of teen space must also take into account "library as place" and the library as "third place," a term coined by Ray Oldenburg in his 1990 book *The Great Good Place*. The *third place* term used in the concept of community building refers to social surroundings separate from the two usual social environments of home (the first place) and the workplace (the second place), where we spend most of our time. (For teenagers, the equivalent would most likely be school.) Third places are defined as locations that have a role between the home and the workplace (or school) that allow people to be around other people without being in a structured setting. More and more libraries are being identified by their customers as their third place. Libraries are incorporating features such as cafés, comfortable seating in living room–like areas, group and quiet study rooms, spaces for community meetings, and public performance venues. Look at the Bookworm branches in China. The Bookworm Chengdu is a library with 5,000 (and growing) books in English, European languages and Chinese, a European restaurant, a full program of poetry and book readings, Scrabble competitions, free wireless Internet access, and more. With increased attention to and accommodation of these characteristics, libraries can become the third place for teenagers. See appendix E for more information.

Just as there is no mistake that children's libraries are intended for young children, there should be no mistake that a teen area or facility is intended especially for teenagers. A first-rate teen space should have the ability to fit into a teen's life, meeting the variety of needs and uses essential for this age group. Just as teens long for separate identities, it is equally important for them to establish a distinct area that allows them to express their individuality, including but not limited to how the space is designed and decorated.

If done correctly, teen space is a useful marketing tool, enabling libraries to draw teenagers into the library and leading them to other library services such as materials, programming, etc. All of these efforts provide a path to increasing current and future library supporters. The future of libraries is tomorrow's adults and, believe it or not, these are today's teenagers.[13]

NOTES

1. U.S. Census Bureau, "Projected Population of the United States, by Age and Sex: 2000 to 2050," www.census.gov/ipc/www/usinterimproj/natprojtab02a.xls.

2. Peter Zollo, *Getting Wiser to Teens: More Insights into Marketing and Advertising to Teenagers* (Ithaca, NY: New Strategist Publications, 2004), 6.

3. Ann Curry and Ursula Schwaiger, "The Balance between Anarchy and Control: Planning Library Space for Teenagers," *School Libraries in Canada* 19, no. 1 (1999): 9.

4. National Youth Development Information Center, "Seven Developmental Needs of Young Adolescents (and Their Characteristics)," www.nassembly.org/nydic/programming/whatis/needs.htm.

5. The Search Institute, "Developmental Assets: An Overview," www.search-institute.org.

6. Kimberly Bolan, comment posted January 20, 2008 on "2006–2007 Teen Focus Group Summary," *Indie Librarian Blog,* http://indielibrarian.blogspot.com.

7. Harris Interactive, "American Library Association Youth and Library Use Study," www.ala.org/ala/yalsa/HarrisYouthPoll.pdf.

8. Council for Educational Facility Planners, www.cefpi.org/welcome.html.

9. Public Agenda, "Long Overdue: A Fresh Look at Public and Leadership Attitudes about Libraries in the 21st Century," www.publicagenda.org/research/research_reports_details.cfm?list=99.

10. Debra Burn, e-mail interview, February 19, 2008.

11. Suzanne Slesin, "Live and Learn," *O at Home: An Oprah Magazine* 4, no. 2 (Summer 2007): 84–93.

12. Gloria Willingham, e-mail interview, December 4, 2007.

13. Kimberly Bolan, "Why Teen Space?" Young Adult Library Services Association (white paper), www.ala.org/ala/yalsa/profdev/whitepapers/teenspaces.cfm.

Chapter 2 | **Ask and Analyze**

Teen involvement is the key success factor in any teen space project. Getting buy-in from adult stakeholders such as staff members and other adults in the community will also ensure success. Making teen participation a priority as well as an ongoing practice throughout the planning, design, implementation, promotional, and maintenance phases of your teen space project and your overall library services is essential. Getting buy-in from teens through hands-on involvement will ensure the space is designed to meet their needs and it will bring fresh, creative, ideas to the table. It will also guarantee the project is successful by giving teens ownership of the space as well as giving the library credibility in the eyes of teens. Not to mention, if done correctly, teen collaboration will ultimately lighten your workload.

Begin your project by talking with teens, staff members, and other stakeholders in your community. Teenagers are not only your target customers; they are the biggest and best resource for the job. Staff members and other adult stakeholders are also vital to the process as they will be your supporters, serving as an additional driving force, and assisting in carrying out the plan. It's important not to waste valuable time and energy devising a plan based only on your personal assumptions. Instead, let teens guide you and collaborate with key adults to cover all your bases and help prevent problems before they occur. Openly share your ideas and ask for theirs. And don't be afraid to educate them about teen space and today's libraries along the way. A variety of outside comments and suggestions will be invaluable in sorting out your preliminary ideas and establishing concrete goals and objectives for the project.

Next, move on to the second phase—the space analysis. This is where you begin to gather tangible data that will be used to support your objectives by measuring and comparing library services and statistics and by taking a complete inventory of the existing space. In the end, the information gathered by following the procedures in this chapter will become the foundation for your space plan.

GETTING INPUT

Communication is an essential component of the design process. It involves not only relaying information but, more important, listening. Getting input from teens and library staff will prove invaluable throughout the project. Focus groups, brainstorming sessions, surveys, committee work, advisory groups, and Junior Friends of the Library are a few simple ways to actively involve key players while gathering valuable information. No matter what methods you implement, remember that the basis for success with teen involvement is open-minded, progressive adults who are open to collaboration and power sharing. To further assist you in successfully collaborating with your teen partners, AtTheTable.org and Youth on Board have identified fourteen points to successfully involving youth in decision making. They are

1. Understanding why you should involve young people
2. Assessing your readiness for youth and governance
3. Determining your organization's model for youth involvement
4. Identifying organizational barriers
5. Overcoming attitudinal barriers
6. Addressing legal issues
7. Recruiting young people
8. Creating a strong orientation process
9. Training young people for their roles
10. Conducting intergenerational training
11. Making meetings work
12. Developing a mentoring plan
13. Building youth-adult relationships
14. Creating support networks[1]

See the Organizational Assessment Checklist (figure 2.1) for additional information and guidance for uncovering hidden issues, understanding the tasks at hand, and working with others to commit to this initiative. Use the checklist as a tool with your board, staff, and teens.

Guidelines for Success

Active recruitment is essential to making teen participation a success. Make a concerted effort to identify and recruit both users and nonusers of the library. Work with colleagues and network with teens you already know to determine participants. Recruit teens where they hang out, and get the word out by using methods such as

post signs throughout the library

distribute fliers

coordinate with students to get information in the school paper or library newsletter

approach teens directly

make phone calls

post information on the library's website, blog, or social networking site

send out e-mails and text messages

No matter which recruitment method you use, be clear about what you want from your participants. Follow these guidelines to ensure your teen group or meeting is a success and generates productive results:

Be proactive and actively recruit. Do not sit back and wait for teens to come to you.

Balance the interests, skills, ethnic and social diversity, and gender of the participants as much as possible.

Figure 2.1 Organizational Assessment Checklist

Use this checklist to help give direction, uncover hidden issues, clarify tasks, and guide commitment to involving youth in decision making. Use it as a tool with your board, your staff, young people, or other people who are participating.

YES = We do this already and don't need assistance

NO = We don't do this yet and want to develop next steps to move forward in this area

N/A = This is not applicable to us / We don't plan to do this

Please note that we are not suggesting that every organization meet all of these criteria.

	YES	NO	N/A
Point 1: Define Decision Making			
Have you clearly identified the ways young people can be involved in your organization's decision-making process?	☐	☐	☐
Do you know which decisions you want young people to be involved in?	☐	☐	☐
Have you considered how your organization will make decisions with young people?	☐	☐	☐
Point 2: Know Why You Want to Involve Young People			
Do you understand how youth involvement can benefit youth, adults, and your organization?	☐	☐	☐
Do you know how your motivations affect youth involvement?	☐	☐	☐
Does your organization have a clear vision, goals, and objectives for youth involvement?	☐	☐	☐
Point 3: Assess Your Organization			
Do you know how to build support for youth involvement in your group?	☐	☐	☐
Is everyone in your organization (board members, staff members, administrators, teachers, and young people) committed to successful youth involvement?	☐	☐	☐
Point 4: Determine Your Approach			
Is your group going to add youth representatives to an existing all-adult decision-making group?	☐	☐	☐
Will your organization involve equal numbers of youth and adults in decision making?	☐	☐	☐
Do you know if an all-youth or youth-adult structure will work best for your agency?	☐	☐	☐
Point 5: Overcome Organizational Barriers			
Are there permanent policies in your organization that support youth involvement in decision making?	☐	☐	☐
Has your organization addressed budget and staff issues related to youth involvement?	☐	☐	☐
Are the terms of office and voting rights equal for young people and adults?	☐	☐	☐

(cont.)

Figure 2.1 Organizational Assessment Checklist (cont.)

	YES	NO	N/A
Point 6: Overcome Personal Barriers			
Are young people involved in all issues, not just those that affect youth?	☐	☐	☐
Have adults throughout your agency examined their own stereotypes about young people?	☐	☐	☐
Are young people engaged as decision makers throughout the organization?	☐	☐	☐
Point 7: Address Legal Issues			
Is your organization aware of the legal responsibilities of involving youth as decision makers?	☐	☐	☐
Does your state have laws that restrict youth involvement in decision making?	☐	☐	☐
Have you explored all the legal options for formalized youth involvement?	☐	☐	☐
Point 8: Recruit Young People			
Does your group have successful recruitment criteria?	☐	☐	☐
Do your decision-making activities attract diverse groups of young people?	☐	☐	☐
Does your recruitment process educate others about youth involvement in decision making?	☐	☐	☐
Point 9: Create a Strong Orientation Process			
Do you have an orientation process for young decision makers?	☐	☐	☐
Has an adult explained youth involvement to parents?	☐	☐	☐
Is there a system in your organization to help young people understand their involvement, as well as the roles they will serve?	☐	☐	☐
Point 10: Develop Young Leaders			
Do you have a peer training system for young decision makers?	☐	☐	☐
Are there opportunities for young people to develop their decision-making skills?	☐	☐	☐
Do you offer a system of support for adult allies?	☐	☐	☐
Point 11: Provide Intergenerational Training			
Is there a formal training process for adults committed to youth involvement?	☐	☐	☐
Does training meet the needs of youth and adults?	☐	☐	☐
Does your organization's culture embrace diverse training interests, needs, and approaches?	☐	☐	☐

Point 12: Facilitate Successful Meetings	YES	NO	N/A
Do you use techniques that engage youth and adults throughout meetings?	☐	☐	☐
Are there opportunities for all members to speak at meetings?	☐	☐	☐
Do you encourage personal and group appreciation during meetings?	☐	☐	☐
Point 13: Foster Youth/Adult Partnerships	**YES**	**NO**	**N/A**
Are there multiple strategies and opportunities for youth and adults to build relationships?	☐	☐	☐
Do you involve parents from the start?	☐	☐	☐
Point 14: Develop a Mentoring Plan	**YES**	**NO**	**N/A**
Do you encourage personal success for youth involved in decision making?	☐	☐	☐
Is there an empowered, accountable resource person committed to helping youth and adults build relationships?	☐	☐	☐
Do young people have substantive connections with adult leaders in the organization?	☐	☐	☐
Point 15: Sustain Youth Involvement	**YES**	**NO**	**N/A**
Are there reflection opportunities infused throughout activities for young people and adults?	☐	☐	☐
Do you evaluate youth involvement activities?	☐	☐	☐
Do you have ways of recognizing success and appreciating people?	☐	☐	☐

Source: Based on Youth on Board's publication *14 Points: Successfully Involving Youth in Decision Making.* Reproduced with permission of Youth on Board, 58 Day Street Somerville, MA 02144, www.youthonboard.org.

Include library users and nonusers. If your group only consists of the same five teens who use the library week after week, you haven't done your job.

Include a variety of ages (grades seven through twelve).

Keep the group size manageable. For example, no more than fifteen participants for a focus group and a maximum of thirty teens for a teen advisory board. Otherwise the group becomes too unwieldy. (The more the merrier when it comes to Junior Friends.)

Actively and openly communicate with teens. Learn each teen's name and use it.

Provide guidelines and set expectations.

Let teens know you are interested in their lives, their interests, and their friends and that they are important to you and the library.

Treat them as adults, but let them be kids.

Encourage the entire library staff to be pro-teen.

Bear in mind that teen groups are as unique as the personalities of the teens involved.

Let teens do the work. (You provide the support.)

Guide; don't dictate.

Use visuals such as presentations, samples and sample boards.

Prepare to incorporate and defend teen input.

Empower them and give them the freedom to assist and make decisions.

When a teen completes a task, praise him or her, and if someone makes a mistake, don't reprimand—everyone makes mistakes.

Libraries that have had success with teen groups and collaboration include the Leominster (Massachusetts) Public Library, Phoenix (Arizona) Public Library, Louisville (Colorado) Public Library, and the Evanston (Illinois) Public Library. Evanston's Teen Advisory Board members were involved in their renovation project from the very beginning, even before the location of the space was decided. Teen preferences determined the location of the teen space (far from the children's room). They met with the architects and the library director on several occasions, and they met regularly with the young adult librarian. During those meetings they were asked many broad and specific questions, such as "What is your dream space?" and "What specific kind of furniture and lighting do you want?" Teens even created the bylaws for the room. When the space opened, they trained to be tour guides. Refer to appendix E for more libraries that have successfully collaborated with teens. For more ideas on teen participation, see the "Teen Facilitations Summary" text box for a summary of a teen input session at the Louisville (Colorado) Public Library.

QUICK TIP

To find teen participants who are not (yet) library users, ask for recommendations from local teachers, coaches, scoutmasters, church youth leaders and other professionals who work with teens.

Avoiding Pitfalls

Equally critical is gaining an understanding of the reasons why teen participation can fail so that you avoid pitfalls. The Innovation Center for Community and Youth Development and the National 4-H Council have defined fives challenges in getting youth involved in decision making. They are

Lack of knowledge. Many youth have not been involved in decision making previously. There is basic knowledge that must be gained to be an effective participant.

Unwillingness to get involved. Because they have not been invited to the table before, many youth are skeptical that their voice and vote will count.

Lack of a support network. Simply bringing youth to the table is not enough. Early on, concerted efforts should be made to ensure they succeed.

Unclear roles. Structure and clarity about responsibilities are essential.

Unique needs. Organizations must also pay attention to the unique scheduling, transportation, and financial constraints that are often associated with being young.

TEEN FACILITATIONS SUMMARY

The Louisville (Colorado) Public Library conducted a teen session concerning the teen space in their facility that opened in August 2006. Forty-one teens were invited to participate for the teen planning and design council, and thirty-three attended. Here are the results:

Purpose

Receive input from teens on what they would like to have in their new library space and their vision for teen council.

Outcomes

1. List of three to five technologies recommended by teenagers for library.
2. List of ideas for future programming, emphasis on middle versus high school desires.
3. List of three to five preferred ways to find out about library programming.
4. List of three to four visionary objectives for a teen council.

Top Five Technology Interests

1. Wireless Internet
2. Laptops
3. Computers in general
4. Game systems (electronic)
5. Music system (individual listening *and* group jukebox)

Décor Ideas

- Neat lamps including lava lamps, colored lights, dimmers
- Plants
- Aquarium
- Open areas
- Individual study areas with good lighting
- Group study
- Air purifiers
- Bulletin board/white board

Programming for High School—Top Five Choices

1. Study groups—Organized tables by subject, student run with phone/e-mail list

2. Movies—Any time is great for movies, movie nights or weekends, teen selected, large screen and projection, snacks
3. Tutoring service that teens would provide to younger kids
4. Tutors for teens
5. Student librarian/volunteer

Promoting Programs for Teens

- E-mail and phone lists
- Bulletin boards in teen areas of library, schools, recreation center, coffee house
- Library website (include on homepage)
- Newspaper, commercials in local media
- Large posters
- Promotion by library staff and teen volunteers at reference desk and circulation desk

Teen Council

Teens listed ideas, which we compiled later since we ran short on time. There was a lot of interest in being involved on teen council; we received a list of student names and e-mail addresses, as well as their interest in teen council and teen website involvement.

Teen Council Top Three Suggestions

1. Should be a small, dedicated group with regular attendance required.
2. Teen council could have fundraisers for the library.
3. Council could plan, run, or volunteer for programs at the library. (See below for individual comments.)

All Remarks about Teen Council

Small group of five to ten members

Dedicated group

Required to attend meetings

Each school and each grade should be represented

Meet two times a month

Have a meeting schedule

Meet only when necessary

Have separate groups for middle and high school

(cont.)

Have meetings open to anybody for comments occasionally

All ideas or additions to room should be approved by the teen council

Have an adult advisor so *real* decisions can be made

Have a cut-off age for membership (no suggestions for this age)

Have a deadline for joining

Have teens as volunteers

Volunteer to help at the library for things teens can do together

Recruit friends to help

Plan programs because teens would come

Run some events

Help advertise items with posters, e-mail, etc.

Council should sponsor fundraisers, brainstorm or raise money for the teen room

There should be a suggestion box for problems

Make a website

Have a teen message board

Suggest items for the collection

Invest in the future

Have a vision for the library

Wide web of contacts with easy access to information and logistics

The results of teen input: a bright and airy space with an industrial ceiling and windows on almost every wall. Furnishings are flexible in configuration, allowing teens to rearrange the seats to suit their needs. Computer chairs are adjustable, ergonomically sound, and on casters so they can be easily moved. Cherry wood appears on the windows and borders the shelving end panels. This works together with the bright colors to create a distinctive blend of style and youthfulness.

FOCUS GROUPS

Focus groups consist of a selected group of people used to test and evaluate a concept or product. Focus groups are generally short-term and can be formed in addition to other discussion forums, such as brainstorming sessions or teen advisory boards. In fact, forming a focus group is a great segue into establishing a teen board. Utilize focus groups to

gather opinions, beliefs, and attitudes about a particular subject

test your assumptions

encourage discussion about a particular topic

build excitement about a topic

provide an opportunity to learn more about a topic or issue (in this case, twenty-first-century library design and services for teens).

Typically, focus groups are conducted by a neutral party such as a library consultant. Because this is not always feasible, a library staff member may conduct focus groups, as

TIPS FOR TEENS: SUCCESSFUL COLLABORATION

- Be open and communicate in a positive and effective way. Share your ideas and skills with your adult library partners.
- Be enthusiastic.
- Know all the possibilities. There are a lot of options for how your library's space can look as well as what your library can offer.
- Be creative with ideas for design, layout, decoration, furniture, flooring, lighting, ceilings, shelving, displays, collections, programs, and technology. *What do you like and need? What would others your age like and need? What would make you want to hang out at the library?*
- Ask questions. What are other libraries around the world doing with their teen spaces? What are the possibilities for your library?

- Do research. Look at bookstores and places you like to hang out. *What is good and appealing about these places and what is not so good?* Go online and look at other libraries and teen-related organizations and businesses. Collect pictures to show library staff.
- Help plan, design, and implement ideas now and in the future. Make suggestions, assist in decision making, and discuss progress and problems.
- Assist in recruiting friends and other people your age to participate.
- Respect others and their opinions. Provide support for one another.
- Enjoy yourself!

long as he or she remains unbiased. Holding a series of focus groups is an excellent way to begin work on a teen space project. Consideration should be given to holding a variety of sessions, such as one junior high session, one ninth- and tenth-grade session, one eleventh- and twelfth-grade session, as well as a session or two for adult stakeholders.

Because a focus group can be such a powerful information-gathering tool, it is important to understand the key elements for success.

Plan, plan, and plan some more. The effort you put in will be reflected in the quality of the output. Refer to the "Teen Facilities: Focus Group Questions" text box for sample questions to help you plan.

Public/school library collaboration is key in high-quality recruitment and attendance. Working collaboratively will go much further than working in a vacuum.

Plan to gather answers, but also use the session as an opportunity to show them possibilities and obtain teen buy-in. Kay Appleby, librarian at the Tekamah Carnegie (Nebraska) Public Library says, "I operate on the 'cook's theory' which means: put plenty out there for others to choose from because you never know what each person is hungry for."

Use visuals to help foster discussion. Create a ten- to fifteen-slide PowerPoint presentation of inspirational teen spaces and related ideas to help teens understand the concept and evoke comments.

Set the tone of the group. Teen participants should have fun and feel good about the session.

Get full answers—not just "we need more computers" but "we need more computers because we wait in line over an hour every day and there are never enough computers with the things we need like MS Word and the Internet."

Keep the discussion on track. Have fun with participants, but also keep the discussion productive. The goal is to answer all or most of the questions you've planned.

Monitor the clock closely; don't exceed time limits. Suggested time frame is between 60 and 90 minutes per focus group.

Make sure every participant is heard; draw out quieter group members by directing questions to them.

Incorporate feedback forms. Since it is often difficult to capture all the input from a group of teenagers, consider supplementing your discussion with a quick and easy feedback form that lists the questions and gives teens room to give a written reply. Collect the forms at the close of the session.

Create and post a follow-up online survey on your library's website. Ask teen participants to encourage their friends to complete the survey. Consider having a prize drawing at the close of the survey to help promote participation, and make sure this is listed at the top of the survey.

Analyze and summarize each focus group meeting. Look for trends and common comments as well as surprises worth noting. Note things that elicited positive, negative, and emotional responses. Did anything generate additional comments or questions? If possible, review the session with another person to make sure all impressions and opinions are accurately captured. Better yet, have teens assist with compiling feedback.

Write a brief report. Focus group summaries can be important supporting documents in a space plan.

Work with architects and designers who want customer input and involve them in the process.

Keep teens informed. Be sure you show them results of their comments and suggestions.

Many of the libraries featured in appendix E have done a tremendous job integrating teen focus groups into their planning process. Librarian Michael Nyerges says two of the most important elements of planning and design for the Canandaigua (New York) Middle School were district support and active stakeholder participation. All stakeholders had a voice, including a variety of teen input through focus groups. "It's important to have the kids talk to the consultant and the planning committee," says Nyerges. Nancy Eckert, assistant superintendent for instruction, highly recommends involving teens in this process. "Student focus groups were the critical piece in how our plans developed. It's a fairly easy process," says Eckert. "The school library media center is the core of the building and at the core of teaching and learning. We need to prepare students for the world they are going to be exposed to and the school library media center needs to be key in the development," she adds.[2] See appendix E and the companion website at www.ala.org/editions/extras/Bolan09690 for additional information.

COMMITTEE WORK

Committee work may include having teen representatives on adult-dominated planning committees. This is a growing practice in many libraries, especially in those that are building new libraries or expanding or renovating existing facilities. Not only does teen participation broaden the perspective of the group, it can also be an efficient way to help distribute the workload. Involving more people in the planning and decision-making process also builds support for the project and the fund-raising effort. Remember, teens have parents and friends (and their friends have parents). A committee is also excellent leadership training ground that readily supports asset development and adult-youth collaboration.

QUICK TIP

Prior to the focus group, make sure you establish a way to take notes to collect comments and suggestions. You can assign a note taker, or record the session, or hand out a blank copy of the questions to participants for taking notes and have them turn in their notes at the end of the session.

A common product of focus group sessions is another type of committee: a teen space committee. Such a committee would consist of a diverse group of ten to fifteen teens. The group should be similar in composition to that described in the focus group section earlier in this chapter. The group should include a few adult collaborators, including at least one staff member from outside youth services. The purpose of this committee is to formally carry out the work started in the focus groups or brainstorming sessions. Teen space committees should be included in the following:

> budgeting
>
> collaborating with staff
>
> working with architects and designers to discuss goals, design, content and collections, sustainability, environment (lighting, etc.), use patterns, ADA compliance, shelving and furnishings, etc.
>
> incorporating additional teen user input
>
> selecting and testing furnishing options
>
> establishing a timetable for the project

BRAINSTORMING SESSIONS

Brainstorming is a useful tool for gathering myriad ideas and perspectives in a short period of time. More important, it is an efficient way to collect ideas from teens and staff members. Sessions can be held in lieu of or in addition to focus groups and committee meetings. For best results, brainstorming sessions should be conducted a minimum of three times with teens and staff members throughout the course of the planning and design stages.

Acknowledgment of staff input is critical in making this project work because they are the ones who will be responsible for supporting the new teen space. Without their support, a well-intentioned teen project will quickly fail. The first staff brainstorming session should be held at the beginning of the project and include a combination of

TEEN FACILITIES: FOCUS GROUP QUESTIONS

Facilitator Introduction (5 minutes)

Staff Note: Begin each focus group with a general welcome and introduction. Talk to the participants about what you are trying to accomplish and why they are there. For example:

> We would like your honest opinions on various questions. There are no right or wrong answers. Everyone's opinion is important. Your answers will be confidential. We will be taking notes and/or recording this session, so it's important that only one person talk at a time.

Questions

Staff Note: When conducting the session spend five to eight minutes per question.

- Please introduce yourself and tell us what grade you are in, what school you attend and what libraries you use.
- Where do you like to hang out?
- How often do you come to the public library/school library, if at all? (every day, once a week, once a month, a few times a year, once a year, never)
- What do you like about the public library/school library? What do you dislike about the public library/school library?
- Why do you visit the library? What would you like to see at the library that would make you and your friends want to use the library? [*Staff note: Talk about the options to get them started. For example: to do homework or research, hang out, look for magazines, borrow materials, read for fun, use computers, the Internet, etc.*]

- What kind of "look and feel" would you like the teen area/school library to have? [*Staff note: Discuss basic design, color, flooring, lighting, layout, etc. Show a few images to spark ideas using a PowerPoint presentation.*]
- What kinds of furnishings and accessories would you like to see? [*Staff note: Provide some examples from other libraries, retail catalogs, etc. Direct the conversation toward furnishings, shelving and display units, and miscellaneous decorative items.*]
- Would you be willing to serve on a teen space planning committee and or a teen advisory board to help plan the new teen area?
- What kinds of materials would you like to see more of in the library? Less of? [*Staff note: This is optional if you have time. If you don't get to it, it can be the focus of future discussion groups.*]
- What kind of activities and programs would you like to see in the library? [*Staff note: This is optional if you have time. If you don't get to it, it can be the focus of future discussion groups.*]
- Are there times (beyond regular library hours) you would come to the library? For example, if we were open Friday night, Saturday night or Sunday night? Any other ideas?
- Do you have any comments, questions, or concerns about the library or this project?

youth services staff and staff members from outside the department, with a maximum of three to five staff. This session should be casual, nonthreatening, and informative for all involved. Begin by briefly describing the purpose behind the meeting and follow up with some ice-breaking questions such as "What was your worst experience with teens in the library?" and "What was your best experience with teens in the library?" Next, ask the group key questions specifically related to the goal of creating a new and improved young adult area. Divide the discussion into two parts: young adult services and physical young adult space.

Refer to appendix B for a Brainstorming Ideas Worksheet. Sample topics are listed in an easy-to-use grid format to simplify organization and note taking. When using the brainstorming worksheet, formulate the discussion so that each topic is asked in three ways.

Where has the library been in relation to _____?

Where should the library be in relation to _____?

Where is the library headed in relation to _____?[3]

This type of questioning will provide focus and direction for the group. Remember to set a time limit so that one topic does not monopolize the conversation. Consider meeting over the course of several sessions, tackling services in one meeting and physical space in another.

Throughout the discussions, encourage participants to be candid about their feelings and be prepared to listen to a variety of viewpoints. It's better to get staff concerns out in the open at the beginning than to be surprised in the middle or, even worse, at the end of the project. Potential areas of concern might include things such as a shortage of staff and time, physical distance of the teen area from service desks for observational purposes, and the possibility of loud talking and rude behavior.

After brainstorming with staff, it is equally important to initiate a similar session with teens. Many of the questions developed for the staff brainstorming session can be used in teen discussion groups. Participants for these sessions can be gathered in a number of ways, including looking to teen advisory board members, teen focus group participants, and collaborating with schools, teachers, and school administrators. Once you've established a core group of diverse teens, there will be countless ideas generated.

GROUP BRAINSTORMING GUIDELINES

Choose a topic.

Assign someone to take notes.

Go around the room and solicit one idea per person.

Think quantity, not quality.

Say "pass" if you don't have an idea.

Do not criticize or discuss ideas.

Good-natured laughter is okay.

Exaggeration is encouraged!

Spend a total of twenty to thirty minutes brainstorming.

When you're finished, discuss the ideas that stood out during the session. Which ideas really work? Which don't work?

SURVEYS

A simple way to find out about teens and to generate ideas for your young adult area and services is to develop a survey. Teens love them, because surveys provide an opportunity to voice their opinions. They are also an inexpensive and easy way to reach a large number of people at a variety of locations. Conduct surveys in writing, online, over the phone, or in-person.

Survey Design

When designing the survey, keep it simple and to the point. Whether online or in paper format, a survey that is too long won't be completed. With print surveys, the format must

Figure 2.2 Sample Paper Survey

We WANT to know...what YOU think!

Are you a ☐ male or a ☐ female?   How old are you? _____

How often do you use the library? (Check **one**)
☐ Once a week   ☐ Once a month   ☐ Once a year   ☐ Only when I have to   ☐ What library?

Where do you like to hang out with friends? (Check all that apply)   ☐ At my house   ☐ At their house
☐ Community center   ☐ Local hangout (What's it called? _____)   ☐ School library   ☐ Public library
☐ Other _____

Where is your favorite place to study?   ☐ My bedroom   ☐ At a friend's house   ☐ At school
☐ At the library   ☐ Other _____
Why? _____

Think of your favorite place to be. What two things make it your favorite place?
1. _____   2. _____

What kinds of things would you like to see in the library? (Check all that apply)
☐ Music   ☐ Stereo system   ☐ Individual listening stations   ☐ VCR   ☐ Videos   ☐ DVDs
☐ DVD player   ☐ Computers   ☐ Comfy furniture   ☐ Comics/Graphic novels
☐ Magazines   ☐ Electronic games   ☐ Board games   ☐ Lots of good paperbacks
☐ Other _____

What two things would you most like to borrow from the library with your library card?
☐ Books (If so, what kinds of books (fantasy, mysteries, etc.)? _____)
☐ Music CDs   ☐ Videos   ☐ DVDs   ☐ Books on cassette/CD   ☐ Games
☐ Graphic novels/Manga, etc.   ☐ Other _____

What do you use computers for?   ☐ Social networking   ☐ Chat/IM   ☐ E-mail   ☐ Play games
☐ Look up fun stuff   ☐ Download stuff   ☐ Make web pages   ☐ Type letters   ☐ School research
☐ Other _____

What types of events and programs would you like to see at the library? (Check your top 3.)
☐ Sports/exercise   ☐ Writing workshop   ☐ Music   ☐ Arts/crafts   ☐ Book discussion
☐ Homework help   ☐ Computer skills   ☐ Dancing   ☐ Babysitting
☐ Job hunting skills   ☐ Movies   ☐ Cartooning
☐ Other _____

What activities, subjects, and/or items are you absolutely passionate about? This can be anything from horses to soccer to science to music and, if you're not into anything, tell that too. (Feel free to write on the back.)

What suggestions do you have for attracting teens to the library? (Please write on the back.)

Would you be interested in serving on a teen council that helps design a space especially for you in the library?
☐ **YES**   ☐ **NO**   **If YES . . .**

Name: _____   Phone: _____   E-mail: _____

or contact us: **[insert staff person's name, phone, and e-mail]**

be eye-catching and visually appealing. Use clip art, attention-grabbing fonts (generally not more than two), and experiment with color. Be creative! Try to stick to multiple-choice questions as opposed to open-ended questions, but always leave room at the end for one open-ended question that invites comments or other ideas. Refer to figure 2.2 for a sample paper survey and see appendix A and the book's companion website for sample online survey questions.

Survey Availability

Next, you need to get the survey out. You can accomplish this in a number of ways:

> Distribute paper surveys in-house, asking participants to put completed forms in a suggestion box.

> With an online survey, advertise to let teens know it's there. (See figure 2.3, and read chapter 5 for more information on successful advertising.)

> Hand out paper surveys in person or distribute reminder cards with online survey information. See figure 2.3 for an example. With paper surveys, make sure there is a convenient place to leave completed forms. With an online survey, make it readily available on library computers. Collaborate with computer lab instructors in schools, asking if they would let students spend a few minutes completing it.

> To get input from nonusers, advertise around favorite hangouts such as the community center, pizza shop, the mall, etc.

> Complete surveys, either paper or online, at group brainstorming and focus group sessions.

> Get out into the community and verbally survey teens. For example, the Lake Hills (Washington) Library staff went to the shopping mall, a transit bus stop heavily used by teens, a city teen council meeting, and a youth detention center. This is a great method for hearing from teens who do not use the library.

Don't forget to set a time limit for your survey (one month is a reasonable time frame). Don't be discouraged if it doesn't work the first time; revamp the survey, rethink your distribution methods, and try it again. Depending on how comfortable you feel with the confidentiality of your survey and the reliability of the teens you work with, consider putting a trustworthy teen in charge of assisting with compiling survey results.

Figure 2.3   Wanted: Teen Perspectives on Libraries and Design

★ WANTED ★

TEEN PERSPECTIVES ON LIBRARIES AND DESIGN

Respond to a brief online survey
and You'll be eligible to win a
$50 gift card to Best Buy!

Survey at: http://indielibrarian.blogspot.com/
Scroll down to "Teen Focus Groups: Wisconsin"

Survey Results

Using the original survey as a master, compile results using the tally method. Record the number of responses for each question above the corresponding answer on the original survey. If you ask for responses to open-ended questions at the end of the survey, list the comments exactly as worded at the end of the compilation. For each answer, divide the number of responses by the number of teens who completed the survey. This will give you

QUICK TIP

To make compilation of your survey results easier—and easier to follow—consider guiding responses to open-ended questions. Rather than ending with "Please include additional comments here," try "What are the top three things you'd like to see in the new teen area?"

a percentage for each answer. (Note that the percentages for each answer should total 100 percent.) If time and resources allow, consider putting results into a spreadsheet to incorporate into your final plan. Post survey results on the library's web page as well as at the library to show teens that you take their comments seriously. Most important, share the survey results with your administrator, and incorporate these new and exciting ideas into your space plan.

TEEN ADVISORY BOARDS AND JUNIOR FRIENDS

Teens want to make a contribution to society, and they need a forum to provide input on those things that directly involve them. Forming a teen advisory board or starting a Junior Friends of the Library (JFOL) are excellent ways for libraries to get young adults involved. They are also great ways for teens to earn community service hours to fulfill graduation requirements.

A teen advisory board (TAB) or teen advisory council (TAC) is a long-term group and is recommended for providing ongoing service for the teen area and teen services. Teen boards tackle a myriad of topics such as advising on library rules and regulations, young adult collection development, and programming such as planning parties, writing original plays, conducting contests, etc. Their duties may also consist of raising money, volunteering for after-school activities and service projects such as children's summer reading program and computer classes, and overseeing special ventures such as a teen space renovation. On average, advisory boards meet monthly, but the number and length of meetings will vary depending on the tasks at hand. See appendix A for a sample TAB application and bylaws from the Roaring Spring (Pennsylvania) Community Library, as well as sample TAB agendas from the Farnsworth (Wisconsin) Public Library. Even schools such as the Coppell (Texas) Middle School West and Lee County (Georgia) Middle School are creating TABs.

A JFOL group is quite similar in nature to a TAB. The primary difference is that members of JFOL pay annual dues. The Union County (Florida) Library also has a supporting business membership category that is open to any organization in the community interested in supporting the efforts of the group.[4] Annual dues are $5 for individual members (grades nine through twelve) and $20 for organizational membership.

Union County JFOL, founded in 2001, began as a group of older middle school and high school students. Eventually the group came to include only high school students, with middle school students welcome at events. Union County JFOL has a blog, a Flickr photo album, and holds meetings on a monthly basis, conducted by a chairperson and run by *Robert's Rules of Order*. The Union County JFOL officers include a chairperson, a vice-chairperson, a secretary, and a treasurer. Officers are elected by a majority vote of all members. Although the Union County JFOL's activities and duties are similar to those of a teen advisory board, the JFOL has more responsibility for fund-raising (comparable to the efforts of an adult Friends group) for new library materials as well as for annual scholarships. The scholarship program, available to JFOL members who are high school seniors in Union County, began as a way to encourage and reward students for pursuing a college education. To raise scholarship money, the Junior Friends hold a number of fund-raisers every year including Karaoke Knight, a medieval-themed karaoke party/dance, Super Awesome Game Nights and Fingers of Fury, Feet of Frenzy, video game parties with Guitar Hero, Dance Dance Revolution and Halo tournaments, movie screenings, and car washes and bake sales. Scholarship dollar amounts vary from year to year, depending on the success of the fund-raisers. Winners of the scholarship receive their money after registering at their college and providing the JFOL with a copy of class registration.

The design elements for your teen space will fall into place once you clearly understand the group for which the area is being designed. Ideas and plans may change many times, but that is part of the process. Take plenty of time and give careful consideration to every idea from your TAB or TAC. Although the following chapters will provide step-by-step basics for designing the ideal young adult area, appreciating the importance of teenagers and recognizing their uniqueness will be the best resource for discovering the key to creating and maintaining a winning teen space.

TEENS AS VOLUNTEERS

According to Youth Helping America, 55 percent of youth ages twelve to eighteen volunteer, which is nearly twice the adult volunteering rate of 29 percent.[5]

SPACE ASSESSMENT

Begin the analysis phase by assessing the physical space of your entire library. Examine essential components such as design, décor, functionality, content/collection, service points, and layout. Having a firm grasp of the overall facility will help form preliminary ideas and supply the initial framework for the teen project. Such components will provide the foundation for the space plan and ultimately create the ideal teen area with optimal services.

Location

Careful thought and analysis should go into location, whether planning a public library teen area or a library within a school. Consider the following factors:

> needs of your teen customers
>
> needs related to the facility as a whole
>
> traffic patterns and accessibility
>
> appearance of the area

Take into consideration that the ideal public library teen space location should have easy accessibility and high visibility. Teens should be able to discern their area when first walking through the front door. This can be accomplished by locating the teen area near the entrance of the facility or by using signage that quickly points them in the right direction. Other factors to consider include

Good traffic flow. Avoid placing teen spaces near congested areas that could cause issues with other customers. Teens should be able to get to and from the teen area with ease and without disturbing others.

Easy access to services and amenities. The location should be near key service areas such as information, computers, audiovisual collections, circulation, restrooms, cafés, etc.

Good staff sight lines. If the area is not staffed, library personnel should still be able to see what's happening in and around the space.

Some degree of privacy. Don't isolate teens, but choose a location that has some seclusion so teens have the freedom to talk, and staff can hold programs there without disturbing others.

Flexibility. Plan a space that is adaptable and has room for growth and change.

Avoid putting the teen area next to or, even worse, in the children's area. Teenagers do not want to be associated with little kids. And last, but not least, always consider the impact the teen space will have on other customers and areas of the library.

When planning a new school, school library planning experts Rolf Erikson and Carolyn Markuson recommend

making the library easily accessible from all learning areas of the school, which often means placing the library in a central location

locating the library away from noisy areas

keeping the library on the ground floor

locating near a building entrance that will allow for extended use of the library during nonschool hours[6]

Although there is rarely one perfect location for a teen area, you'll do well to follow these guidelines and incorporate them into what works best in your library environment and suits your teen customers' needs. Always compare the strengths and weaknesses of several locations before making a final decision.

Function

A key rule to keep in mind throughout the planning and design process is that form follows function. Having a solid grasp on how teens use the library and on how the space will ultimately operate will help you better plan the aesthetics of the space. Whether choosing a location, purchasing furniture and materials, or laying out the space, all design elements will ultimately come back to the question of, "What best supports the functions of the space?"

To get started, make a list of all activities planned for the teen area. Include everything you can think of such as studying, socializing, meetings, after-school activities, homework assistance, and programs (small group and large group). Once you have generated the list, determine what will be needed in the physical space to accommodate such activities. Will you need to consider multiple spaces (i.e., study area and a lounge area, a separate meeting room or quiet study room, a computer area, and an office space for staff)? These are more pieces of the puzzle that will help you shape the space and the overall direction of the project.

Inevitably, considering the functions of the space will raise questions which in turn will lead to answers that can point you in the right direction. For instance, you might ask, "Should a teen area be for educational purposes or for entertainment?" and "Should it serve as a quiet study area or a central meeting place?" At its best, the ideal teen area should not be limited to only one purpose; instead it should serve as a multifunctional space: for studying, reading, hanging out, socializing, meeting after school, using the Internet, listening to music, being entertained, getting help with homework, or simply relaxing. All libraries must strive to build such a space for their teen customers; however, some libraries will have more freedom, funding, space, and flexible management than others do. The most important thing to remember is that anyone can have a teen space that is everything to its teenagers, as long as the planners keep open minds and have a willingness to try. The key is to include as many functions as possible for each library's situation, and the rest will fall into place. If you are located in a small library and don't have room for separate areas, strive to make your entire facility teen-friendly.

Content

The content of a teen area includes all those items that will assist in defining the physical space. Fundamentals include

> the collection, including materials of all formats (books, audiovisual items, graphic novels, magazines, games, etc.)
>
> furniture and fixtures (tables, task chairs, soft seating, shelving, display units, room dividers, etc.)
>
> equipment (computers, printers, listening devices, gaming equipment, televisions, etc.)
>
> signage
>
> accessories (decorative elements such as clocks, posters and artwork, etc.)
>
> any other physical components of the area

Begin to create a list of items you envision in the space. What items can be derived from the function list? For example, if a function of the area is that it will be used for hanging out after school, then this will determine what kinds of furniture you'll consider. This function might also suggest purchasing more browsable materials, such as graphic novels and magazines, or looking into incorporating listening stations or stereo equipment into the area. If a function will be to provide computer access and assistance on a regular basis, then this would imply additional computer purchases for the space and improved literature and signage to show where teens could find help.

Staff

The element of staffing is not always as evident as the other components, but it is equally as important. Just as shelving, lighting, flooring, and books are a part of a new space, so are people. Analyzing the staffing situation beforehand will enhance the final space plan. A library's staffing situation will guide both the location and the layout of a teen area.

After all, staff will be the ones responsible for working with teens and maintaining and promoting young adult services.

From day one of the project, take into account who will be involved with the final space. For example, a small or medium-sized public library is less likely to have a separate desk staffed by a young adult specialist. Therefore, for a small public library, the decision about where to locate key service points in relation to the entire teen area will be crucial. In a school or large public library, the decision of where to best locate the service desk within the space and how to staff it will be a guiding factor. In all situations it's vital that staff members be readily accessible to teens so there is no question about where they can find help. It is also important that staff members who will assist teen customers be friendly, approachable, and knowledgeable. In all actuality, a library can be stylishly decorated and filled with great materials, but if the staff is unapproachable and rude, teens won't want to use the area. Thinking about your library's staffing situation at the beginning of the project, rather than at the end, will be one of the best moves you will make in developing your young adult space.

Size

It is crucial that you appropriately size your teen facility based on community and student populations for ages thirteen through eighteen. The square footage of your teen area should be based on *demographics and need,* not personal bias. Strive for a ratio where the teen area square footage to the overall library square footage is equal to the ratio of the teen population of the community to the overall population of the community. (See figure 2.4.) For further analysis, compare ratios of the population for ages infant to twelve and the square footage of your children's area, as well as that of your adult population and adult allocated adult space. How do they measure up? The Farnsworth (Wisconsin) Public Library teen population makes up approximately 7 percent of the overall population. Their teen area is 9 percent (764 square feet) of the overall square footage of the library (8,100 square feet). Libraries such as the Bedford (Massachusetts) Public Library, the Springfield-Green County (Missouri) Library— Republic Branch, Newark (New York) Public Library, Reuben Hoar Library (Massachusetts), and the East Brunswick (New Jersey) Public Library all re-evaluated space allocations for their overall facility to accommodate their growing population of teen customers. The Republic Branch's reference area was redesigned to house its teen space. (Their previous teen area consisted of a bookshelf.) Bedford and Reuben Hoar downsized their reference collection and swapped their reference and teen spaces. The former teen area at Bedford (432 square feet) is now the reference area and the former 1,200-square-foot reference area is now the teen area. That's a 768-square-foot gain for teens! The Newark and East Brunswick public libraries reallocated staff space and other adult spaces to reconfigure for their teen customers.

Another way to get started is to utilize an instrument such as Anders Dahlgren's Space Needs Worksheet. Dahlgren's method uses estimates for determining collection, seating, staff work, special use, and other spaces. It is best used for obtaining an approximation of a library's space needs based on its underlying service goals. Generally, this process is used for

Figure 2.4
Square Footage Ratio

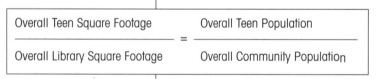

planning an entire library facility, but it can easily be adapted to teen space planning. For a downloadable copy of the worksheet, visit the website for the Wisconsin Department of Public Instruction at http://dpi.wi.gov/pld/plspace.html. Follow the guidelines as outlined on the web page, because they will provide a clear understanding of the entire process.

To complete the Space Needs Worksheet, enter all relevant information, skipping over those sections that do not pertain to the project. The purpose of this worksheet is to calculate square footage and to evaluate space based on collection growth and design population (i.e., the population that the expanded or improved young adult facility is expected to serve). For public libraries, collaborate with your schools. Local school districts are an excellent resource for gathering demographic information on teens including population growth projection.

Once the worksheet is complete, you'll be left with a thorough space analysis and a representation of the gross area based on the existing facility. Depending on the size of your project, it might be helpful to go back through the steps a second time, but this time input your projected or proposed figures to get an idea of the square footage necessary for your ideal teen area. Compare your new figures with the actual square footage of the existing space. Compare your calculated square footage with your square footage ratio. How does everything measure up?

Everyone faces similar questions and concerns when starting to examine their teen areas. Looking at and analyzing the numbers are only one piece of the puzzle.

THE ANALYSIS

Now that you are on track gathering data as well as input from teens and staff, the next step is to make a thorough analysis of your existing teen area. A successful teen space analysis must address the following issues:

> motivation—an explanation of the drive behind the project
>
> comparison with other library areas—how young adult services stack up against the other departments and services, including general information pertaining to the area as well as a detailed comparison of the teen area with other areas of the library (e.g., children's services, adult services, etc.)
>
> a detailed inventory—an outline of the existing space's furnishings, fixtures, collection, etc.
>
> a listing of strengths and weaknesses—the positives and negatives of the existing young adult space—to help generate a needs assessment and list of priorities as you move into the planning stage

Each of these steps is crucial for organizing ideas and, ultimately, keeping the project on target. If clear and well thought out, the resulting analysis will provide the necessary framework for a teen space plan that is both well-received and truly functional.

Motivation

What is the drive behind your teen space project? Is the project an independent redesign introduced by the teen or youth services department? This type of endeavor is generally initiated because the current teen facility is nonexistent or in desperate need of improvement. When a teen space project falls into the *independent redesign* category, the emphasis should be on building a persuasive plan compelling enough to convince decision makers that the project is a necessary and worthwhile endeavor meriting the investment of both library time and money. Your attention must focus on selling the idea.

If the project does not fall into the independent redesign category, then it is most likely a component of a larger undertaking such as a new building, expansion, or renovation. A large-scale project such as this is usually initiated by administration for the good of the entire facility. In this case, it is a given that some sort of teen space change will ultimately take place. The question now is, what kind of change will that be? It is up to the person in charge of teen services to influence those decisions. Space plans and proposals must have that wow factor that will convince administration that the teen area deserves as much (if not more) funding, space, and attention as the other areas of the library.

Teen Services Compared with Other Services

Begin this stage by noting fundamental information about the library as a whole. Include specifics such as demographics of the community broken down by age group, library service hours, door counts (i.e., how busy the library is), a staff roster for the entire library (names, titles, and statuses), the date the library was built, and dates of other facilities projects. (These may directly coincide with the last known update in the teen area.) Also gather information about each department's collection sizes, circulation statistics, programming statistics, and technology-related information (e.g., number of computers, website statistics, etc.). For comparison, collect similar data specifically related to teen services. Comparative data will prove essential when attempting to obtain support or funding for a project of this nature. Once it is clear how teen services rank in relation to the rest of the library, you will be able to gradually start building your plan. Use the Public Library Comparison Worksheet in appendix B.

In compiling your comparative data, consider these factors: verify demographic data for children and teenagers by calling your local school district for an estimate. Then, look at how the young adult collection compares with the other collections. Break it out into books, magazines, audiovisual materials, online resources, or whatever is appropriate for your situation.

Taking Inventory

Taking an inventory involves evaluating the space and furnishings of the teen area. Never make assumptions about what you think makes up the area; it's important that you check the space firsthand with a critical eye. If feasible, ask someone from outside the library (perhaps a colleague from another library, someone from the local recreation department, or a community member with an eye for design) to view the space with you. You'd be surprised at the insight and perspective a fresh eye will bring to the project. Participation of members of a teen facilities planning group or teen advisory board would be another excellent resource during the inventory analysis.

During the inventory process, it's essential to keep detailed records with as much information as possible; use the Inventory Checklist as a guide. (See appendix B.) It is also important to keep in mind that a thorough inventory should include *what is not there* as well as what is. The following sections provide definitions of terms used in the inventory.

When working with teens during the inventory process, hand out a blank checklist to each person before walking through the teen area as a group. Use the master Inventory Checklist as a general model. Pull out the key questions, keeping the sheet to one or two pages. Briefly explain the checklist and what each person is expected to do. As the group progresses through the space, introduce the inventory components one at a time, giving each person time to jot down his or her reactions and ideas. Collect everyone's sheets at the end. Compile the data—potentially with the assistance of a teen or two—and then get together a few days later to review the data as a group. To keep things orderly, bring up one component at a time, and elect a secretary to take notes. Add the notes to the initial data and findings.

FUNCTION AREAS

When laying out your space, think about dividing the space into function areas. Areas to consider for all public and school facilities include

- lounge/soft seating/recreational
- Small group
- Computer
- Quiet and individual study
- High-interest and popular/new display
- Collection/stacks

Additional areas of consideration for larger public and/or school facilities:

- Service (for check-out, informational assistance, etc.)
- Small group conference
- Staff work room
- Instructional
- Vending or café

Layout

The foremost thing to remember when considering layout is that it's not the amount of floor space a library has that matters; it's what you do with the space. The smallest of library spaces can be the most creative, well-designed place for teens as long as it is arranged with careful consideration to its users and functions.

Begin by obtaining a floor plan of the entire library or school facility as well as a separate plan of the teen area or school library. A good floor plan shows the entire area and the space that each piece of furniture occupies, and will serve as an invaluable tool and visual aid throughout the design process. If a professionally drawn floor plan of the library is not available, create a simplified version.

Start the layout analysis by looking for *potential*. Examine all the possibilities for the space by considering each of the key components (location, function, content, staff, and size) and how they tie together. Each will have a significant effect on the ultimate presentation of the space. Additional elements to consider include

- smooth traffic flow and handicap accessibility (i.e., space between aisles, the height of tables, etc.) (See appendix C for resources on obtaining a copy of *ADA Standards for Accessible Design*.)
- logical arrangement of and easy access to all materials
- equipment placement that is easy to locate by teens as well as easy to monitor by staff

decorating elements including lighting, signage, and wall treatments (Refer to chapter 4.)

division of space into task or function areas (See the text box for sample function areas.)

When deciding the layout of a teen area, experiment with the space using a scaled floor plan and cutout furnishings or an online tool. There are also a variety of professional design products and space planning tools on the market. (See appendix D for details.) As you go through the process, consider the traffic pattern of the space as well as the activities that will take place there. Delineate function or task areas. The arrangement should enhance, not hinder, the area's accessibility and atmosphere. Pay close attention to balance and how a focal point such as a mural ties into the rest of the space. Place large pieces of furniture or shelving in the space first. Be aware of the light in the room when placing pieces associated with studying or reading. Keep pieces of similar scale together, but remember that something a little off-balance and unusual is oftentimes better than that which is too symmetrical. Creative furniture placement or the addition of room dividers such as folding screens or office panels can instantly separate an area into distinct spaces. Depending on the features and design of the area, a rail or curtain rod and some fabric might work well to divide a large area.

A floor plan provides a foundation for the design project, presenting a reliable overview of how things are arranged within and around the space. A floor plan allows a designer to explore options before spending time and money implementing them. An accurate floor plan will allow you to determine if you have room to include features that you want in your new young adult space. Having the floor plan on hand throughout the inventory will prove invaluable.

For examples of a professionally rendered floor plan, refer to figures 2.5 through 2.9. and see photographs of these spaces on the companion website at www.ala.org/editions/extras/Bolan09690. If you don't have a professionally rendered floor plan, make your own. When creating a floor plan from scratch, be as accurate as possible. Follow these tips:

1. Keep the drawing to scale (e.g., 1/4 inch = 1 foot).

2. Measure the wall length starting at one corner of the room and working in a clockwise direction. Draw the walls and their measurements on graph paper. Write the dimensions in one direction so you don't have to keep turning the paper to read them.

3. Measure the width of the doors as well as the distance of the doors from the ends of the walls, and draw the measurements on the graph paper.

4. Measure the width of any existing windows or other miscellaneous openings, and note it on the floor plan.

5. Include all architectural elements in the plan such as pillars, lights and light switches, and outlets (telephone jacks, cable and electrical).

QUICK TIP

Make multiple copies of your floor plan and experiment with filling in the furnishings and other features. Measure each piece of furniture and shelving, draw the outlines to scale on colored construction paper and cut them out. You can then arrange them and rearrange them on your plan. When you have a layout that works, tape the "furniture" in place.

6. Incorporate any furniture such as tables, chairs, shelving units, and computer stands, and make a rough sketch of their placement and dimensions.

7. Attach any photographs of the space for additional reference.

Figure 2.5   Canandaigua Middle School Floor Plan

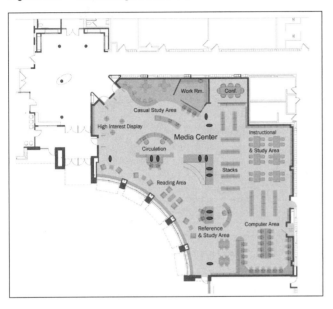

Source: Courtesy of Canandaigua (New York) Middle School.

Figure 2.7A   Campbell County Public Library System Floor Plan

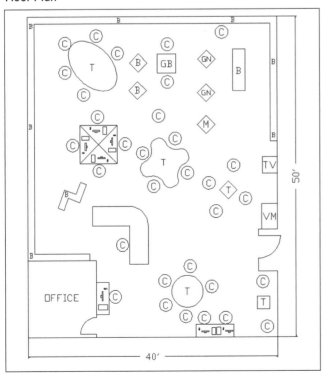

Source: Floor plan courtesy of Campbell County (Wyoming) Public Library System.

Figure 2.6   East Brunswick Public Library Floor Plan

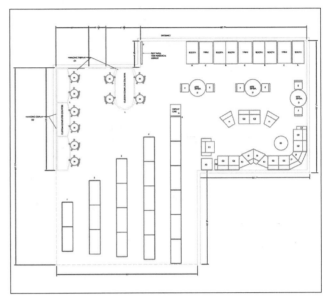

Source: Space designed by Kimberly Bolan of Kimberly Bolan and Associates, DEMCO Library Interiors (DLI), Carol Phillips, and the teens of East Brunswick, NJ. Floor plan courtesy of DLI and East Brunswick (New Jersey) Public Library.

Figure 2.7B   Campbell County Public Library Basement

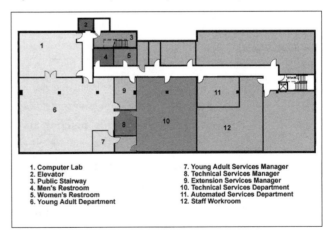

1. Computer Lab
2. Elevator
3. Public Stairway
4. Men's Restroom
5. Women's Restroom
6. Young Adult Department
7. Young Adult Services Manager
8. Technical Services Manager
9. Extension Services Manager
10. Technical Services Department
11. Automated Services Department
12. Staff Workroom

Figure 2.8 Port Jefferson Public Library Floor Plan

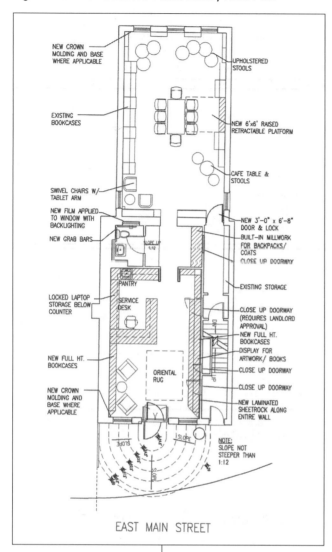

EAST MAIN STREET

Source: Floor plan courtesy of Port Jefferson (New York) Public Library and Janko Rasic Architects.

Figure 2.9 Farnsworth Public Library Floor Plan

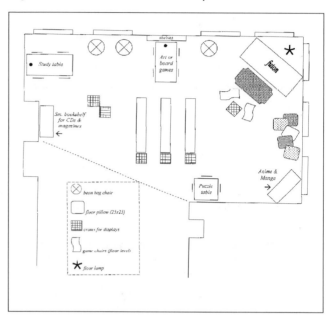

Source: Floor plan courtesy of Farnsworth (Wisconsin) Public Library.

When analyzing your layout and floor plan, consider the following questions:

Is the teen area or school library a distinctly separate space?

Where is the teen area or school library in relationship to other service points, departments, etc.?

Where is it in relation to the entrance of the building?

What is the overall feel of the space? Is it overly crowded with no room for expansion of materials, seating, etc.? Or maybe it is too spacious and there's ample room for materials and seating, but the contents are out of proportion compared with the space itself—a warehouse feel.

How are the contents of the space arranged?

Is there any privacy and can teens be social without disturbing other customers?

Overall, is the physical and psychological environment of the existing teen space both appropriate and appealing to teens?

How much floor space of the library is devoted to teens and how does it relate to the entire square footage of the building?

As the design process progresses, use the floor plan to refine the layout to reflect new ideas and proposed changes for the space.

Furniture

Furniture, for inventory purposes, consists of the area's furnishings including tables and chairs, soft seating, ottomans, occasional tables, etc. Working from your master inventory, look at what types of furnishings are in your library's teen space. Consider the following questions.

> How many people can be seated simultaneously in the entire teen area?
>
> Is there room for group seating? For individual studying? For socializing? For program activities?
>
> Are there any furnishings available to the individual browser or studier?
>
> Are there furnishings conducive to group study?
>
> Is there lounge-style, comfortable seating?
>
> Are furnishings flexible and portable to accommodate the program?

In a teen space, a variety of seating options is necessary for accommodating the needs and general nature of customers. The overall appearance of the furnishings and how they tie in with the rest of the space is also crucial. To attract teens, it is vital to keep comfort and social needs in mind as well as the certainty that stylish, up-to-date furniture will grab their attention. At this point in the process you'll want to start making a discard versus keep list, dividing furniture and shelving, etc. into two categories: items to throw away and things to reuse or refurbish. Have this list handy as you move into the planning stages.

Shelving and Display

For the purposes of this book, this category consists of shelving units, paperback racks, and display units. Evaluate the following aspects:

Listening station, comfortable seating, and the teen study room (separate, but attached to the teen area), which has a conference table for four, a white board, and a magnetic wall. Kent District Library (Michigan) Cascade Branch also has soft seating and an ottoman for socializing, café tables and chairs for studying, metallic silver walls, and blown glass pendulum track lights. The collection and computer area are attached to the teen area.

Does the space have adequate shelving for all materials? Make sure to count the total number of shelves that are currently in use.

Are shelves empty or jam-packed? Is there enough room for displays and face-out merchandising at the ends of the shelves?

Are there display fixtures such as book easels or slatwall panels in the area? What are they used for?

Do the shelves and display fixtures adequately and appropriately accommodate the format? Do the items stand up properly or do they fall over? Can they be easily browsed by teens?

At this point you will also want to consider how items are merchandised to the customer. Ask yourself

How are teens exposed to library materials?

Is the collection presented in an eye-catching manner?

Is there use of face-out merchandising, or is everything spine out?

Are new and high interest materials highlighted?

Are thematic displays used?

Are the walls, pillars, end panels, and ceilings used to their maximum potential?

Are materials not physically present in the teen area marketed in the teen area?

Are there point of purchase displays at key service points throughout the library? (Point of purchase means promotion of materials through interior displays, annotated booklists, window presentations, or other face-out merchandising, especially near the circulation desk, that encourage customers to impulsively borrow an item.)

In order to ensure that you plan enough space for your collection, it is important to use a few basic formulas. First, determine the number of shelving units that will be required. Divide the size of the collections by the capacity per shelving unit.

collection size / shelving unit capacity = no. of shelving units required

For example, if the capacity for fiction volumes is 400 volumes per shelving unit and the on-shelf collection size is projected at 4,000 volumes, then ten shelving units are needed. Next, determine the total collection space (or square footage) required:

no. of shelving units × square footage per unit = total square feet required

For example, if the number of shelving units is 10 and shelving unit is 14 square feet, then the total square feet required for shelving is 140. Capacity calculations should account for shelves that are only 70 to 75 percent full. Capacity will also vary based on the type of collection housed on the shelving.[7]

volumes per linear foot × shelf length (width) × no. of shelves = no. of volumes per shelving unit

To determine the number of volumes per linear foot for cantilever-style shelving, see figure 2.10.

Figure 2.10   Shelving Capacity for Cantilever-Style Shelving

Teen material type	Recommended shelving depth (inches)	Unit or volumes per linear foot of shelf
Audio CDs and DVDs	8–10	30
College and careers	10–12	6
Classics	10	8
CliffsNotes	10	35
Fiction	10–12	10–12
Graphic novels	10–12	30
Magazines	12	1
Nonfiction	12	10
Paperbacks	8–10	16
Textbooks	12	8

Source: Adapted from Earl Siems and Linda Demmers, "Library Stacks and Shelving" (Libris Design Project supported by the U.S. Institute of Museum and Library Services under the provisions of the Library Services and Technology Act, 2001), www.librisdesign.org.

The Collection

A good teen collection consists of fiction and nonfiction books, graphic novels, comic books, magazines, audiovisual items (audiobooks, DVDs, music), online resources, and games including board games and electronic games. When analyzing your teen collection, refer to the collection data gathered through your inventory and Space Planning Worksheet. View the collection in terms of selection and variety.

> What teen materials actually reside in the teen space? What resides outside the space?
>
> Is the teen collection up to date?
>
> Is the collection diverse? Does it include a variety of genres and formats?
>
> Does the collection need weeding?
>
> Does the library offer alternative formats (graphic novels, videos, DVDs, music, audiobooks, and video games) for teens? If so, are there any restrictions on audiovisual materials? Can teens check out these materials?
>
> Are materials attractive and fresh?
>
> How are materials arranged? Are materials grouped by genre or designated by a spine label (e.g., horror, science fiction)? Are they easy to find?
>
> Are there children's titles in the young adult area? Conversely, are there young adult titles in the children's collection? If either situation exists, it may be time to talk to the children's librarian about collection development policy and, possibly, relocating age-appropriate titles.

At this point it's also helpful to start looking at bookstores to see how they merchandise items for teens. (See chapter 5 for more information.) During your shelving and collection analysis, keep in mind that an attractive, clearly labeled, and effectively merchandised area will surely pique teen interests.

Technology

Technology includes anything electronic including computers and audiovisual devices such as listening stations or domes, DVD players, MP3 players, and gaming equipment. It also encompasses online resources such as databases, Internet access, and electronic games. When first starting a technical inventory, begin by examining your computer situation.

> Are any PCs designated just for teens? If so, how many? If not, why, and are there any immediately adjacent to the area?

> What do these computers have access to? Online catalog? The Internet? Research databases? Games? Microsoft Office, or comparable software?

> Are there age restrictions on accessing the Internet?

> Is Internet access filtered for teens? If so, what is the cut-off age?

> Is there restricted use of the Internet (no e-mail, no chatting, no downloading, no social networking)?

> Are there notebook computers that can be checked out?

Pay attention to electric and data resources. Are there ample outlets throughout the space? Be sure to locate wall-mounted outlets where they are easily accessible. Install floor outlets for instructional, listening, and viewing areas. Locate electrical outlets (each with a dedicated circuit if possible) at all computer workstations. If appropriate for your space, install proper wiring for telephone systems, ceiling-mounted projection units, and video surveillance. In addition, pay attention to technologies beyond computers.

> Are listening stations, sound domes, or other sound systems available for teens to listen to music, audiobooks, etc.?

> Are there MP3 players that can be checked out?

> Are viewing stations or a television available for teens to game on or to watch television or movies?

> How does this information assist in planning for a more effective teen library facility?

Technology is a teen magnet, and to create the ideal teen library space, technology must be a vital part of the space plan. According to the Pew Teens and Technology Report from 2005, the number of teenagers using the Internet grew 24 percent in just four years, to a total of 87 percent. Compared to the previous four years, teens' use of the Internet intensified and broadened as they logged on more often and did more things.[8] Teens log on most frequently to the Internet at home, with school and a friend's house close behind. (See figure 2.11.)

Figure 2.11   Where Teens Log On: The Places Where Teens Have Ever Gone Online and Where They Go Online Most Often

	Ever (%)	Most often (%)
Home	87	74
School	78	17
A friend's house	74	N/A
Library	54	N/A
Community center, youth center, house of worship	9	N/A

Source: Reprinted with permission from Pew Internet and American Life Project, *Teens and Technology* (July 2005), www.pewinternet.org.

School Internet usage has increased from 64 percent in 2000 to 78 percent in 2004. Library numbers aren't too far behind and have also shown increases: 54 percent of teens have logged on at the library as compared to the 36 percent reported in 2000. Knowing this information, ask yourself, "How can my library create a positive environment that is conducive to constructive Internet use so teens log on at the library?" See chapter 5 for more information on technology.

Staffing the Area

By now you should have a good idea of the staffing situation in your library. Additional issues to consider during the analysis phase include the following

> Are there staff directly or indirectly assigned to teen services? If so, how many? Part-time or full-time?

> Does the library use adult volunteers to work with teens? If so, how many? How many hours per week?

> Is there currently a service desk within the area? If not, is a service desk nearby?

> Is it easy to discern where a teenager can find assistance? (It is crucial that help be readily accessible to teens, especially since most will not seek out someone for help.)

> Are staff members friendly, approachable, and knowledgeable?

Over and over again, teens everywhere stress the importance of warm, open, and friendly people. After all, one negative experience is all it takes to turn a teenager away. For additional information on staffing, refer to chapter 6.

Additional Items for Consideration

Once you have examined your situation with furnishings, shelving, and fixtures, the collection, technology and staff, consider miscellaneous elements including lighting, flooring, food services, signage, climate control, electric, safety, ADA compliance, and overall décor. Items include, but are not limited to

GEORGE SCHOOL, PENNSYLVANIA

The staff at the George School (Pennsylvania), a boarding school of approximately 540 students in grades nine through twelve, have found that understanding the needs of teenagers, including their technology needs, results in students who respond to adults who treat them with respect, talk to them with genuine interest, and admit when they've made a mistake. Kids are often in the building when library director Linda Heinemann arrives at seven-thirty in the morning. They are finishing homework, just waiting for class, checking e-mail, or sleeping.

- Students can come and go in the library as they please. When they do not have class, they can be anywhere on campus and the library is one of their favorite places.

- The library is often noisy, with lots of active collaboration taking place; sometimes teens just hang out with friends.

- They do not limit what students do in the library (within reason, of course—kissing in the basement is discouraged!) Ms. Heinemann says, "We try very hard to create a pleasant and inviting space where students want to be."

- Two rooms for quiet study are available and are monitored by the teens themselves.

Full access to the Internet is offered. There is no blocking or filtering of websites on library computers, except for the two hours of study hall during the evening when social networking sites are blocked so kids will do their homework. Library staff walk around, ask students how they are doing, and have a sense of what is going on. "I also trust the students to use information in a responsible way, and am willing to talk to them about any issues or concerns I might have. Games, Facebook, MySpace and YouTube are all popular," adds Ms. Heinemann. She believes that if you can get the kids in the door and build a good relationship with them, then they will come to you for help when they need it.

Lighting. Consider the amount of artificial and natural light in the space. Discussion includes access to, control of, and amount of lighting.

Windows. Natural light can be an important piece of the puzzle, so be sure to plan for an adequate number of windows. Consider window treatments that reduce glare and protect materials. If doors are present, make sure they are conducive to good traffic flow. They should be lightweight enough to be opened easily.

Flooring. Think about the range of functions that occur in the space and how various types of flooring would enhance or hinder these activities. Does the space warrant a single surface or multisurface design? Options should also enhance the look and feel and comfort of the space. Avoid having thresholds that people may trip over.

Acoustics and sound. If noise is an issue, plan on installing elements to reduce sound such as carpeting or other sound-absorbing flooring, ceiling baffles, insulation, and interior barriers such as walls, strategic placement of shelving, and other large fixtures. The teen center at the Hercules (California) Public Library is acoustically insulated from the rest of the library.

Storage. Plan for adequate space and equipment for storage in staff areas and in the teen area proper.

Food services. Consideration should be given to food service for teens, whether healthy vending, a nearby café, or the ability to bring in their own food and drink. If not offered within the space, accommodations should be in close proximity.

Climate control. If you are in a school or large public library, consider separate climate controls for heat and air. Place return air vents high on walls or in the ceiling to allow for maximum wall space for shelving.

Safety and security. Make sure you have an understanding of fire code and basic safety guidelines. If a security system is important, protect computers by locating the security system away from them. Better security can also be achieved by positioning high-demand materials near service areas or creating good sight lines.

Accessibility. Be sure your space is compliant with the Americans with Disabilities Act (ADA). Issues to be addressed include aisle width, lighting, shelving, signage, table height, and technology.

Signage. When evaluating signs and way-finding methods, look at stack signs and labels, directional signs, promotional signs, and electronic signs.

Use the master Inventory Checklist (appendix B) as a guide to check these elements and more.

Strengths and Weaknesses

After completing the information gathering and analysis stages, immediately begin classifying your information into either a plus or minus category. Dividing the inventory in this manner is an easy way to instantly organize and prioritize a wide range of elements. When proceeding through this step, remember that there are always pluses, regardless of how bleak it may seem. Figure 2.12 is a list of strengths and weaknesses compiled for a fictional library. The simplest way to initiate the plus and minus process is to go through your inventory list and for every element ask the following questions:

Is this beneficial to teens and service to teens, or is it a hindrance?

Would this make a teenager want to hang out here? Why or why not?

Once you've reviewed the strengths and weaknesses, begin to ask general questions such as

What is there about the space that could be used to attract teens? What could you get or do to make the space grab their attention?

What makes the area attractive and comfortable—or ugly and unpleasant?

Can a teenager entering this library find the teen area or easily locate needed materials and key service points? Why or why not?

Are there hindrances to good service? If so, what are they? If not, what is attractive about the services currently offered?

All data gathered up to this point should work to support your objectives and shape your final space plan. Active teen participation, open communication with staff, thorough and well-thought-out data gathering, inventory, and analysis will ensure that the next step of formalizing your plan and proposing it to decision makers will be a smooth and painless process.

Figure 2.12   Strengths and Weaknesses of Library Z's Teen Area

Strengths	Weaknesses
Good-size space with room for tables and chairs and soft seating as well as teen computers	Located in the back of the library (hidden) and next to the children's department
Located adjacent to college and career information, adult/teen audiovisual collection, and information desk	Existing tables and chairs not attractive and in poor condition; no comfortable, lounge-style seating currently available
Extensive collection of teen paperbacks, multiple copies of popular authors and titles, and a good teen magazine collection	Cement floors; makes wiring for teen computers difficult
	Books all spine-out, with no face-out display
Attractive (and potentially reusable) paperback racks	Teen hardcover fiction and nonfiction collection is dated and in rough condition; needs weeding
Ample wall and ceiling space	Teen magazines and graphic novels located in the adult area
	Very little signage; boring and small signage

NOTES

1. Youth on Board, "14 Points to Successfully Involving Youth in Decision Making," www.atthetable.org/resources.asp.
2. Michael Nyerges and Nancy Eckert, phone interviews, May 10 and 11, 2005.
3. Created with assistance from Renée J. Vaillancourt, "YA Assessment Outline" (Parmly Billings Library, Billings, MT, 2000).
4. This model is based on the Junior Friends of the Library started by Nick Burke at the Union County Public Library, Lake Butler, FL.
5. Corporation for National and Community Service, "Building Active Citizens: The Role of Social Institutions in Teen Volunteering, Brief 1," in Youth Helping America series (Washington, DC: Corporation for National and Community Service, November 2005), 2.
6. Rolf Erikson and Carolyn Markuson, *Designing a School Library Media Center for the Future* (Chicago: American Library Association, 2007), 23.
7. Earl Siems and Linda Demmers, "Library Stacks and Shelving" (Libris Design Project supported by the U.S. Institute of Museum and Library Services under the provisions of the Library Services and Technology Act, 2001), www.librisdesign.org.
8. Amanda Lenhart, Mary Madden, and Paul Hitlin, *Teens and Technology: Youth Are Leading the Transition to a Fully Wired and Mobile Nation* (Washington, DC: Pew Internet and American Life Project, 2005), www.pewinternet.org/pdfs/PIP_Teens_Tech_July2005web.pdf.

Chapter 3 | **Plan and Propose**

All space and facilities projects should include a well-thought-out written plan, including short- and long-range planning for teen space and services. During this process, continue to get buy-in from all stakeholders, including teens, staff, faculty, administrators, and the community. Equally important, continue to think about what teenagers *need*, not about what adults *want*. After you have thoroughly assessed your situation and arrived at a sound idea of where you're headed, concentrate on working out the details—bringing everything together into a workable plan. In addition to using the worksheets provided in this chapter and in appendix B, you should start a design file early in this process. For more on creating a design file, see chapter 4.

A space plan will combine all issues related to budget, design, furnishings and shelving, equipment, collection, technology, layout, and staffing into one document that will serve as a manual to guide you through the process. This document is valuable for several reasons:

> It is the catalyst for getting a project accepted and keeping it on track, serving as the primary tool used in presenting project information to staff, administration, and key decision makers.

> It assists in organizing ideas and components of the project.

> It will be the blueprint for everyone involved, serving to transform the library into a teen-friendly space.

A well-received space plan must be flexible and easy to understand, describing what you want to do as well as the steps you will take to get there. A strong space plan will include

> goals and objectives

> a plan for improvement, including action steps and an explanation of how the project will add value to teen services or library services on the whole. See figure 3.1 later in the chapter for a sample Space Planning Worksheet—Value-Added Plan.

> an outline of the resources—both money and people—necessary to carry out the project

> a budget

> information on furniture, shelving, equipment, collection, and technology

> location and layout information

> teen, staff, and professional design and/or architectural input

staffing information

an estimated time frame for completion

By including each of these elements, you will be left with a solid plan that is ready to sell and ready to implement.

GOALS, OBJECTIVES, AND ACTION STEPS

What is your library's or school's mission and vision? Is there a long- or short-range plan in place? If so, what goals and objectives have been determined? How do these mesh with the goals and objectives for the teen space project? In the simplest terms, *goals* mean desired outcomes and should clearly identify what you are trying to achieve. For instance, one broad goal for this project might be "The library will remodel its existing teen area/school library, creating a new, fully functional space for teenagers." Others might be "The library will build a new young adult area focusing on the recreation and academic needs of teenagers in the community" or "teenagers (grades seven through twelve) will participate in designing and creating a new and improved teen area for the library," or "High schoolers will participate in designing and creating a new and improved school library for the school."

QUICK TIP

To help ensure buy-in from administrators, model the stated goal(s) for your teen space project on the library's current mission or value statement. Pick up some of the language and phrases to mirror that statement, and you'll reinforce that the proposed teen space will dovetail with the library as a whole.

Next, define the objectives for this project, or the way the library will measure its progress toward reaching its goals. Examples of objectives incorporating actions and measures might include the following:

Double the floor space of the existing teen area by a specific date.

Hire a professional designer by a specific date to consult with library staff to design a new teen area.

Train all staff in the area of customer service by a specific date to deliver friendly and knowledgeable assistance to teens with homework, personal research, and recreational needs.

By a specific date, increase the number of items in the teen collection by 30 percent, including adding new formats such as graphic novels, magazines, and DVDs.

Increase technology by purchasing four new computers; relocate two old computers from the adult area into the teen area; and incorporate listening stations and a television—all with specific deadlines.

A strong, well-thought-out teen plan takes into account young adult elements as well as the entire facility, its functional requirements, overall vision, and inherent characteristics. Ask, "Does the library's or school's plan coincide with the teen space plan?" If so, it is imperative that you illustrate how the two work together and make a point of highlighting it in your final space plan. If the two don't seem to agree, ask, "How could the teen space plan be altered to better complement the facility as a whole?" Don't compromise your ideals; simply try to work them into the bigger picture. The more your ideas relate to the library or school, demonstrating an understanding of how the teen space piece fits into the entire puzzle, the stronger the plan will be.

PLANNING TIPS

Public and school librarians and administrators across the country offer the following tips for successfully carrying out a teen space project:

Develop a process to identify priorities and goals. Equally important, develop an evaluation process.

Understand what the goals are for the administrators you work with and align your priorities as closely as possible to theirs.

Establish a stakeholders' committee and planning group, including teens, and include them throughout the process.

Gain administrative, community, staff, and district support.

Take your planning group on at least five to ten site visits to other libraries (for public libraries, include schools and vice versa for schools). Take photos and be sure to note things you like and don't like.

Read *Teen Spaces.*

Give attention to traditional and new ideas and resources.

Be flexible.

Ask the teens about everything and involve them in the process as early as possible. Lisa Tharp, librarian at Phoenix (Arizona) Public Library says, "Having watched that process and the way the popularity of Teen Central has grown, I really believe this is the key."

The information gathered in the inventory and analysis stage will be used as a springboard for creating a to-do list or list of action steps. Action steps must be as specific as possible and serve two purposes: (1) to outline the proposed ideas in a clear, succinct manner, and (2) to serve as a support mechanism for goals and objectives.

Appendix B has a Teen Space Planning Worksheet to record your action steps. Examples might be similar to those shown in the first column of figure 3.1. (The other columns are discussed throughout this chapter.) During this process it is essential to continually refer to your goals and objectives to ensure that every action supports them and that all goals and objectives are addressed in the plan.

To determine your action steps, think about all the things that you would like to add, modify, or improve in your current teen area. List everything you deem necessary for creating that ideal teen space, from the obvious to the minuscule to the outrageous. Be prepared to change your mind several times during the process, but don't be afraid to aim high. Everyone's ideas seem out of reach at first, but with a little perseverance many of them can become a reality.

Physical Space

Two important action steps are determining where the new teen area will be and how much physical space it will occupy. The location might have a lot to do with the square footage needed to carry out the plan. Intrinsic to these decisions is whether you want to relocate the teen area entirely, expand on the space you have, or simply improve the existing area. Regardless, remember that a successful teen area must be appropriately sized by demographics and need, easily identified by customers, easy to get to, and located near key teen-related library areas.

Making a decision on location and size will have a direct impact on the remaining action steps and will clearly announce the importance of teenagers to the library. Historically, organizations reveal what and whom they value through spatial design.[1] Even with teen demographics increasing, most libraries continue to undervalue teenagers by giving them less floor space than any other user group. Refer back to chapter 2 for determining what is appropriate for your facility.

Figure 3.1   Sample Space Planning Worksheet

Action Step	Value	People	Money	Time
Location and Layout				
The teen area will remain in its existing location, but will be slightly expanded to include 1,500 square feet of space. Rearrange the floor plan of the existing teen area to create a well-defined space with a more comfortable and welcoming feel.	Will give teens an appropriately sized, identifiable space of their own Will allow them to gather and socialize without disturbing others	Designers (teens and library staff)	$200 (staff time)	10 hours
Furniture				
Improve the feel of the space by painting and incorporating comfortable seating Purchase new soft seating (six lounge-style chairs) Purchase two tables with eight task chairs on casters	Will add character and a much-needed identification of the space helping to define the variety of functions of a thriving teen area Will increase flexibility of the space to accommodate various needs of the teen program Will increase teen participation in library	Selectors (teens and library staff) Painters (teens) Designers and selectors (teens and library staff) Installers (vendor)	$300 (staff time) and $5,000 (cost of new furnishings)	10 hours to plan, discuss, vote, and purchase décor and furnishings 12 hours to paint space
Shelving and Display				
Rearrange existing shelving and the collection; move three 48"h × 36"w × 12"d and two 72"h × 36"w × 12"d shelving units Purchase a new portable display rack for graphic novels Purchase face-out magazine shelves for existing shelving units (accommodate thirty new titles with one year each of back issues)	Will assist in defining and separating the physical teen space Will encourage teen self-sufficiency in finding materials Will improve the look of the area and the advertisement of its goods and services Will increase teen participation in library	Weeding and shelving (teens and staff volunteers) Movers (maintenance staff) Designers (library staff and teens)	$200 (staff time) $400 (graphic novel display) $500 (magazine shelves)	3 hours to relocate shelving 5 hours to select and purchase display rack and magazine shelving
Miscellaneous				
New directional signage to the teen area and new stack signs within the teen area	Will increase efficiency of how teens use the library and its services	Sign designers (library staff and teens)	$200 (staff time)	20 hours

50

Action Step	Value	People	Money	Time
Miscellaneous (cont.)				
Improve use of wall space (purchase message board, posters, teen artwork, etc.) Improve lighting by adding two floor lamps	Will improve circulation of materials Will increase teen participation in library	Selectors (teens and library staff) Sign installers (teens, library staff, and maintenance as needed)	$200 (posters, message board) $100 (lamps)	
Collection				
Weed hardcover and paperback teen fiction based on automated circulation report and shift collection accordingly Relocate teen magazines from the adult section, reevaluate title selection, and establish a popular teen magazine display Incorporate new formats into the teen area including a circulating video game collection and non-circulating board games Collaborate with audiovisual library staff to allocate more funds and materials purchases to teen-related DVDs and music	Will enhance the attractiveness and teen appeal of the collection Will increase circulation of library materials Will increase use of the space by teens Will increase teen participation in library	Library staff to weed collection with assistance from teens Selectors (library staff with assistance from teens)	$600 (staff time) $900 to start gaming collection ($500 to be funded by Friends) $3,000 (recurring annual charge—suggest 20 percent increase in budget for next year)	16 hours to weed collection 20 hours for evaluating and selecting other formats
Technology				
Purchase three new computers and one printer The three new PCs will have access to the online catalog, the Internet, research databases, and Microsoft Office products Add licenses for Office software Purchase sound dome and install over soft seating	Will increase usefulness of the library to teens Will help encourage school-library cooperation Will improve the overall appeal and use of the space	Technical staff and teen librarian to purchase and configure equipment (teen tech assistant to help with setup and configuration)	$250 (staff time) $3,000 (computers) $250 (printer) $500 (licensing) $600 (sound dome)	12 hours

All action steps share one common denominator: they must all somehow relate back to the physical space of the teen area. For example, when evaluating the content of your young adult materials collection, you might want to improve the collection, weeding old materials and adding new formats. This is a great action step, but take it a step further by viewing the collection in relation to the area in which it's housed. How does the collection influence the space? How would the space improve the presentation of the collection? Another example would be the functional requirements of the area. You might decide that the focus of the area needs to be more recreational. An action step would be to incorporate comfortable seating. Be specific about how much and what types of furnishings are to be added. Consider the activities that will take place and how the space will accommodate them.

Problems and Limitations

As you create your list of action steps, look for any immediately recognizable problems or limitations. It is always better to recognize potential roadblocks at the beginning rather than being unpleasantly surprised once the project is well under way. Keep in mind the inherent characteristics of the overall facility and how they might affect the action steps of your plan. For instance, you might want to build a loft in a renovated teen area but the construction of the library makes it impossible, or maybe the library is located in a historical building that has specific guidelines for renovation and design. Another desired action step might be to relocate the teen area to a back corner of the library, but you know that library administration and staff have expressed legitimate concerns about being able to monitor this space. These are roadblocks that you must be prepared to address. Always have an alternative to your ideal plan; the point is to consider everything.

VALUE

To ensure your project's success, you need to attach meaning to your action steps and add importance to your plan. Decision makers will better realize the merit of a project if they are shown the value of your proposed ideas. The second column in figure 3.1 shows specific examples of value-added action steps.

Researching public and school teen space projects at other libraries will provide additional, substantial value to your plan. Begin by looking at the model teen spaces featured throughout this book (including those listed in appendix E). Spaces such as these are great idea generators, motivators, and confidence boosters. Perhaps there is a library near you that has recently renovated its teen area. Take a field trip—set up an appointment to visit the space and to talk to the person responsible for overseeing the project. This is one of the best steps you can take to help determine your action steps and point out their value to your plan. Any evidence you can provide that demonstrates how this type of project has been successful at other locations will encourage support in your own library. If possible, include before and after photographs from other sites as well as statistics showing increases in young adult circulation, library use, and program attendance. This type of data and firsthand information provides concrete proof that teen space projects are well worth the investment. Look at projects similar in scale to yours, but don't be afraid to present something a bit larger to wow your stakeholders and help illustrate your points.

STANDARDS

During this action step and value process, take a look at how the space plan corresponds with young adult library standards for your local library system, state or national library organization. Supporting your ideas with standards such as these will add strength to your case. The Young Adult Library Services Association's (YALSA's) *Competencies for Librarians Serving Youth* is an excellent place to begin.[2] State and local standards may be more difficult to locate, but they are out there. Seek them out because the resulting information could be essential in presenting your case. For instance, the New York Library Association's *Nothing but the Best: Professional Standards for Youth Services in Public Libraries in New York State* dictates that every public library should have a separate area for teen use that is located away from the children's area, and that teens or a teen advisory board should be consulted on new construction and redesign projects.[3] The *Massachusetts Library Standards for Public Library Service to Young Adults* is even more specific, stating that the area should be accessible to all adolescents, easily visible, functional, and flexible in design. It should be an environment that is comfortable and arranged to accommodate noise and movement to make young adults feel welcome. The decor should make it evident that the area is for teens. Young adult involvement is essential in establishing an effective, dynamic young adult area. Details are provided for space, furnishings, infrastructure, and web presence.[4]

RESOURCES—PEOPLE, MONEY, TIME

To complete your library's teen space plan successfully, all aspects of the project must be considered. Those resources necessary for consideration include people, money, and time.

People

The most valuable resource of any design project is people. Whether teens, staff, contractors or designers, people will be responsible for carrying out the project from start to finish. Go through each action step one by one. Determine who will be responsible for each task, whether an individual or a group. Assign tasks to people immediately, so you can quickly learn where you have adequate support and where you need assistance. (See the third column in figure 3.1.) By considering this now, you leave yourself ample time to recruit volunteers and hire outside assistance if needed. However, don't worry if the assigned people and responsibilities change as the project unfolds—that is expected.

TEEN VOLUNTEERS

It's no secret that teens will be your biggest asset throughout the project. The challenge is to decide exactly how and to what extent they will be involved. The important thing is to include teens in every step of the project. As you've seen, there are many ways to include teens in the planning stages. You will also want to consider how to involve them in the implementation. How much work will teens actually put into the project? More significantly, how much responsibility will they have in terms of money, creativity, and hands-on involvement? Look carefully at your action steps and begin thinking about assigning duties to teens based on their individual strengths, interests, and talents. As with anything, certain tasks may not be suitable for certain people, and this goes for teens as well as for adults. No matter how and when they are involved, teens will have the opportunity for self-expression and skill building whether they are organizing, budgeting, designing, or simply expressing their opinions, all of which will be useful to them for the rest of their lives.

PROFESSIONAL OUTSIDE ASSISTANCE

If the project is too overwhelming or if you feel you need additional expertise, consider hiring or collaborating with outside help such as a consultant, a local interior designer or architect, or a library vendor who offers free or low-cost design services. This is especially critical in renovation or new building projects as this could be a full-time job, especially in large public libraries and school libraries. Hiring professionals is not a sign of inadequacy, but a sign of intelligence as the cost of assistance will be far less expensive than construction and renovation costs and may help you avoid costly mistakes and make better decisions.

A sample job description for such a consulting position might include one or more of the following:

review the library's mission, vision, goals, and plans

assess existing space(s) and services

visit other teen spaces in newly constructed and reconfigured facilities

conduct focus groups and other input sessions with teens, staff, and other key stakeholders

develop a plan to facilitate the creation and maintenance of teen space

design and implement teen area

train staff to plan, create, and maintain effective and exciting teen space

instruct staff in teen collection development, programming, and marketing for teens

Carol Phillips, head of Youth Services at East Brunswick (New Jersey) Public Library, says:

> The best thing we did for our project was to hire a consultant who was able to give us her expert advice, work with the teens as an unbiased party, put together a design plan, help us in our dealing with vendors, and keep the project on track. We handled many of the details on our end, but needed the expertise of someone who had done this kind of thing before. I have never been part of a building project like this. What an exciting experience! Using the services of a consultant greatly enhanced our building remodeling project. It was an invaluable investment of our time and money.[5]

Partnering with a local interior designer or architect can also be a great benefit. The Waupaca (Wisconsin) Public Library staff enlisted the help of an architectural designer and architect to work with Student Library Advisory Group (SLAG) members to design their new space. A local designer donated her skills and designed the Annex at the Palos Verdes (California) Library. She also assisted with the acquisition of specific furniture pieces. Collaborating with library vendors who offer design services is another way to obtain expertise while saving money. Oftentimes these services are offered for free—as long as you order your furnishings, shelving, etc., through that vendor.

No matter what outside services you choose, professionals can help can you make the best possible use of every inch of space, offering your teen customers an inspiring environment. See chapter 4 for more examples of collaborating with consultants and designers.

Money

No matter what the size of the project, you must prepare a budget or indicate the general cost. A budget is essential in providing guidance, thus helping to better determine the overall scope of the project as well as the feasibility of the proposed ideas. This process may also assist in addressing previously overlooked details as well as help tackle big issues such as the ability to hire outside assistance. When putting together a budget, make it somewhat flexible because the figures being gathered are cost estimates, and at some point during the course of the project, they might need to be revised. (See the "Money" column in figure 3.1 showing cost estimates. Note that these figures are for illustrative purposes only.)

When drafting your project budget, review the data collected in chapter 2 during the analysis stage. Compare the existing teen budget or school library budget with the overall library or school budget as well as other departments of the library or school. It is important that you include all budgetary findings in your final proposal, being careful to point out your awareness of the overall library or school budget and how your project can effectively and affordably fit. How does your project measure up? Is there any flexibility in your existing materials, programming, or other budgets? Could you apply any of your regular annual budget to project costs? Are there any hidden or unused monies in the overall library budget that you might be able to use, such as capital improvement funds? Investigate any budget information available from comparable projects. For example, has the teen area or school library ever gone through a redesign or renovation? If so, how long ago did it occur, and how much did it cost? Have any other depart-

GOING GREEN

During the information gathering and planning phases, you will want to consider going green. Terms such as *sustainable, green, high-performance, recyclable, renewable,* and *LEED* keep coming up again and again. If you're not familiar with this topic, no doubt teens are, and most are very passionate about the issue. In short, the goal of green design is to produce places, products, and services that reduce the use of nonrenewable resources and minimize environmental impact. Whether working on a new building or renovation, explore options for green design at the outset of the process. Although you can research much of this information yourself, this would be a good time to consult with a professional such as an architect or LEED (Leadership in Energy and Environmental Design) Accredited Professional. Benefits to sustainable design can include

- reduced operating costs
- improved air quality
- better staff performance
- improved library customer comfort
- increased library support and elevation of the library or school's standing within the community

Depending on your situation you may choose to pursue LEED certification from the Green Building Council or you may choose to do without certification, selecting green design options suited to your library and its needs.

ments gone through a similar project? If so, how much was spent? Take a look at design projects at other libraries in your state and out of state. Find projects similar in scale so the costs are comparable.

Producing a detailed budget proposal will be a key element in gaining support and persuading administration that its money will be invested well. No matter what size the project, if a budget has not been outlined, don't wait for someone to tell you what you have to spend. Go ahead and start preparing a budget of your own. Your initiative and organization might just influence administration decisions.

ESTIMATES

Undoubtedly, your level of involvement with finances will be entirely based on the size of your project. With small-scale ventures, where only a few hundred dollars are involved, you might be able to use existing library funds or outside donations. With a larger scale project, such as a renovation or expansion, more extensive budget work is required. In the latter situation, is your project large enough that it will go out to bid? With larger projects it is also quite common for budgetary guidelines to be predetermined by administration. If so, you may have to fight for the funds necessary to create the space you want.

You will find that written estimates are essential when gathering costs for a budget. Most organizations have procedures for collecting and comparing estimates. For example, the procedure might state that for items or services over $500, a minimum of three quotations must be collected. No matter what guidelines your organization uses, it is important that you understand and follow them. At the same time, keep in mind that it never hurts to gather multiple estimates for everything. Because you will be able to compare information from multiple sources, you will get a better understanding of what you are looking for and, ultimately, end up with a more accurate proposed budget.

When gathering estimates for each item or service, choose one vendor to deal with for the initial quotation. Draft the request with as much detail as possible. Once the vendor returns the estimate, look it over to make sure that it is accurate and that it includes exactly what you're asking for. Don't be afraid to make modifications or to send it back for clarification. When the estimate is finalized, use it as a model to draft requests to two or three more vendors. This way each vendor receives the same request so you can compare apples to apples. When at all possible, try to avoid gathering quotations by telephone because there is a greater chance for miscommunication. Get everything in writing, perhaps through e-mail or fax. Attach copies of the estimates to your budget worksheet for easy reference.

ACTION STEP BUDGET

The best way to begin estimating project expenses is to determine the cost of each item outlined in the action steps of your space plan. Figure 3.2 shows a sample action step budget. When completing your action step budget, make sure that you include all action steps and that everything adds up to 100 percent. (For your convenience, an Action Step Budget Worksheet is provided in appendix B.) The notes section should include information such as the company that provided the estimate and specifics of what was quoted. Attach written estimates and any informational notes. As you proceed through your own budget worksheet, categorize each action step, breaking each out into as much detail as possible and gathering estimates for each item listed. Your action steps will take on a new form, moving from a narrative description to a more detailed listing.

Figure 3.2 Action Step Budget

Action Step	Current Budget	Proposed Project Budget	Difference	% of Project Budget	Notes
Location & Layout					
Rearrange existing shelving and the collection, moving three 48"h × 36"w × 12"d and two 72"h × 36"w × 12"d shelving units	—	—	—	—	Shelving moved by library personnel. No additional costs for labor or materials. Materials will be moved by teen volunteers.
Furniture					
Purchase new soft seating (six lounge-style chairs)	—	$5,000	$5,000*	31	Estimates noted were received from companies A, B, and C. See attached estimates for more details.
Purchase two tables with eight task chairs on casters					*The teen advisory group is looking into fund-raising ideas or sponsorship opportunities to fund the furniture.
Shelving & Display					
Purchase a new display rack for graphic novels	—	$900	$900	6	Graphic novel and magazine shelves as specified by company D. Estimates noted were received from companies D, E, and F. See attached estimates for more details.
Purchase ten face-out magazine shelves for existing shelving units					
Miscellaneous					
New directional signage to the teen area and new stack signs within the teen area	$50	$300	$250	1	Estimates noted were received from companies D, E, and G. See attached estimates for more details.
Improve use of wall space (purchase message board, posters, teen artwork, etc.)					Recommend increase in annual budget to $300 per year for miscellaneous items
Improve lighting by adding two floor lamps					
Collection					
Incorporate new formats into the teen area including a circulating video game collection and noncirculating board games	$3,600	$5,700	$2,100**	35	58% increase in budget for teen-related audiovisual materials
Collaborate with audiovisual library staff to allocate more funds and materials purchases to teen-related DVDs and music					**$900 to start a new circulating video game collection ($500 to be funded by Friends the first year)
Technology					
Purchase three new computers and one printer	$1,000	$4,350	$3,350	27	Computers to be purchased on contract #1234 from company H.
Add licenses for Microsoft Office software					Estimates noted were received from companies H, I, and J. See attached estimates for more details.
Purchase sound dome and install over soft seating					Software to be purchased from K (academic pricing). Sound dome purchased from company L. Estimates noted were received from companies L and M. See attached estimates for more details.
Total	**$4,650**	**$16,250**	**$11,600**	**100**	

CATEGORIZED BUDGET

A good budget will include all anticipated expenditures. In addition to basic materials expenses (furnishings, fixtures, computers, collection materials, etc.), your budget may also include estimates for the following items:

> professionally rendered drawings or plans
>
> in-house personnel costs, for example, additional staff hours to help move materials and furnishings
>
> consultant fees or miscellaneous outside labor charges (professional design services, movers, painters, and contractors)
>
> rental equipment (stack movers, extra book carts, carpet cleaner, and painting gear)
>
> wiring (cost of additional or new electrical outlets, network drops, and telephone lines)
>
> insurance coverage (for large-scale projects and for volunteers who will be moving books and heavy items)
>
> recurring charges such as telecommunications fees and software upgrades
>
> long-term budget adjustments (for example, additional funds necessary for maintaining new collections, increasing programming, and adding staff)
>
> packing materials (boxes and labeling materials may be necessary if you are planning an extensive move where storage is involved)
>
> publicity

Once all the potential expenses have been outlined, prioritize the budget items, listing items in order of their importance to the project. What absolutely has to be done first? Can anything wait? Can you divide the project into phases so it's not so monetarily overwhelming? Can anything be revised to better fit the budget? Is there anything on the list that you absolutely cannot afford? If so, what are the alternatives? Can something be scaled down, or is outside funding for big-ticket items an option? Highlight items on the list that require an alternative funding source and make note of whom to contact.

To help illustrate the financial projections, calculate budget percentages for each action item. This will show what part of the budget will be directed to each item on your list. It might also be helpful to divide the project into general budget categories, such as furniture/fixtures, consultant fees, and materials, so you can see how the funds are being allocated. Figure 3.3 is an example of a categorized budget used to determine what funding will be needed for a project. The difference column in particular provides a total budget figure based on the difference between the current and proposed budgets. The percent column shows exactly where the money is going and how the expenses are divided. This column may also prove helpful during your presentation, so be prepared to provide explanations regarding distribution of funds (i.e., why more money is being spent on one category over another). (See appendix B for a Categorized Budget Worksheet.) Once your figures have been firmed up, consider creating a graphical representation of the numbers represented in the category worksheet. (See figure 3.4.) Illustrations such as graphs add a nice touch to a final presentation; they present numbers clearly as well as add variety and color.

Figure 3.3   Categorized Budget

Category	A. Current Budget	B. Proposed Project Budget	C. Difference	D. Percent of Project Budget (B / Total of B)
Architect/Designer and/or consultant fees	—	$1,500	$1,500	7.5
Furniture, shelving, display, décor, etc.	$50	$6,200	$6,150	30
Labor (staff time, movers, etc.)	—	$1,750	$1,750	8
Supplies (attach list)	$300	$300	—	1.5
Rental equipment	—	—	—	—
Technology	$1,000	$4,350	$3,350	21
Collection development	$3,600	$5,700	$2,100	28
Miscellaneous long-term expenses (i.e., additional staffing, software license, telecommunications cost, etc.)	—	$500	$500	2.5
Publicity	$200	$300	$100	1.5
Total	**$5,150**	**$20,600**	**$15,450**	**100**

Figure 3.4
Budget Graph

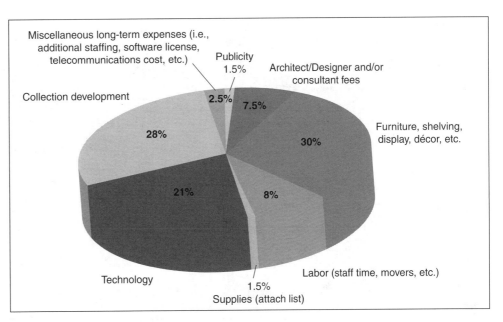

FINANCIAL ASSISTANCE

For financial assistance, consider applying for a grant, looking to private or corporate donations, sponsorships, or allocating funds in the following year's budget. As a result of a full-day teen spaces presentation, the Nebraska Library Commission promoted teen spaces as one of the two areas of focus for their Youth Grants for Excellence. The total amount available for youth grants each year was $50,000 in state funds. Grants funded in 2004 included $39,336 for 21 teen spaces grants; and in 2005, eight teen spaces grants were funded for $12,788. The Tekamah (Nebraska) Carnegie Public Library was one library to receive $2,000 in grant funds. Tekamah also received an additional $500 from their library foundation. When the youth librarian published a news article in their weekly newspaper, a former resident, a retired woman living in California, promptly donated an additional $500.[6] A new building project at the Taylor (Pennsylvania) Community Library was 90 percent (of a $1.8 million project) funded by a waste management landfill company.[7] Springfield-Green (Missouri) County Library—Republic Branch was made available through the Missouri State Library grant program. The Roberto Clemente (New York) Middle School was funded in part by a $150,000 grant from their borough president. The new school library features areas for reading, playing games, and a staging area for poetry readings and presentations. A row of booths is also available for students planning and discussing research projects. One seventh-grader said, "Last year, I came to the library only once. There were books all over the place and it was yellow—kinda ugly. Now, I think more people will come here."[8] The London (Ontario, Canada) Public Library had great success with teen space due to a Library Strategic Development Fund grant from the Ministry of Culture (Province of Ontario). They were also awarded the Minister's Award for Innovation for their work with youth. See the text box for details on their project. For more information on applying for local, state, and national grants, contact your local library system, consortium, or state youth services consultant. For additional funding resources, refer to appendix C.

Roberto Clemente (New York) Middle School Library includes a reading corner, booths (the Book Nook), and a game area. Photos courtesy of DEMCO, Inc.

Alternative financial sources may include Friends and/or Junior Friends of the Library, the library foundation, private donations, and corporate sponsorship. A staff brainstorming session may produce additional ideas for fund sources. The Palos Verdes Library District's Annex is a partnership between the Palos Verdes (California) Library District and Freedom4U, a local nonprofit that supports healthy living for teens.

Teens can also be instrumental in raising money for their libraries, teen space, and teen services. Following are a few examples of how teens have been actively involved:

The Teen Advisory Board members at the East Meadow (New York) Public Library wrote letters to local politicians and businesses asking for help in obtaining funds to furnish the new room.

The Longview (Washington) Public Library's new teen space, which opened May 2007, was built entirely with donations and grants, $5,000 raised by teens.

Teens at Roaring Spring (Pennsylvania) Community Library helped their library reach a $5,000 benchmark in its fund-raising efforts by recycling soda cans and donating $67 to the library.

Farmington (New Mexico) Public Library's teens received a $17,000 grant from ConocoPhillips to start their own zine. Teens did all the work, from developing the marketing plan, to writing the proposal, to doing the presentation. See chapter 5 for more information on this project.

Even library staff can be creative in their fund-raising techniques. How many librarians do you know that would dye their hair blue to raise money for their teens? Kelaine Mish, youth paraprofessional/teen coordinator, did just that for her teen customers at the East Grand Rapids Branch of the Kent District (Michigan) Library. She raised enough money to purchase games and a rug for their teen area.

BUILDING BIG ON A SMALL BUDGET

If library funds are limited, don't be discouraged. If you are smart, you can create an absolutely wonderful teen space on a small or even nonexistent budget. But before putting together your proposal, make sure you have tapped all potential resources. Consider all funding sources as well as free materials or resources from the community and within your own library. Another way to help reduce initial costs is to consider dividing the project into phases. In this way you can distribute the cost over a multiyear period. Carol Eshleman, teen librarian at North Platte (Nebraska) Public Library, says:

> After I attended Kim Bolan's teen spaces workshop, I decided it would be of no value unless I made use of the information, so I went to my director, shared the ideas, and was prepared to ask for a small amount of money—perhaps $200. Before I got to the amount, my director responded that the ideas were so good I could spend up to $500. And so the process began. When I started my job in June of 2002, I had a very small area with one four-foot shelving unit with four shelves on one side. My area has been expanded to five eight-foot shelving units (and I get to use both sides for more and more good books). My area has more than doubled in size since I started and I am pleased that my director and staff are welcoming teens into the library.[9]

THE TEEN ANNEX AT LONDON PUBLIC LIBRARY

The London (Ontario, Canada) Public Library received $35,000 from the Library Strategic Development Fund (LSDF), managed by the Ministry of Culture, for their LOLLYPOP (Learning, Literacy and Leadership for our Youth POPulation) program. Based on community needs and research, it was identified that leadership and literacy skills among youth ages twelve to eighteen needed to be addressed in unique ways at the library. Objectives of LOLLYPOP were to

- create a comprehensive and integrated youth services strategy for the library which actively engaged youth in all aspects of the project
- use new and emerging technologies (e.g., MySpace page, Flickr, YouTube, etc.) to capture the target audience
- create an inviting space by adding a drop-in center at the central library and two computer homework centers in branch libraries where there was a highly identified need for the service
- increase literacy and leadership skills of youth by weaving together creative expression, leadership development, and community building
- forge partnerships and collaborate with youth services providers in the city of London
- use this project as a pilot at the central library which can be rolled out to all sixteen branch locations

As part of the project, they also created a brand and a logo, which are used at all locations and for all publicity and promotion of teen programs and services. A graphic designer worked with teens to create the logo. She also taught them about graphic design, color, font, and brand use and recognition. As a point of interest, the name of the space, the brand, the logo, and the choice of colors in the space were all chosen by teens who are part of the teen advisory group called the Teen Annex Committee who regularly meet to help shape teen programs and services.

The Central Branch Library's Teen Annex was launched in January 2007. The Teen Annex pilot project was so successful they expanded their teen services to create a Teen Annex in each of their other branches, which include libraries and communities of various sizes and types. The project galvanized staff at all levels and engaged youth in all aspects of planning and implementation. They told the staff what they wanted and staff listened.

Overview of the Teen Annex at London (Ontario, Canada) Public Library's Central Library Branch. Large, multifunctional space located on the main floor adjacent to the library café. An interior designer worked with teens and staff to teach them about design elements, color, and creating anchors. See the book's companion website for photos of their branch spaces. One branch is an anchor at a local mall and another branch shares a building with a YMCA and a small community center.

An *urban expressionism* mural on the side of an escalator in the Teen Annex titled "Know-U-Turn" by young local artist Bryan Jesney.

TEEN SPACES BY LOCATION (AND COLLECTIONS HOLDINGS)

Each location is very distinct and varies in size and focus; however, there is a Teen Annex in every location, regardless of size.

Central Library	95 × 40 feet	3,800 sq feet	6,112 items
Beacock Branch	12 × 15 feet	180 sq feet	1,343 items
Byron Branch	9 × 11 feet	99 sq feet	988 items
Carson Branch	3 × 5 feet	15 sq feet	397 items
Cherryhill Branch	11 × 15 feet	165 sq feet	1,324 items
Crouch Branch	21 × 6 feet	126 sq feet	1,179 items
East London Branch	6 × 9 feet	54 sq feet	968 items
Glanworth Branch	one shelf		100 items
Jalna Branch	20 × 17 feet	340 sq feet	1,768 items
Lambeth Branch	15 × 15 feet	225 sq feet	418 items
Landon Branch	11 × 8 feet	88 sq feet	1,045 items
Masonville Branch	21 × 17 feet	357 sq feet	1,531 items
Northridge Branch	6 × 6 feet	36 sq feet	337 items
Pond Mills Branch	10 × 10 feet	100 sq feet	1,317 items
Sherwood Branch	13 × 18 feet	234 sq feet	1,545 items
Westmount Branch	8 × 12 feet	96 sq feet	1,530 items

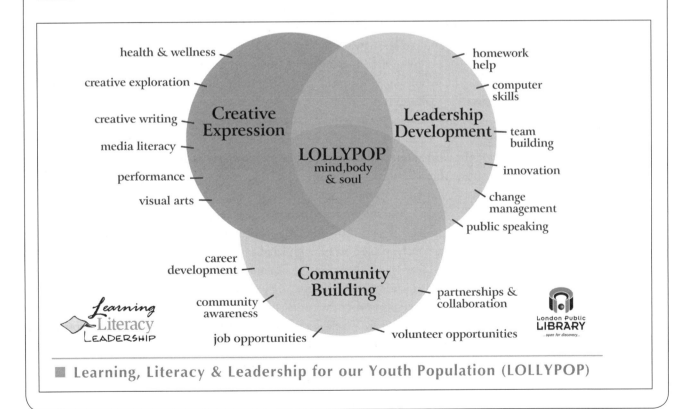

health & wellness
creative exploration
creative writing
media literacy
performance
visual arts

Creative Expression

LOLLYPOP
mind, body & soul

Leadership Development

homework help
computer skills
team building
innovation
change management
public speaking

career development

Community Building

community awareness
job opportunities

partnerships & collaboration
volunteer opportunities

Learning Literacy LEADERSHIP

London Public LIBRARY
...open for discovery...

■ **Learning, Literacy & Leadership for our Youth Population (LOLLYPOP)**

Corte Madera (California) Regional Library's teen nook.

If you're still not convinced that you can renovate a teen area on a small budget, take a look at the quick, low-budget revamps of model teen spaces in appendix E, and see the text box on Tekamah Carnegie (Nebraska) Public Library in chapter 4 and the photos of Corte Madera (California) Regional Library's teen nook shown in this chapter.

Time

It is always wise to think of your plan in terms of time. Devising a schedule can help make your project more manageable by assigning reasonable time allotments to each task. Begin creating a timetable by going back to your Space Planning Worksheet and arranging the action steps in the order they need to occur. Next, jot down a general time estimate for completing each event. (See the "time" column of figure 3.1 for an example of time estimates.) Some tasks may take days; others may take weeks, months, or even years depending on budget, project size, and staffing. For larger projects, it could take six months to one year to create a plan and begin the process. Total implementation could take anywhere from one to three years depending on budget.

When assigning deadlines and time frames to activities, be sure to take into consideration the people you've assigned to perform those duties. As with everything else in this project, be realistic, but don't be afraid to aim high when setting goals for yourself, the project, and the people participating. Once a schedule has been devised, add everything together to get an overall estimate for completion of the project. Some design projects might be carried out within months, but others might take a year or two before they are finished. After overseeing a 750-square-foot teen space renovation for the Schaumburg Township (Illinois) District Library, teen coordinator Amy Alessio says that a clear project time line and deadline are crucial, especially when using an outside designer. Because her library hired a design company that was in great demand, the library had to wait almost a year for the project to be completed.

If it is not feasible for the project to be completed all at once, perhaps the action steps could be divided into phases. This may be especially useful for small budget, long-term (i.e., those that will occur over the course of a year or more), or large-scale projects. If the project is of significant size, consider using a software program such as Microsoft Project to help create and manage your schedule. No matter what size your project, once the timetable has been devised, it is essential that you try to adhere to it as much as possible, but be realistic—updating and revising are allowed.

EFFECTIVE LONG-RANGE PLANNING

In 2003, the Newark (New York) Public Library's staff started their incredible teen space journey. After realizing their teen population was in desperate need of a place to call their own, the library's director and youth services librarian started a small teen advisory group to convert a staff area in their basement to a 230-square-foot teen center. Five years later, the space has grown to over 1,000 square feet. Circulation figures are also growing. In 2006 teen materials accounted for 4.47 percent of the library's overall circulation. In November 2007 it was up to 5.43 percent.

While teen involvement has changed, with kids growing up and their demands changing, the most important activity that the teen advisory board engaged in was the direct involvement in hiring the new youth services librarian. There were ten teens involved who interviewed candidates for this professional position. They asked predetermined questions and then engaged candidates in conversation and rated them. Staff and teens then sat down and discussed their impressions. "I think this made them feel a real part of the process," library director Elly Dawson explains. Currently, teens also assist in materials selection and have input on what goes in the room. In the past year the library has incorporated two public access computers and one ten-minute e-mail express computer into the room. They also started staffing the space. "It's a great way to help people find things and familiarize staff with what is in there and who the kids are," says Dawson. She also

notes that financial and emotional support for teen service has grown over the past five years, including Friends and community support for furnishings, décor, and computers. Dawson feels strongly that, "If you build it, they will come. If it works, people will support it." Truly passionate about serving this age group, Dawson adds, "We don't want to lose these people."[10]

Overview of Newark (New York) Public Library's teen space, which began as a 230-square-foot area and has grown in just five years to a 1,003-square-foot teen center.

The Big Picture

When creating your proposal, consider long-range planning. Having a long-range, strategic plan in place will assure decision makers that you understand the big picture and have thought about the longevity of your project and teen services. A long-range plan takes into account the future as a consequence of present, short-range, and intermediate-range events. Generally, this plan will include the next three to five years.

Since the first step in a long-range plan is information gathering and understanding your population served, you should have more than adequate information to formulate a plan for the future. (Refer to the information gathered in chapter 2.) Keep in mind that the variables are always changing. As with the project proposal, get buy-in from *all* stakeholders and consider the entire facility when planning. When outlining your long-range plan, make sure you account for a long-term budget. In particular, account for regular expenditures for furniture, maintenance, and other décor-related purchases. This will be a small percentage of the annual budget, but nonetheless needs to be accounted for.

On a related topic, including teen space and services in long-range and strategic planning for the entire library or school is critical. In public libraries, teen service has traditionally received minor representation in long-range planning and oftentimes school library service is loosely included in a school's plan. Having a seat at the long-range planning table is critical for successful service to teens. To ensure your seat at that table, be proactive in your approach by preparing supportive data, and present goals and objectives with an action plan outlining resources, budget, and time frames.

A long-range plan should not be locked in a filing cabinet; it should be a living document that is constantly referred to and updated annually. It is an effective management tool that assists in gaining recognition, funding, and support. When compiling information for a long-range plan, be sure to

explain the teen program

create a clear sense of purpose

identify priorities, strengths, and weaknesses

articulate the relationship with the larger organization

provide a blueprint for future development

PRESENTING THE PROPOSAL

As with the other aspects of teen space planning and implementation, get teens involved in the presentation process. Consider choosing one or two teens to co-present with you. Before making any formal presentation, look over all your findings and ideas. Make certain you are familiar with every part of the plan and can enthusiastically discuss any questions that arise. Create a narrative, supporting it with data, worksheets, focus group feedback, etc. Take a look at your original goals and objectives, double checking that they are clearly represented and defined in the space plan. If you discover any last-minute gaps in your plan, fill them in, even if they seem nominal. Never go into a presentation unprepared or with an incomplete plan or you will find yourself with a quickly fading project. You are the authority on this topic, so be prepared and be confident. If you are sincere and passionate about the project, it will show in

QUICK TIP

Practice your proposal a few times, just as you would a public speech. Reading through your entire presentation once or twice in front of a friend (or a mirror) can help you practice the pacing, see where you may need more (or less) information, and see how long the presentation takes. If necessary, you can cut or lengthen it to fit a prescribed time limit. If co-presenting with teens, include them in the rehearsal.

the presentation. However, no matter how much you prepare, it is always possible that someone may touch upon a topic for which you don't have the answers. If this happens, be honest. Say that you'll have to look into it and get back with an answer.

Any worthwhile teen space presentation should include handout copies of the space planning worksheet, action step and categorized budget worksheets, graphs, and any other key materials you deem worthy of presenting—but be wary of handing out too much paperwork. Focus on a few essential items. The rest of the plan can be presented using flip charts, posters, a PowerPoint presentation, or any other creative method you want. You might also consider incorporating and highlighting the following items somewhere in your presentation:

> supportive comments and quotations about the project from staff, teens, and teachers
>
> interesting ideas generated from staff brainstorming sessions, teen advisory meetings, and focus groups
>
> two or three of the most exciting or innovative action step items with sample drawings, photos, clippings from catalogs, or quotations
>
> the results (both statistically and photographically) of comparable projects from other libraries

Use presentation boards to help illustrate ideas and provide inspiration. (For more information on presentation boards, see "Design Boards" in chapter 4.) The most successful sales pitches always have that visual wow factor. Ideas must be sold, and seeing is believing.

Regardless of how great your plan and proposal are, you must be prepared for rejection. It's an unfortunate reality, but not all plans are approved (at least not right away). So, what do you do if the initial plan is rejected? Do you go back to the drawing board and start from scratch? Of course not. Simply make the necessary alterations—whether that means scaling down the project a bit, revising the budget, or doing more research. When you are satisfied with the changes, go back and present it again. It never hurts to ask those reviewing your proposal to give you feedback for future reference. Don't give up, and don't get discouraged.

Spend time creating a space plan equipped with a clearly outlined, value-added strategy for improving the space consisting of careful allocation of resources including money, people, and time. Stepping into a presentation with this quantity and quality of information along with a few added extras will surely impress decision makers and start the wheels turning. More important, you will reap the benefits of all your hard work when you begin the design and decorating phase.

NOTES

1. Anthony Bernier, "On My Mind: Young Adult Spaces," *American Libraries* 29, no. 9 (October 1998): 52.
2. See www.ala.org/ala/yalsa/profdev/yacompetencies/competencies.cfm.

3. New York Library Association, Youth Services Section, "The Key to the Future: Revised Minimum Standards for Youth Services in Public Libraries of New York State," www.nyla.org/content/user_12/NYS2006Standards.pdf.

4. Massachusetts Library Association, Youth Services Section, "Massachusetts Library Standards for Public Library Service to Young Adults," www.masslib.org/yss/mlayastandards.htm#facilities.

5. Carol Phillips, e-mail interview, January 30, 2008.

6. Kay Appleby, phone and e-mail interview, May 10, 2005.

7. Loretta Heffernan, e-mail interview, December 1, 2007.

8. Tanyanika Samuels, "Roberto Clemente Middle School's Library One for the Books," *New York Daily News,* November 20, 2007, www.nydailynews.com/ny_local/education/2007/11/20/2007-11-20_roberto_clemente_middle_schools_library_.html.

9. Carol Eshleman, series of e-mail interviews, January 31, 2008, and February 1 and 2, 2008.

10. Elly Dawson, e-mail interview, February 3, 2008.

Chapter 4 | Design and Decorate

Now that the plan is in order, avoid the temptation to go out and start shopping. With the endless choices in today's marketplace, jumping headfirst into a furniture or paint purchase without preparation can be both intimidating and frustrating. Before you make any purchases, it is essential to figure out what you need as well as what decorating items you want. Whether you're doing it yourself or working with the assistance of a professional designer, begin by finding an inspiration, move on to developing the style and character of the space, and then start experimenting with the layout and décor.

Throughout this phase, keep in mind that a truly teen-friendly space is comfortable, colorful, interactive, flexible in design, and filled with technology. Equally important, remember that *teen-friendly* is not synonymous with unruly, unreasonable, impractical, or tacky. Don't make assumptions or let personal biases impact decision making when selecting furniture, shelving, flooring, lighting, paint color, or signage. Items should be welcoming, have visual impact, be versatile, and encourage positive, independent use of the library.

WORKING WITH ARCHITECTS AND DESIGNERS

At this point, you will have determined whether the project will be done in-house or with the assistance of a consultant, architect, designer, or a combination. Such professional assistance can come in many shapes and sizes including private, local practices in your community, independent library consultants, and library-specific design services such as DEMCO Library Interiors (DLI), Highsmith, and Brodart, to name a few. (See appendix D for additional information.) No matter whom you're working with, it is an opportunity for collaboration as well as learning—for you and for the design professional.

The Interview Process

When searching for and selecting professional assistance, interview multiple consultants, designers, or firms. Someone with library design experience is good, but don't limit yourself to only those professionals. Seek professionals you are comfortable with, who are eager to listen to you and your customers, who are open to collaborating with staff and teens and are enthusiastic about new ideas and incorporating features you and your teen partners suggest.

Equally critical, before making a selection, make sure they understand twenty-first-century library design concepts, and are free of library stereotypes and outdated concepts of library planning and design. Those who have worked with professional designers feel that a truly good designer is one who incorporates the library's ideas into theirs and enthusiastically involves the teens from the beginning.

BE PREPARED

During the interview process be prepared to answer and discuss the following types of questions:

> For whom is the space being designed?
>
> What is the vision for the space?
>
> What activities will take place in the space?
>
> Are you remodeling or building from scratch?
>
> How long will you occupy the space? Five years, indefinitely, or something in-between?
>
> What is the square footage?
>
> What is the time frame of the project?
>
> What is the budget for the project?[1]

If you are prepared and organized and can communicate clearly, you'll be well on your way to finding a successful design partner. See the "Working with Professional Designers" text box for additional tips.

If you are interested in working with a professional but have a limited budget and can't afford the full services of a consultant or interior designer, consider exploring a more limited role with a professional. Options such as long-distance mentoring based on hourly rates are often available. Another option is to seek out a local designer who will provide discounted work on an hourly and daily basis instead of for the duration of the project. Another idea is to ask a design company if you can purchase the initial concepts or drawings and then find the furniture and accessories and do the decorating on your own. Yet another option is to consider what design services library vendors might provide free of charge with furniture and other product purchases. Any of these options can save a significant amount of money. The décor and layout of the Reuben Hoar (Littleton, Massachusetts) Library teen space was greatly helped by a local interior designer who led a workshop for teens where they selected color palettes for paint and upholstery fabrics. The designer was also instrumental in facilitating a pillow sewing workshop, designing floor plans for the area, and presenting to the board of trustees.

INTERVIEW QUESTIONS

When interviewing architects and other design professionals, schedule appointments with each and ask them to prepare a 20- to 30-minute presentation for you and other stakeholders, including teens. At the end of the presentation, allow time for a question and answer period. In addition, present each candidate with a copy of the written questions and have them respond to each question in writing after the presentation.

Consider the following:

> What kinds of design services do they offer? For instance, will they prepare floor plans, CAD drawings, design boards, color and finish recommendations?

Is there a charge for these services? If so, how much?

If working with a designer or company that provides products (e.g., furnishings), will they provide design services for free if the products are purchased through them? If the majority of the items, but not all are purchased from them, will they still provide the service?

Are there any limitations to their design services?

Who from their company will oversee the project?

Can they get furniture, shelving, etc., beyond what they've shown in their presentation? What are the possibilities? Limitations?

Are there any installation costs for furniture, shelving, etc.?

Can they provide assistance in estimated shelving needs?

Can they provide products, fabrics, and finishes that go beyond what was presented?

Will they provide samples of furniture before purchase?

Are they on state or government contract? If so, which one(s)? If not, do they have any discounts to offer?

What are the warranties on their products?

What is their service policy? In other words, how do they handle problems? What if the library doesn't like something once it's installed? Is there a restocking charge?

What is the general time frame on design work? Furniture installation? Shelving installation?

Are there storage fees if the library is not ready to install furniture or shelving when it arrives?

QUICK TIP

Assign a teen to take minutes at design meetings. Have teens also assist you with distribution and action item follow-up.

The Three Cs

Once you've selected an architect, designer, or consultant, it is essential to have effective communication, both verbally and in writing, throughout the entire project. Always practice the three Cs of communication: be clear, concise, and consistent. Don't expect a designer or consultant to read your mind. Be prepared to ask lots of questions and to take notes as well as to present samples of items and ideas from photos and drawings. The more you put the three Cs into practice, the better the designer will be able to understand and interpret your ideas into a final design plan. To further develop a successful working relationship with a designer or consultant, keep the following procedures in mind:

Define your priorities and convey your expectations.

Understand the scope of the agreement.

Share your expertise in a positive way.

Review codes, ADA requirements, etc., before the project gets too far along to avoid disappointments if an idea doesn't meet requirements.

Educate yourself in the language of design, architecture, engineering, and technology. (See figure 4.1 for a little help.)

Figure 4.1

Architectural Symbols. Familiarize yourself with basic blueprint reading and symbols to help you better understand and communicate with design professionals.

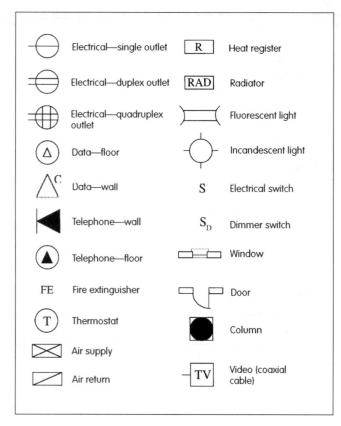

Source: From Rolf Erikson and Carolyn Markuson, *Designing a School Library Media Center for the Future,* 2nd ed. (Chicago: American Library Association, 2007).

WORKING WITH PROFESSIONAL DESIGNERS

- Know your stuff—do your homework and be prepared.
- Be confident—you know libraries and your teen partners.
- Encourage collaboration on all levels, especially when it comes to teen input.
- Don't use library jargon when communicating (e.g., YA, circ, etc.).
- Use visuals—architects and designers are very visual, so utilize photos, drawings, and other illustrations to relay your ideas.
- Educate professional designers—teach them about new concepts in library service and design; show them the possibilities.

Develop a relationship of trust and respect.

Remember that professional consultants or designers are compensated based on their time, so use that time wisely.

Take minutes at each meeting and include action items at the end of the minutes. Note the persons assigned to follow up on each item. Distribute minutes to all participants for review and follow-up.

Communicate, communicate, communicate.

GETTING INSPIRED

A successful design begins with a flash of inspiration. Inspiration is an integral part of design; it sparks creativity and imbues teen spaces with personality and teen appeal. Inspiration could come from one's background, surroundings, or personal interests. In fact, the best inspiration for a new teen space comes from teens themselves. However, before scheduling any meetings with teens, consider devising one or two ideas of your own just to get thought processes started. Draw inspiration from other teen spaces and other places teens like to be. Draw a comparison between those places and your library, and then begin to formulate a design plan that incorporates what you've observed.

TEEN ENVIRONMENTS

Now more than ever, it is imperative that you become familiar with the places and things most important to teens. Teens like the comfort and softness of their beds and pillows and the warm, relaxed atmosphere that allows them to listen to music ... igning a ... elements ... because ... oming to ... ot neces- ... Central ... pal Mike ... gensen go by the philosophy, "It's not about us (the adults), it's about them (the kids)." See more about their philosophy and their library in chapter 6.

Creating the ultimate space for teenagers means looking for alternatives, being creative, and resisting the temptation to go with what adults like or with traditional library furnishings, ideas, and policies. It's about searching for something a little different and making teens feel at home. A good teen-inspired design includes a place for them to study comfortably as well as an area for them to hang out and do the things they like to do such as talk, listen to music, and have fun. After studying the places where teens hang out, solidify your teen perspective by browsing through teen magazines, retail catalogs geared toward adolescents, and teen-related websites. Also take a look at a few general decorating and design resources such as television design shows and decorating-related websites, books, and magazines. This will give you the much-needed design perspective and a basic understanding of decorating principles, materials, and concepts. (See appendixes C and D for sample resources and vendors.)

GIVE TEENS OWNERSHIP OF THEIR SPACE

Tekamah (Nebraska) Carnegie Public Library knew that, at a glance, a teenager had no clue where he or she belonged at their 1916 facility. "While we moan and groan that our kids reach junior high age and grow away from us, we have, in fact, failed to provide a specific place or resources for their academic and recreational nourishment," said Kay Appleby, youth librarian. "What happened to our young adults? They came regularly to our story hours, loved our summer reading programs and had wonderful reading appetites until they reached junior high. We watched this age group leave us with regret, but without a peep, hoping they would return as adult readers one day," adds Appleby. So how did Tekamah get teens in to the library? Here is their formula for teen success:

Step 1: Clean, paint and clear an 11 × 13 foot area in the lower level of the building for the new teen space. This area was originally an overflowing storeroom.

Step 2: Form a charter council of five teens and a part-time high school staff member.

Step 3: Ask teens for suggestions on the teen area. The teens selected a vibrant décor theme of purple, black, and lime green furnishings, as well as the name Teen Text for the space. The focal point is a lime flokati area rug which begs a good book and a floor pillow.

Step 4: Conduct a junior-senior high student survey at the local school asking what teens would like to see in reading materials, programs, and activities.

Before and after photos of Tekamah (Nebraska) Public Library's teen space, which was once an overflowing storeroom.

Once you have one or two ideas in mind, immediately discuss them and any potential concerns with your director. Talk about how the teen area or school library will coordinate with the rest of the library or school. Ask if it is acceptable for the space to differ from the main library or school in style and décor. Be very clear about what determines when a decorating scheme or design idea has surpassed what is permissible by your standards and the administration's standards. Once everyone is in agreement regarding these boundaries, get teens involved as soon as possible.

Teen Design Groups

Include teens in planning committees or focus groups involving the design of your space. (See chapter 1 for recruitment ideas.) Although the number of teens involved won't make or break a project, try to involve at least ten to twenty teens. As with anything else, include a variety of ages, library users and nonusers, and males and females. If you grab their attention and intrigue them at the first meeting, you won't have any problem getting them to come back. When scheduling meetings, be consistent (i.e., hold meetings the same day of the week and at the same time of day). Present a general written agenda for each session. Review the tasks at hand, presenting any ideas that have transpired since the previous meeting, and then open the floor to discussion. Depending on the size of the group and the topic, allow fifteen to thirty minutes for brainstorming. Because it's crucial to keep good records, assign one member to record the minutes of the meeting and another member to list the ideas from the brainstorming session on a board or large flipchart at the front of the room.

Following are a few ideas to help plan the meeting agendas. Depending on the size of the group and scope of the project, you might want to divide these meetings into multiple sessions.

QUICK TIP

Whenever possible, divide large groups into small work teams. Assign teams different tasks, and ask them to present their findings to the group. For consistency and fairness, let them know they will be expected to participate for the duration of the project.

MEETING 1: INTRODUCTION AND GROUND RULES

Explain the purpose and scope of the project, and ask teens what they would like to see in the library that would make them and their friends visit the library regularly. Prepare a PowerPoint presentation of other teen library spaces to begin educating them and inspiring them about possibilities. This meeting is crucial because it is your first chance to enlighten them and to let teens know that they are a vital part of the project and that you want them to freely express their ideas. It is a huge public relations opportunity as well as a prime chance to get them excited and educate them about today's libraries. Before moving ahead, lay the ground rules of the project so participants are clear about what's expected of them and outline the vision of the project and any limitations. Without a doubt, it will be easier to present guidelines at the outset rather than have to veto ideas once everyone is excited. At the end of the meeting, consider asking participants to create a collage of their ideas. Collages would consist of pictures that illustrate their

LIBRARY TEEN

Lounging in the comfy green chair
I sit around the clock
Books are everywhere
Right, left, all around
Aquarium in the entrance
Rocking chairs
You could enjoy

This library
Entertains and
Employees are nice too
Ne'er-do-wells

By Amanda, Josh, Chris, and Mellie, teen customers at the Fresno County Public Library, Clovis Regional Branch. Notice that the first letter of each line spells out *library teen*.

ideas. Sources may include magazines, the Web, furniture vendors as shown in appendix D, and teen spaces photos from the book's companion website. Have participants bring their work back to the next meeting to share with the group.

MEETINGS 2 AND 3: INSPIRATIONS

Have teens share their collages with the group. Share your collage and any additional inspirational resources you found. Ask for their opinions. For the next session, think about taping a series of decorating programs to show. The point here is to expose teens to a variety of resources to inspire them and give them options. At this point, you might also begin to discuss the location of the new space and any other immediate concerns or issues that have popped up.

MEETINGS 4 THROUGH 7: DESIGN AND DECORATING

Use these meetings as springboards for discussion of potential color schemes, furnishings, shelving, location, layout, other design and décor issues, as well as technology, etc. Limit discussion to one or two topics per meeting. Show samples or photos of furnishings, paint and other wall treatments, flooring, lighting, materials, accessories, and so forth, and have teens discuss or vote on what they like best. See appendix A for a sample Design Feedback Sheet. If you are working with a professional designer, have him or her visit the group, present ideas, and show samples. Planning buying trips would be another welcome component of these sessions.

MEETING 8: THE FINAL DESIGN

Present and discuss the final floor plan, renderings, models, furniture samples, etc. This would also be a good time to discuss the name of the new area, if applicable. (See the naming and signage section at the end of this chapter.)

MEETINGS 9 AND ON: COLLECTION DEVELOPMENT, PROGRAMMING, PROMOTION, AND MORE

Let teens be a part of what happens after the space is complete. Give them a voice in what materials will be included in their new space—books, graphic novels, magazines, music, movies, games, etc. Get them involved in program planning and implementing, marketing and promoting the space, and policy development. (Refer to chapters 5 and 7 for more ideas on this topic.)

When the Park Ridge (Illinois) Public Library redesigned their Young Adult Loft in 2007, they actively involved teens in the process. This group met several times to

TEEN PLANNING MEETING

The Park Ridge (Illinois) Public Library conducted a teen space planning meeting to jumpstart the design of their new teen area. The group consisted of nine middle school teens, two boys and seven girls. For the first part of the meeting, teens brainstormed what they liked in places they already hang out. Favorites included their bedrooms, coffee shops, and friends' houses. Then the group looked at seven pictures of various spaces captured from decorating and vendor websites and rated them using the Design Feedback Sheet found in appendix A. They judged the space on color, layout, furniture, and overall look and feel. After the meeting, the librarian prepared a written summary of the overall findings including a detailed breakdown of discussions by picture with the photo to the left of the notes.

For example: Teen comments on pictures they liked included "Looks comfy." "Looks cool." "Everything I love." "Love the floor rockers. Like the iChairs." "Maybe décor higher on walls?" "Maybe different color walls?" "Like contrasting colors and idea of having a rug." Comments from the least favored pictures included "Too open." "No warm colors." "Cramped." "Don't like long-backed chairs." "Don't like stripes." "Too much like school."

Opened in June 2007, the contemporary, coffee shop–like space called the Young Adult Loft overlooks the rest of the library.

Before photo of the Park Ridge (Illinois) Public Library's teen area.

Close-up of seating area and graphic novels. The 840-square-foot space is informally divided into task areas using strategic placement of furnishings and large shelving display units on casters.

brainstorm wants and likes for the room. They evaluated pictures of other teen rooms and developed a list of criteria for what the room should contain. They also reviewed the designer's proposals and gave feedback. Teens worked with the library director, head of reader services, and the young adult librarian who served as the redesign committee and oversaw all decisions about the room. Their head of maintenance did much of the work on the room and helped oversee and find any outside contractors. For more information, see the text box.

Kelly March, youth services librarian, formerly with the Corfu (New York) Free Library and currently at the Richmond (New York) Memorial Library, had a "Changing Spaces" theme for her teen summer program in Corfu. Each week the teens made a craft for their bedroom as well as worked on a total redesign of their less than 75-square-foot library space. March brought in an interior decorator to get them started thinking about colors, space, window treatments, and textures. The teens chose the colors and the Friends of the Library gave them a $100 budget. March reports that the kids were great and came in a couple of nights a week to get the project completed before school started. As things progressed, more kids wanted to help, and more adults were willing to contribute money to help with the finishing touches (chairs and a lava lamp) and pizza and soda for the teens. Every teen that helped put their handprint on the end of the bookshelf with their signature. "It's amazing what can happen when part of the library is sectioned off and customers get to watch teens volunteering their time to improve their local library," says March. "This project was the catalyst for the library's teen advisory group," adds March.

Look and Feel

Unfortunately, although teen space design and decoration has advanced, many adults have not advanced in their understanding of library teen space. The most successful teen spaces have a teen look and feel. This means that the space is warm, inviting, and comfortable for teens. Teen space has an easiness about it; it's flexible in design and accommodates the overall program, promoting a variety of collections and activities. Equally important is understanding what teen look and feel is not. Teen space is not stuffy or rigid in design or service. Teen space is *not* necessarily synonymous with bright colors, beanbag chairs, and neon signs. It has evolved. It can be sophisticated as well as classic. There is no one style that defines teen design and décor—that is why it is critical to get teenagers involved in the process. When shown the possibilities and given the chance to contribute, teenagers will rise to the occasion and help create dynamic, teen-friendly spaces that meet their needs and wants as well as connect to the bigger picture of the library or school.

When developing a look and feel for your teen area, look at the entire library or school. What interesting features does it have? What colors and design elements come into play? What are the design and décor strengths and weaknesses? How can the teen design incorporate, improve, or enhance those elements? For example, does the library have stained or frosted color glass windows? If so, what colors does it include? How can these colors be incorporated into wall color for the teen area?

Public and school libraries across the county have positively demonstrated the variety of teen look and feel. For example, the Ames (Iowa) Public Library's 575-square-foot area spruces up plain white walls and creates warmth by incorporating color through furnishings, artwork, and area rugs. The Port Jefferson (New York) Free Library's Young Adult

Port Jefferson (New York) Public Library's Young Adult Center at Goodtimes opened in August 2007.

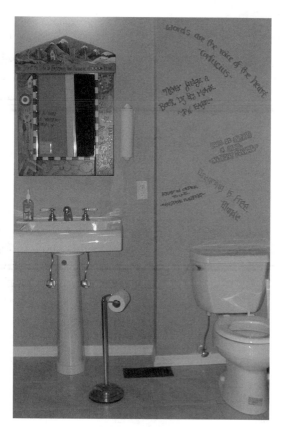

Even their bathroom is teen friendly.

A view from the inside looking out over the built-in shelves and chalkboard paint walls.

Center at Goodtimes resides across the street from the main library in a retail rental space. The teen area is a 620-square-foot room in the rear of the building. (The Friends of the Library occupy part of the front room with the teen services librarians—what a great example of adult-youth collaboration!) This eclectic space was designed collaboratively with teens, staff, and an architect. It includes maple wood, painted fluorescent lights as well as track lighting, two couches, three lounge chairs, four tables with chairs, and built-in shelving units with a large amount of display space. For a diverse portfolio of public library and school teen spaces refer to appendix E and the book's companion website.

Themes

A theme is a main idea that provides focus for a space Themes can be direct or subtle, serious or whimsical. Whatever your theme is, it will say something about the people

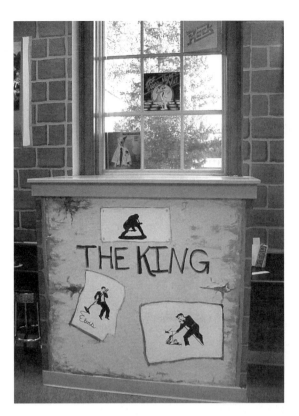

The Teen Beat–themed space was designed and implemented by teen customers at Deschutes (Oregon) Public Library's Redmond Branch.

for whom the space is designed. The possibilities for themes are endless. However, there is one small caution: stay away from trendy themes that involve concepts that will date quickly or involve permanent or costly items. Although it is important to choose something that teens will like, it is equally important to work with an idea that will endure the test of time (or at least last until you can afford to revamp the teen area again). Trendy ideas and elements are definitely a double-edged sword because it's no secret that *trendy* attracts most teens. Therefore, don't disregard that which is all the rage; instead, turn it around and think of ways to mix in the practical and long-lasting. Teens and staff at the Deschutes (Oregon) Public Library's Redmond Branch incorporated a successful musical theme in their Teen Beat space. The jukebox entrance, retro musical theme, and teen-created mural all work to create a unique space that can easily and affordably be transfigured in the future.

Be prepared for the theme of your teen area to be influenced by the overall style or décor of the library facility. Many times a library may have specific guidelines for renovation or interior decoration.

When investigating thematic options for your space, consider more subtle elements such as three-dimensionality. Incorporate a variety of 3-D objects into a one-dimensional mural; hang items from the ceiling or, even better, mount them directly on the ceiling. Use everyday, fun objects as pieces of sculpture—big and small. Focus on images and elements based on their shape, not their context. Include them in the space because of the similarity in the way they look, not for their continuity in meaning (or vice versa for an entirely different look). Another idea would be to use repetition throughout the space. Display a shape, an idea, or a popular motif (a repeated figure in a design) over and over again in different combinations, sizes, and colors. Color in itself could be thematic. Incorporate various shades and hues through different mediums. This is a highly effective method for adding personality and life to any space simply by being imaginative with paint and accessories. Notice that these ideas can be easily updated and changed from year to year without tremendous budgetary impact. No matter what approach you take, it is essential that you involve teens in this entire process because you might think you have the best idea in the world, but teenagers might have a totally different opinion.

DECORATING 101

Teenagers and their interests and tastes can be impulsive and unpredictable. Therefore, it is imperative that libraries decorate for teens in a versatile, interesting, and persuasive way. To be fully effective in achieving the goal of creating the ideal teen area and meeting teen needs, educate yourself about decorating concepts and practices. Pass along this information to teens so they too can make well-informed decorating decisions for their library space.

John Toppe, architect with Toppe Consultants Inc. (Florida) works with a lot of public school media centers and finds he is often challenged with beige rectangles with standard school carpet, acoustical ceilings, fluorescent lighting and sturdy uncomfortable furniture. "Very often furniture, flooring, colors, accent lighting, and graphics are suggested (if not actually chosen) by teens through focus group meetings. When given a choice, teens suggest colorful sofas, booths for group projects, and computers with clusters of chairs. With a modest additional budget, enhancements such as themed graphics, neon and display walls can be customized and incorporated. Acoustical treatment and isolation are also essential as is a lot of glass to assure visibility and a sense of supervision," says Toppe.[2]

To get teens involved, coordinate a series of field trips to other libraries with teen spaces, a mall, local bookstore, home remodeling center, a paint/wallpaper shop, or furniture store. On each trip, have each teen carry a clipboard that includes a simple questionnaire appropriate for each space visited. If possible, hand out disposable cameras so they can take pictures. If funds are short, have small groups share a camera. Have teens answer each questionnaire completely. The kinds of questions on each questionnaire will vary depending on the purpose of your visit. Refer to appendix A for a sample questionnaire. When visiting teen spaces or local stores, ask questions such as items 1 through 5. When visiting stores to pick out materials, have teens make note of specific items they liked. (See questions 6 through 8 in the sample questionnaire.) Give them guidelines and be clear about what you want. Collect questionnaires at the end of each trip and have a trustworthy teen volunteer compile the results to be presented and discussed at the next focus group or advisory meeting. (Count all design meetings and field trips as young adult programs.)

Design Tools

Having the proper design tools readily and easily available is an important part of successfully planning and designing a space. Begin by creating a design file to store all the information and ideas you have gathered. In fact, you may find that parts of the file, if you had started it at the onset of the planning stages, could be used as a visual enhancement in your proposal. The purpose of a design file is to help you organize the project. It is an excellent way to illustrate ideas to architects, consultants, decision makers, and teens and is invaluable for making purchases and staying on top of the entire decorating phase of the project.

THE FILE

The physical file or container can be almost anything—a three-ring binder (items may be hole punched when appropriate, topics can be separated with tabbed dividers, and file pocket may be inserted), an accordion-style folder with pockets, or a medium-sized file box with dividers. Use a tool or a combination of tools that suit your personal working style and the style of your teen collaborators, can be easily transported and simply organized, and can accommodate a variety of samples and ideas. Also consider creating a design kit that will hold essential design tools such as a tape measure, notes, pens and pencils, and a writing tablet, paper clips, and a variety of envelopes for quick storage of samples and other small items.

Include the following items in your design file:

the latest floor plan

pictures of the space, including before shots and photographs throughout the course of the project from all angles

inspirational items: colors, textures, photos, images, and ideas (Include pictures from magazines, photocopies or scanned images from books, Internet printouts, and photographs of other inspirational teen spaces including library spaces, stores at the mall, and favorite teen hangouts.)

samples of paint, wallpaper, fabric, flooring, and finishes (Staple or tape a small section of the sample to a piece of cardboard or cardstock for easy, organized access.)

a calendar to keep track of important dates and deadlines

DESIGN BOARDS

A design board is a tool used to display a collection of samples, photographs, or images of the actual materials being used on a project including color schemes, furnishings, finishes, fabrics, wall coverings, flooring, and shelving. (Professionals often refer to this as a presentation board or a color board.) Most are presented on 36-inch-wide × 24-inch-high boards because they are easy to store, transport, and handle. Smaller, 8½ × 11 inch or 20 × 30 inch boards are fine too. Large projects may require several boards. Materials such as foam board, illustration board or gator board will work best. Images and photographs can be dry mounted, and samples can be applied with almost any type of glue or double-sided foam tape.

QUICK TIP

Create an e-design file using tools such as Google Docs, Flickr, etc. Start a teen space design blog to post images, foster discussion, and collect input.

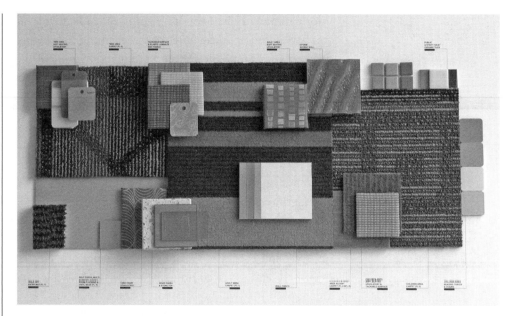

Design board courtesy of Integrated Design Group (New York) and Queens (New York) Library.

Ask a teen volunteer to assist in constructing the board. Consider creating mini-boards for the decorating file. If you are using the presentation board to make large group presentations, a larger format is most effective. Design boards are excellent tools for presenting decorating plans to staff, administration, and teens at focus group and planning meetings. A professional designer should include this service in their contract.

Focal Point

Once you have determined your overall design and style, start thinking about establishing a focal point—something that will serve as the heart of the area, ultimately tying the space together. To begin, think of the plans for the area and the existing features of the space, as well as current and future elements. What are or will be the most impressive components of the space? Your focal point should be the first thing that people notice when entering. It should also be something interesting to look at and something that will accentuate the area's best qualities. Many times a focal point will be the largest element, but it could also be anything from a window to a piece of furniture to an entire wall. It could even be a breathtaking view. As you proceed with this process, consider the other elements of the area (walls, ceilings, floors, color, lighting, furniture, fixtures, accessories, and layout). They will work together to frame the focal point.

Walls and Ceilings

No rule says that walls and ceilings have to be white or boring. You might consider painting the ceiling the same color as the walls or, for a completely different effect, go a shade lighter. Since many libraries have suspended ceilings, attempting to be creative with ceilings might be somewhat of a challenge. For those who are lucky enough to have a drywall ceiling, try something different with paint, decorative (and functional) baffles, or 3-D objects. Wallpaper borders and other wall graphic products are another easy and inventive way to enliven walls and ceilings. (See appendixes C and D for resources and vendors.) Create your own borders and oversized graphics with teens by cutting out designs from scrap wallpaper, magazines, or whatever comes to mind and then attach them directly to walls and ceilings. If your library has high ceilings and you want them to appear lower, create the illusion of a lower ceiling by placing a wallpaper border or wide color stripe directly on the wall several inches below the ceiling, or paint the ceiling a darker shade of the wall color. By the same token, you can create the illusion of a higher ceiling by placing a border or stripe at the very top of the wall where it meets the ceiling or by painting the ceiling a light shade (but not necessarily white).

COLOR

Whether addressing the topic of walls, ceilings, floors, or furnishings, one of the easiest and most dramatic ways to create an impact in a space is to use color and texture effectively. Both elements reflect personality, mood, and interest, setting the scene for any area. Don't be afraid of color and texture, especially when it comes to decorating for teenagers. Choose colors and textural items that excite and motivate you and your teen partners. At the same time, consider the surrounding library or school facility. Play off of surrounding color and textures.

Color represents energy, and energy is a necessary component of the ideal teen space. School planning expert Sheri Thompson says:

> Choice of color can either enhance or impair learning. Generally, red and orange are stimulating, yellow is cheery, and blues and greens are calming. Warm and cool colors make people perceive temperature differently, either warmer or cooler as their name implies. In addition, cool dark colors seem to recede, whereas bright warm colors seem closer. Libraries don't need to be dreary, dull spaces. Actually, using color to warm and brighten these spaces encourages students to read. Walls and stacks lined with books can be energized with the use of colorful wall graphics. Frequently, libraries also contain computers, so remember to select colors that help reduce glare and eyestrain.[3]

Betsy Ricciarelli at Lucas Stefura Interiors who worked with staff and teens on their renovation project at the Leominster (Massachusetts) Public Library says, "I like to throw some tasty colors in like greens, plums and tangerines—with touches of black. The laminate for the diner tables is my favorite—Formica Atomic Orange!"

Color can have an impact. It can also assist with the proportions of a space, making it feel bigger or smaller than what it truly is. To give the illusion of a larger space, use a monochromatic, light, cool-color scheme or patterns with small print. Blue is a good choice when attempting to increase the feeling of space. Use dark, bold, warm colors or prints to create a cozy feel. Produce a similar comfortable feeling by choosing the same color (something other than white) for both the walls and the ceiling. The greater the contrast in color, the smaller and cozier the room will look. To make a ceiling look higher, use white paint or a

QUICK TIP

If you simply cannot get away from white walls and white ceiling, experiment with a palette of bright colors for trim work, accents, and accessories such as posters, wall graphics, and area rugs.

light color. The more intense a color, the more it is noticed. You can add a glaze or glossy finish to a surface to make a color look even brighter.

When choosing colors, don't be afraid to experiment with multiple shades and patterns, but be cautious about choosing too many colors for a single space or it could result in an unbalanced effect. (A maximum of three colors for each space is good practice.) It can also be fun to explore different avenues by mixing your own paint colors, keeping in mind that it's easiest to mix colors in the same color family. Before making any final selections, always view wall colors and treatments vertically against the wall and floor colors and treatments flat on the floor. Look at the samples at various times of the day and evening to make sure the patterns and colors work well in the space at all times. When using a fabric swatch to help determine wall color, the background color of the fabric is generally a good choice. A lesser, even more predominant, color in the swatch would be a better choice for accents or furnishings. And, remember, when it comes to color, a can of color paint costs the same as a can of white paint. The more you learn about the benefits of color and how it can breathe life into a space, the more difficult it will be to accept the traditional library idea of white walls, white ceilings, and white everything.

QUICK TIP

If you're on a tight budget, ask your local hardware or home store to donate the cans of clearance paint—the paint that people returned.

TEXTURE

Texture pulls a space together, stimulates the eye, adds depth to an ordinarily flat space, and creates an exciting and interesting overall effect—exactly what the ideal teen area needs. Texture also provides variety and contrast and accents the colors and overall feel of the space. It can be introduced to an area through wall treatments, fabric, carpeting, and elements such as wood, tile, glass, and metal. Such elements not only add texture but also convey atmosphere. For instance, due to its tone and grain, wood suggests a warm and cozy feeling. In contrast, hard, glossy finishes can impart a more modern feeling. When incorporating texture into a teen area, consider what textural elements could be incorporated to better convey it. Textural variety can be achieved in so many ways, including flooring, fabric selection, and faux painting. Select items with interesting surfaces and fabrics and you'll never go wrong.

The Oxford (Michigan) Public Library's 1,200-square-foot teen space presents a good mix of interesting colors (plum, purple, sage green, and sunshine yellow) and textures. The contemporary design has an organic feel with spiral designs throughout for a retro-modern twist. The area is carpeted in five complementary patterns, including a spiral, two geometrics, and a solid. There is a curved soffit above the shelving with track lighting on both sides. Most walls are curved to emphasize the spiral concept, one wall is brick, and one wall has three sheets of spiral patterned Plexiglas. The furniture is very versatile and movable. Curved sectional seating upholstered in spirals can be rearranged to make new seating groupings. Curving triangular shaped tables topped with yellow and purple Marmoleum interlock to make larger tables. Comfortable chairs are on casters and there is a café table and a large computer table with ergonomic purple computer chairs. Three skylights, can lights, fluorescent lights, and halogen track lighting with occasional blue or green glass shields light the space. There is shelving on casters that step up to follow

Overview of the teen area at Oxford (Michigan) Public Library. Going from a 180-square-foot space to a 1,200-square-foot space completed in December 2005, this area presents excellent use of color, texture, and flexibility in overall design.

the curve of the soffit and face out shelving for new books and magazines. See the photos of Oxford Public and figure 4.2 to see how their new teen space increased circulation statistics during and after the renovation.

Figure 4.2   Teen Circulation Statistics, 2005–2007, Oxford (Michigan) Public Library

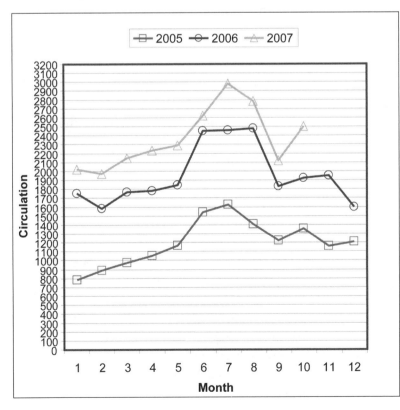

Don't put off color and texture decisions until the end of the project; start collecting ideas and samples right away. Look for images and items that decoratively motivate you and your teen collaborators. Ideas could originate from a picture in a magazine, a swatch or sample, a crayon, or maybe even from a preexisting element in the library. Keep samples, swatches, and photos of inspirational items readily available when shopping or meeting with vendors or designers.

Paint and Other Treatments

Since paint is inexpensive, easy to apply, and easy to change, it is the most common decorative finish used in design projects. Paint can completely transform a room in minutes. Paint finishes and techniques are numerous and can be used for walls, furniture, ceilings, and even floors. Using special techniques such as stenciling, sponging, color washing, rag rolling, combing, stippling, pouncing, dragging, and mural painting are also great

COLOR GUIDE

Colors can convey a wide range of feelings, ideas, and meanings. When choosing a color scheme, plan creatively. To do this, it's important to acquire a basic awareness of the nuances of color and the effects that can be created with it. Here's a quick guide:

Red, yellow, blue are known as primary colors. They cannot be produced from a combination of other pigments.

Secondary colors are a result of mixing two primary colors. That is, red and yellow make orange; yellow and blue make green; blue and red make purple or violet.

Colors beyond primary and secondary colors are known as tertiary colors.

Complementary colors are those colors that are opposite each other on the color wheel. For example, red is a complement to green, and yellow is a complement to purple and vice versa. (Color wheels can be readily located in many paint and decorating books and web pages.)

Neutrals include white, black, variations of gray, and beige tones.

Yellow, red, and orange are considered warm, lively colors.

Blue, green, and violet/purple are regarded as cool, calm colors.

Soft colors generally relay quiet contemplation, sophistication, and relaxation.

Bright colors normally stimulate and communicate a modern and playful mood.

ways to add interest, color, and texture. Treatments such as wallpaper and professional design graphics are usually more expensive and can be more difficult to apply than paint, but they have the potential for creating tremendous impact. A similar concept to wallpapering, decoupage (the art or technique of cutting out pictures or designs from paper or other material and applying them to a surface) is a method for adding bursts of color and interesting detail to a space. Unlike wallpaper, it is relatively inexpensive and can be applied to practically any surface. Regardless of the treatment, always think in terms of the desired style and atmosphere of the space, and never be confined to one technique, pattern, or color.

PAINTING

Paint is readily available in thousands of colors, and can be applied to most any surface as long it is appropriate for the surface and the surface is prepared properly. Plan to make a final paint decision in conjunction with the other elements of the teen area (flooring, fabrics, and furnishings). When selecting a paint color, have your design file handy so you can easily refer to swatches from the other elements of the room. If you don't have a professional with whom to consult, ask a salesperson at the hardware, paint, or home improvement store for advice. In addition to giving helpful paint tips, many of these stores also offer custom color mixing, which enables a customer to bring in just about any color reference and have paint mixed to match. Websites are another easy resource for general paint information and advice. For more details, see appendixes C and D.

As with any wall, fabric, or floor treatment, before making a final decision about a paint color, it is wise to do the following:

1. Tape a selection of your favorite paint chips directly on the wall in the teen area. A strip of paint chips is generally best because there are multiple shades of a color on one card. This is helpful in viewing underlying tones and providing a good overall assessment of the color.

2. Once the selection is narrowed down, purchase sample bottles or pints of your colors, and paint test patches on the wall in the teen area (generally a 12- or 48-inch square will do). For a less permanent test, paint the same size square on a board, and hang the board on the wall. This test will provide a true idea of what the colors will look like in their environment. When testing paint (or

any decorating element for that matter), it is important to live with it for a few days to make certain it looks the way you want it to look. Remember that the larger the painted area, the more intense the color will seem.

3. Make sure the paint dries thoroughly before approving or rejecting it. Paint always looks different when it's wet than when it's dry.

4. Always double check paint colors against the other elements of the space, including fabric samples and floor coverings.

5. When the sampling is over, if the color is not right for the space, simply choose another color and try again.

Paint color alone can be a pretty powerful decorating tool, oftentimes perfectly conveying the theme of a space and providing a brilliant end result, but for those times when the area demands something beyond color or a bit more unusual, consider trying a special painting technique. Blackboard or magnetic paint can turn a wall or part of a wall into a nonpermanent canvas for teen creativity. Fluorescent paint or metallic finishes might be a bit too much for an entire room but work well as accents. Sponging, rag rolling, crackling, and stenciling are all great for adding texture and interest to any space. They are also excellent for concealing imperfections on walls and furnishings alike. (Refer to appendix C for helpful decorating resources and appendix D for a selection of vendors.)

Once a paint color and technique are chosen, estimate how much paint you will need to complete the job. Multiply the length of each wall by its height and add the products of all walls to find the total number of square feet. Divide the total square feet by the number of square feet a gallon of paint will cover to determine the number of gallons needed for one coat. Theoretical coverage per gallon is 200 to 400 square feet, but oftentimes first coats and primers may only cover 150 to 200 square feet. Be sure to consult your paint label for specifics. It's more than likely that two coats of paint will be necessary, and three coats may be required depending on the color choice and condition of the walls. Take into consideration that this method of figuring gallons needed may differ slightly if you are applying a faux finish or using a special painting technique.

MURAL ART

A mural is a painting that exists on a large, permanent surface. Murals can be full wall panoramas or a series of smaller images throughout a space. Although usually applied to large surfaces such as walls, ceilings, and floors, mural art can also work well on furniture, doors, and steps. The key is to work with teen volunteers or art students to create your masterpieces. One mural style is trompe l'oeil (a French term that means "to fool the eye"), which creates the optical illusion that painted objects really exist, instead of looking like a two-dimensional painting. For example, if there aren't any windows in your teen area or school library, you could paint a corner of the space to look like there is a window or a gaping hole through which you can see what's outside the building.

An overhead projector is an excellent tool for mural projects; it enlarges the images so they can be traced and then painted. Have students create their drawings in art class and then transfer the images to transparencies and project them on the walls, ceiling, etc. This will allow you to be creative with placement and size before anything is permanently painted. Once it's been determined where the images will reside, students can trace the art in pencil and then paint it. Freehand work is always an option as long as the idea is well planned and the images are penciled in before painting.

If permanence is an issue, create paintings on a large, stretched canvas or boards and hang them on the walls or from the ceiling or at the end of shelving ranges. Again, this has potential for a class project or an after-school art club undertaking. Have teens work with the teacher to develop a theme or a general idea for the mural. Each student can be responsible for developing a different piece of the mural. Always have a long-range plan for your murals (and other decorative elements). Colors will fade, ideas and themes will become old, and the teens that created the art will grow up and move on. Regularly updating the artwork and involving new teens in art projects is a great way to add excitement and interest and keep your teen area up-to-date.

WALLPAPER AND WALL GRAPHICS

Wallpaper is traditionally more expensive and time consuming to apply than paint, but it is also a terrific decorating tool that can dramatically change a room's appearance overnight. Like textured paint and various painting techniques, wallpaper is great for covering up a multitude of imperfections or an existing wall treatment that is less than desirable. If the walls of the teen area are covered with paneling and it's out of the question to remove it and redo the walls, then wallpaper could be the option for you (although paint works well in this situation too). If you like the look of wallpaper but are on a limited budget, consider wallpapering one wall as an accent wall or use wallpaper borders as a less expensive alternative to wallpapering an entire room. Consider asking teens to make their own wallpaper by cutting out shapes or images and decoupaging them to the wall either in a fixed pattern or in a collage style.

Other options include decal applications such as adhesive vinyl wall graphics and letters. These self-adhesive, removable decals allow anyone to quickly and easily create decorative patterns or custom wall murals. The Santa Monica (California) Library worked with teens once the new Teen Lounge was open to choose temporary wall art to coordinate with the carpet motif. As with paint, choices can be overwhelming. When selecting and ordering wallpaper or wall graphics, keep the following in mind:

Color and pattern will always be the most important deciding factors.

Consider products that are durable, washable, and easy to apply.

Collect a variety of samples and take them back to the teen area to tape on the wall. This will give you an idea of what the colors and patterns will look like in their new environment.

Large-print wallpaper and graphics will make a room seem cozier.

Vertical patterns make ceilings seem higher.

In old buildings, the walls, windows, and doors are often not plumb or perfectly straight. This makes wallpapering more difficult, so try to stay away from vertical patterns in these instances.

Before ordering wallpaper or graphics make sure to carefully and accurately measure the area.

Wallpaper is sold in double-roll bolts, but measuring and ordering are done by single-roll increments, generally 15 feet long. Roll width varies from 20½ inches to 35 inches. Make sure all the rolls have the same lot number. Before hanging the paper, always compare the color of rolls to make sure they match. For best adhesion, use diluted paste when hanging pre-pasted paper. Begin hanging wallpaper in the most inconspicuous corner and work around the space in one direction.

With wall graphics and letters, beware of more complicated designs. They can be tricky if you don't follow the instructions.

For helpful resources on selecting wallpaper and other wall treatments, see appendix C.

Computers and Blik wall graphics in the Santa Monica (California) Public Library's Teen Lounge

Floors

The flooring found in most libraries is fairly typical of business flooring. It's made to be durable and to hide the dirt as much as possible. Flooring options include but aren't limited to carpet (preferably carpet squares), hardwood, laminate, vinyl, recycled rubber, cork, painted or polished concrete, and area rugs. If you are constructing a new facility, define the teen area or school library using a different color or patterned carpet or flooring treatment from the rest of the facility. Carpet tiles are a good option if there are concerns about future stains and wear because individual tiles can easily be replaced. Also, if designed properly, tiles laid out in a pattern will do wonders for hiding dirt and wear. Overall, carpeting is a good choice for a teen area because it lends itself to imagination, and it is definitely the most comfortable of floor treatments. (Teens need the option to be able to spread out on the ground.)

If you're looking for an alternative to carpet or you're considering using a combination of flooring types based on different function areas, consider recycled rubber, laminate, vinyl, or polished concrete. Area rugs are another great option when working solely with hard surface flooring or when trying to define a functional area such as a soft seating area. Besides making great accent pieces, area rugs are affordable, add color and variety, and can be used in conjunction with any other type of floor treatment. You can also easily make your own area rugs by painting canvas or using carpet remnants. (See text box for more details.) To prevent tripping, always firmly secure area rugs with carpet tape.

As with any flooring type, consider the following elements when making a selection:

Overall look and design. Does the flooring match the space and the overall concept?

Functionality and flexibility. Is the flooring appropriate for the various functions that will occur in the space such as computing (chairs on casters), sitting on the floor, events and programming, eating and drinking?

Cleaning and maintenance. What is involved in daily, monthly, and annual maintenance? Are there special cleaners or solutions that need regular application? Do you need to purchase additional supplies or equipment (e.g., rotary machine) to care for the floor? All of these add to the expense of the flooring.

MAKING AREA RUGS

A number of libraries have created painted canvas area rugs for their teen areas. They are durable and very affordable. To find larger pieces of canvas, visit your local hardware store or art supplies store. Once you have your canvas, fold the edges underneath and fasten with a heavy-duty tape. Next, use a roller to paint on a coat of primer or gesso and allow it to dry overnight. Once the primer has dried completely, paint your base coat. Note that darker colors and patterns will hide dirt better. Once that has dried, paint your design over the base coat. Look to area rug vendors online to get design and pattern ideas. A great resource for design inspirations and ideas are design television shows and websites.

On HGTV, designers Kitty Bartholomew and David Dalton demonstrate how to make a custom rug out of a carpet remnant. They suggest using a tight-weave carpet, not a shag, loop, or berber, to keep raveling to a minimum.

- Decide on the shape and draw it onto several sheets of butcher paper that have been taped together.

- Turn the carpet face down and trace around the template with permanent markers. (Tape the template to the carpet with double-stick tape, if necessary.)

- Be sure to work on a surface that can't be damaged with a utility knife. With the knife (use a new blade) cut around the shape, then turn it over and trim the raw edge with scissors. (Or, have it professionally bound.)

- If you wish to add a second color (for example, a flower center), cut a template for the second piece and cut the shape out of the appropriate area on the rug already cut. Then cut out the second color and fit it into the first, securing it with carpet tape. Use double-stick carpet tape to keep the new rug in place on the floor.[4]

Safety. Is the flooring slip resistant? Are there any issues with transitions and tripping hazards between multisurface flooring (i.e., transitions from carpet to hard surface)?

Price. What is the overall price per square foot? What other items add to the pricing? If using carpeting, does it include padding? Are installation fees included? Are there any other fees involved? Are there any long-term maintenance products and equipment that need to be purchased?

See appendix E for a complete listing of all the *Teen Spaces* resource libraries.

Furniture

Furniture can make or break a teen area (or entire library, for that matter), and it should rank high on your list of priorities for teen space design. Teens certainly have a great deal to say about furniture and this is distinctly reflected in their ideas and feelings about library spaces. This is an exciting time for teenagers in the library as well as in the furniture marketplace. Similar to libraries, more and more furniture companies are looking to teenagers and what they need and want; as a result, many new lines have been developed specifically for this age group. More choices mean more inspirational, inviting, and unique spaces for today's libraries.

In Wanda Higgins's article, "What Do Young Adults Want in Their School Library?" she mentions first and foremost, "The library should be a place with comfortable furniture and a welcoming atmosphere, where students can feel safe, secure, and relaxed."[5] She suggests that the school library should have areas designated for different functions, and it's important that one of those areas be a place with overstuffed chairs, pillows, and low tables—a place where they can lie on the floor and stretch out like they do at home. In *Designing a School Library Media Center for the Future,* Rolf Erikson and Carolyn Markuson add:

> Certainly one must look for sturdy and serviceable library furniture, but these attributes can be as easily found in furniture that is pleasing to the eye as they can in furniture that is mundane. Some library planners advocate buying plain, sturdy, serviceable furniture . . . arguing that contemporary design will soon go out of fashion . . . but good design is timeless.[6]

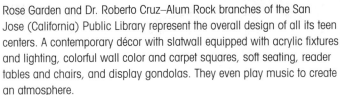

Rose Garden and Dr. Roberto Cruz–Alum Rock branches of the San Jose (California) Public Library represent the overall design of all its teen centers. A contemporary décor with slatwall equipped with acrylic fixtures and lighting, colorful wall color and carpet squares, soft seating, reader tables and chairs, and display gondolas. They even play music to create an atmosphere.

Several model libraries reported that having comfortable soft seating, study tables that are large enough to spread out at, and task chairs that are comfortable enough to sit in for long periods of time are essential. Being able to sit comfortably on the floor is equally important. Take a look at what the San Jose (California) and the St. Louis (Missouri) Public Libraries have done at their branches: as part of an extensive system-wide branch expansion program in San Jose, they've replaced old cramped buildings with lively and attractive spaces, including enclosed dedicated teen centers. St. Louis redesigned teen spaces at several of their branches through funding from a Library Services and Technology Act (LSTA) grant from the Missouri State Library. See photos in this chapter and the companion website for more images.

Shelving

A number of items fall under this category: shelving units, paperback spinners, display racks, freestanding and mobile display units. Once you know how many shelves you need in the space (refer to chapters 2 and 3), start thinking about how each will decoratively fit into the space. For example, traditional metal library shelves can be combined with lift-up shelves for magazines, end-of-the-range displays for merchandising, and bookstore-like units such as slant shelving and zigzag shelving. If new shelving is out of the question, try painting your existing shelves with a good quality metal paint; in fact, the end panels are great places for murals. If you have the budget, go for something completely different. For example, the Phoenix Public Library's shelves are 66 inches high and made of fiberglass and stainless steel. The fiberglass shelves are yellow, orange, and grape to coordinate with the rest of the room. (Refer to chapter 5 and to appendix D for fixture tips and vendors.)

Walnut Park Branch (before)

Baden Branch (before)

Walnut Park Branch (after)

Baden Branch (after)

The Walnut Park Branch of St. Louis (Missouri) Public Library went from having no defined teen space to 70 square feet. The Baden Branch grew to 180 square feet.

Criteria

When selecting new furnishings including shelving for a teen area, consider the following:

Appearance and style. Choose items that enhance the overall design of the space. Look for products that are welcoming. Look to a variety of suppliers for options. (See appendix D for suggestions.) Don't settle for only what you see in catalogs, especially when it comes to library vendors. Ask what other options are available; you'd be amazed at what's out there.

Comfort. Teens want comfortable furniture for hanging out as well as for computing, studying, reading, etc. Consider ergonomics, size of furnishings, distance between furnishings, and fabric options, all of which play a role in comfort.

DESIGN

The Kent District (Michigan) Library wanted its eighteen branches, whether small, medium, or large, old, new or in-between, to be great destinations. They developed the DESIGN method to implement design trends at all of their locations. They have successfully used this process not only in teen services, but also for signage, merchandising, library living rooms, early literacy, and senior services projects. The steps of the process are as follows:

Develop the philosophy or concept.

Establish a checklist.

Shop the library.

Introduce new elements (with an order list and funding initiative).

Grant funds to select, purchase, and install.

Now let the customers enjoy!

The idea behind this process is to

Educate staff about this trend, service, and design concepts.

Engage customers through surveys to determine what types of improvements to make to enhance the library environment. In terms of teens, focus groups were utilized to plan teen space.

Involve staff in providing feedback to improve or reassess the ideas.

Make things easy for staff and energize them by providing simple tools such as checklists (they used the Teen Spaces Checklist from the first edition of *Teen Spaces* for their teen checklist) and order lists. See the figure below as well as the Shopping Order Form Template in appendix A.

Utilize teamwork to create peer teams to visit branches and complete checklists.

Provide funding options such as grants or matching grants and standard budgets for each branch.

Share customer comments and before and after photographs with the public, staff, and boards and administration.

Visit the book's companion website at www.ala.org/editions/extras/Bolan09690 for a complete teen space order form sample and for photos and more information about Kent District Library.

Sample Teen Shopping Order Form   Library: _____

	Quantity	Color (circle)	Item	Vendor	Cost
<Insert item description here>					
<Insert image of item here>	<This is where staff insert quantity ordered>		<insert item name here>	<insert vendor URL here>	<insert item price here>

Functionality and portability. Take into account the variety of activities that will take place in the space. Does the furniture accommodate them? Can furnishings be easily moved and rearranged to accommodate a variety of setups and functions?

Durability and maintenance. If all goes as planned, your space will get a lot of use, so plan for items that can withstand heavy use with little maintenance. Avoid poorly constructed products. This is why testing furniture before purchasing is so critical. When purchasing products you want to last, make sure upholstery or fabric is durable. Use the fabric *double-rub* rating to guide you. In general, fabric for commercial spaces would not be less than 100,000 double rubs. Fabrics with a lower double-rub rating can often be treated with a seating protection product such as Gore to increase their life. Items should be easy to clean and reupholster if necessary. Consider treating furniture or fabric with an antimicrobial product. If you opt for more temporary furnishings, devise an annual plan for refurbishment or replacement. Be sure you have good product warranties. If warranties aren't satisfactory, don't be afraid to negotiate.

Safety. Avoid furniture and shelving with sharp edges and other potentially hazardous features. Also consider flammability standards.

Variety. When space allows, include a mixture of furniture including soft seating, tables with comfortable chairs, and small, portable pieces.

Price. Quality and price often go hand in hand in furniture and shelving, but this is not always the case. Examine a variety of products at an assortment of price points before making a decision. Ask for samples of the product so you can test them in the library. Acquire warranty and pertinent maintenance information to determine quality and true price.

Items need to be durable as well as functional and visually appealing. Opt for furniture that will look fresh and up-to-date for a significant period of time, and select items based on what teens are actually asking for, not on what you perceive they want. Pieces chosen should help define and enhance the theme or style of the area, not distract from it. Be wise with purchases, and don't be afraid to invest in good quality furniture. Making good choices now will help build a strong, long-lasting foundation for the space. See the photo of the Pablo Creek Branch of the Jacksonville (Florida) Public Library.

Bookstore-like shelving, portable seating, and a slew of interesting design elements enhance this teen area at the Pablo Creek Branch of the Jacksonville (Florida) Public Library. Photo courtesy of DesignGroup.

To get started, think back to those things teens most want in their library, the general nature of teens, and their love of lounging. A combination of both lounge-style seating and study furnishings is a requirement for the ideal teen area. No matter how small the space, there are nearly always ways to incorporate both. Adding comfortable furniture doesn't have to mean that you squeeze in a couch. If you are limited on space or funds, come up with alternative solutions like incorporating small, nontraditional library tables for studying and futons or butterfly chairs for lounging. If there is no possible way to fit in both types of seating, concentrate on comfort in the teen space proper and encourage studying in an adjacent area. Better yet, look around your library for a niche or room that doesn't get much use and transform it into a teen lounge. Keep in mind—it's all about being inventive and resourceful.

Tables and chairs traditionally designated as study furniture should be purchased with the intention that teens will use them to sit by themselves to study or to sit in small groups to work together. Study furnishings are a tricky topic because research indicates that teens prefer to study in comfortable furniture, but there are instances when they need traditional tables and chairs. Following are the most important things to keep in mind when selecting study furniture:

- Select chairs that are comfortable to sit in and tables that are easy to work at. When choosing computer furnishings, make sure they are easily accessible and ergonomically designed.

- Choose items that go along with the décor of the rest of the space. Select study furniture that complements the lounge-type furniture. For example, traditional, hardwood library furniture generally does not work well in a space with a contemporary design.

- Look to library vendors such as Gaylord, Brodart, DEMCO, or Highsmith, but also consult with nonlibrary vendors when making purchases. Home furnishing and large chain stores are great furniture resources. (See appendix D.) Also, don't forget about garage sales and consignment shops for low-cost, creative ideas.

SPACE STRETCHING

If you're short on space or simply want to make your teen area as flexible as possible, try one of these helpful space-stretching ideas.

- Purchase furniture, shelving, and display units that are on casters for easy portability.
- Mount small display fixtures at ends of shelving ranges and on windows, walls, or pillars with suction cups or heavy duty adhesive.
- If you're short on wall space, utilize windows or create wall space with portable room dividers.
- Create dimension and flexibility with small, portable fixtures such as crates or storage cubes that can be stacked and easily relocated within the area.
- Use the ceiling as much as possible. Suspend three-dimensional objects such as art and posters. Cut a piece of foam board to match the size of the item, dry mount the images on both sides of the foam, and suspend the board from the ceiling with the appropriate weight fishing line. The same principle applies to three-dimensional objects: attach the fishing line to the object and suspend it from the ceiling with hooks.
- Regularly weed the collection.

Accessories

Strategically integrate accessories and other decorative elements to enhance a teen area. These added extras are an easy and inexpensive way to add interest to any space. Include elements that energize the overall look and feel of the space. Accessories may include

Art. Whether purchased reproductions or teen-created originals, incorporating art into a teen space is an excellent way to create presence. It is also a great way to actively involve and draw teens into the library. When purchasing art, choose items that teens relate to and that complement the colors and style of the space. When working with teen-created art, the sky's the limit. Set aside a wall or corner of the area to serve as a gallery space. Consider laminating or dry mounting two-dimensional pieces and hanging with clips on a line (or a picture hanging system). For more of an art gallery feel, have art matted, purchase simple frames, and hang on a rail mount hanging system. Incorporate track lighting for a polished look. When incorporating sculpture, locate more fragile elements on top

Graffiti created by teens at Phoenix (Arizona) Public Library as part of urban art graffiti project.

Portrait by Charles Ward, teen patron of Phoenix Public Library.

The Terrazas Branch of the Austin (Texas) Public Library effectively accessorizes a small space.

of bookcases out of reach, or purchase a wall-mounted or freestanding showcase. Work with art teachers and volunteer the library to serve as a gallery for traveling art shows. Teen advisory board members curate the Kent District (Michigan) Library's East Grand Rapids Branch Teen Art Gallery, which features drawings, photos, and art created by local teens. The Peabody Institute Library at Peabody (Massachusetts) partners with their local school's art teacher to create rotating student art displays. The Phoenix (Arizona) Public Library framed and laminated a selection of teen-created urban art pieces and comics to travel around for display in teen areas in all their branches. See photos from Phoenix. For information on Phoenix Public Library's teen art programs, see chapter 5.

Sculpture and three-dimensional objects. Items may include teen works or everyday objects such as sports equipment, teen toys, fish tanks, and knickknacks.

Posters. Versatile and inexpensive, posters are affordable (or free if you work something out with your local video store or movie theater) and can be changed regularly to reflect new styles and interests. Use double-sided tape or frames to hang them on walls, on the ends of stacks, and even on the ceiling. Arrange posters at angles, overlapping in a collage, or side-by-side in a long row to create visual interest. Movie theaters are a great source of inspiration.

THE BOB

The Bob (or Robert Cormier Center for Young Adults) at the Leominster (Massachusetts) Public Library broke ground on its library renovation and expansion project in July 2005. The project took approximately two years to complete with its grand opening taking place in June 2007. One of the first libraries to create a model teen area during the late 1990s (see the first edition of *Teen Spaces*), Leominster staff and teens know how to accessorize to create a teen look and feel. "Both of my teen groups, the Red-Eye Writers and REACT (our high school book discussion group) were consulted at various points in the planning process for input and feedback on the new and expanded Bob," says Diane Sanabria, young adult services coordinator. One comment Leominster staff heard over and over again was "We're still going to have a loft, right?" (Their original teen area had a reading loft.) The architects rose to the occasion, creating a ramp leading to a raised platform lined with an assortment of accessories including

  large, comfortable body pillows

  shelving for board games and some books

  magnetic poetry panels

Other teen space accessories in the Bob include

  a scrolling electronic message board

  a collection of toys and knickknacks for the young adult librarian's desktop.

  console gaming

framed movie posters, an autographed poster of the Dropkick Murphys, and a "Death Note" manga scroll wall hanging

charcoal portrait of Bob Cormier created by local artist Louis Charpentier (it was a gift from Cormier's family)

a neon sign incorporating Cormier's actual signature

an inspirational quote from one of his newspaper columns that teens chose to have framed

a mural created by the students of the Leominster High School Art Club with their advisor/art teacher. It commemorates Cormier's life and work and features Leominster landmarks and his typewriter.

the Kit-Kat clock (This is an accessory from the former space that now hangs proudly by the new diner booths.)

The increase in teen circulation statistics at Leominster from 2000 to 2007 is quite dramatic. In 2000, total circulation for young adults was 5,415, compared to 27,953 items in 2007. (This even takes into account the fact that they were closed from April 16 through June 9, 2007, to move into the new building.) After the grand opening of the new Bob, total circulation from July through October 2007 was 16,406 items. See the book's companion website for additional photos.

Overview of Leominster (Massachusetts) Public Library's Bob opened in Summer 2007.

Close-up of the librarian's desk filled with toys and knick-knacks. Photos by Chris Brault.

Boards. Whether using tackable surface such as pinboard and corkboard or decorative boards such as magnet boards and whiteboards, these surfaces are decorative and functional. Use them in small areas or cover entire walls; they're perfect for posting teen art, photos, fliers, and teen-related information and provide a surface for magnetic poetry creations, creative writing, and even temporary graffiti. Consider combining multiple types of boards to create an interactive wall space.

Baskets, bins, and crates. Alternatives to traditional shelving and displays, they can serve as terrific accents for storing magazines, board games, and more. (These may not be sturdy, so consider collection type and weight.)

Wastebaskets and office supplies. The essentials: a place to throw trash and containers for pencils, pens, paper, staplers, tape, hole punch, markers, etc. The Gloucester Lyceum and Sawyer Free (Massachusetts) Library has a file cabinet designated as a school supply and game cabinet for use by teens only.

Miscellaneous items. Includes everything from clocks to mirrors to pillows.

Something Old, Something New

Looking at your discard versus keep list created in chapter 2, what are your plans in regard to new versus old furnishings and shelving? Are you considering reusing existing pieces? Is there something from another department or in storage that you'd like to relocate or revamp for the teen area? Even if your initial plans included all new purchases, you might change your mind after considering the possibilities for recycled furniture. If you are on a limited budget, it helps to be a scavenger. Look for things elsewhere in the library that could be transplanted to the teen area. Keep your eye out for items in unexpected places.

Reupholstering and adding a fresh coat of paint or finish can make items look like brand new, and these improvements can be quite affordable. Think about using leftover pieces from larger projects (e.g., countertops and carpet remnants). Giving life to old furniture can be a creative and rewarding undertaking for you and teen collaborators. Many would assume that furniture face-lifts are reserved for those on a small budget, but reusing fixed-up furniture can be equally beneficial for larger, well-funded organizations. It's all about tapping the imagination of teens and drawing on their talents to breathe life into old, tired furniture and fixtures. Teen services at the Newark (New York) Public Library thrives on teen imagination and revamping their space on a limited budget. Because of their thriftiness and creativity, they are able to regularly give their teen area a face-lift.

Tabletops are the perfect canvas for a mural or a collage. They can also be converted into game tables by purchasing or painting game boards on tabletops and protecting them with a custom-cut piece of glass or Plexiglas as they did at the Schaumburg (Illinois) Township District Library. Phoenix (Arizona) Public Library, the William K. Sanford Town Library (Loudonville, New York) and numerous other libraries were quite successful in using decoupage to revamp old tables. If you're stuck with soft seating that is dingy, dirty, worn out, and outdated, consider reupholstering items. Either budget to hire a professional or do it in-house with the assistance of teen partners and a local expert. A little fabric in the right colors and prints can give a space a whole new look. If money is tight, consider having one or two items done at a time.

Another option for fixing up old furniture is to collect pieces from flea markets, thrift shops, and garage sales. You might want to leave some things just as you bought them. Others will have to be touched up, painted, or decoupaged—whatever teens can dream up. Buying secondhand furniture is quickly gaining popularity with librarians who want to do something with their teen area but are on a limited budget. Even well-funded libraries have discovered that flea market finds can lead to great interactive projects for teens as well as add a lot of interest to teen spaces. What a great outing for a teen advisory council or focus group: spending a Saturday afternoon learning how to be resourceful and looking for the perfect bargain, with the idea that they will be able to use their creativity to turn the items into treasures for the new teen area. For other budget-conscious ideas, check with an organization such as Gifts in Kind International to find out about obtaining free furnishings, accessories, and supplies for nonprofit organizations. See appendix C.

Lighting

Lighting is one of those decorating elements that often gets overlooked. Most people do not immediately recognize the importance and effects of a good lighting plan. Lighting should be functional for studying and reading, but it also creates atmosphere, which directly affects the mood, appearance, and function of a space. For instance, lighting can play a key role in making a small room appear larger. If this is what you want in your library, plan on incorporating a combination of as much natural and artificial light as possible. Mirrors are also quite effective in creating the illusion of a large space. The Waupaca (Wisconsin) Public Library was quite creative in incorporating mirrors to create light and the illusion of more space in their 1,000-square-foot windowless teen area.

The center of the Waupaca (Wisconsin) Public Library's Best Cellar includes a large red and black sectional couch and numerous display options. A separate program room with a large-screen TV is attached to the space. It features cupboards, a refrigerator and microwave, and folding chairs and tables. The space also incorporates a booth with a listening dome, computers, gaming equipment, and furnishings.
(See the companion website for more photos.)

Reading is the most important task in libraries, so proper lighting is crucial. Good lighting design in library buildings is the result of both technical skill and art on the part of the designer. This is particularly true in newer buildings where visual tasks are more diverse and technology poses new types of lighting requirements.[7] A combination of lighting is generally used in library design including fluorescent, incandescent, high-intensity discharge, and natural light. In focus group discussions, teens often express a dislike for fluorescent lighting.[8]

Consider general, accent, and task lighting as well as the various functions to take place in the teen area. Different lighting solutions may be necessary for stacks, reading areas, lounge areas, computer spaces, and so on. Consideration should also be given to motion-activated lighting when appropriate. Fixtures may include

track lighting

recessed ceiling mounted lighting

pendant lights

wall-mounted sconces or other decorative fixtures

floor lamps

table lamps

The variety of lighting fixtures and styles are enough to overwhelm anyone and can have potential for a great deal of planning. Because of the overwhelming number of fixtures and the intricacies of creating a good lighting plan, it is a good idea to acquire the services of a professional if you are planning any major lighting renovations. It will be that person's job to suggest the most appropriate and effective lighting options for a teen area based on its functions. If you have already hired a professional design company, a lighting plan will be included in its services. If you have decided not to hire a professional, consider paying for a consultation with a contractor or a lighting designer—it will be worth the money. If your budget precludes you from hiring a lighting expert, get the input of a specialist at a lighting or home improvement store. A good solution for a small-scale lighting project is to incorporate freestanding lighting fixtures such as lamps for ambient lighting and do-it-yourself up-lights for work-oriented lighting.

Although practical lights are essential, don't forget about novelty lighting. Such items would include belt lighting (theater marquee look), neon lights, lava lamps, string lights, and rope lighting. Teen Central at the Burton Barr Central Library of the Phoenix (Arizona) Public Library incorporated fiber optic lighting that changes color throughout the ceiling. Generally speaking, it all comes down to the mood you want to create in combination with the practical application and function of the space.

QUICK TIP

Model sites such as the Bob in Leominster (Massachusetts) Public Library suggest suspending fluorescent lights at unconventional angles for visual appeal, incorporating multiple types of lighting (e.g., pendant lights over seating area, track lighting in the loft area, and recessed lighting over the computer counter). All lighting in the Bob, with the exception of the track lighting, is motion activated and shuts off automatically.

SIGNS

Signage is one of the most important ways to convey your message to teen customers. To begin this process, walk through your teen area or school library with a few teens, looking at things through their eyes. What message are you sending? Can you find where you want to go? Are you getting these directions across effectively? Good signage will attract teens, providing just the right amount of information. Bad signage can quickly ruin any space, especially when it's unattractive, too small, and filled with jargon. It's especially distressing to see a beautiful teen area or school library with great potential spoiled by disproportionate signage.

Any sign displayed in a teen area—whether stack signage, the name of the space, service signs, interior directional signs, or promotional signs and fliers—need to be well-planned, interesting, eye-catching, and appropriately scaled. Think about how signs are displayed and incorporated into the space and into the collection. Browse through magazines, observe retail signage, and look at vendor websites and catalogs to get ideas. Unclear and unattractive signage is confusing to customers and sends a negative message. Common problems include use of library jargon, too many signs, not enough signs, confusing messages, or signs that are not appropriately scaled and difficult to read. Be careful of using words that are out of date. Today's word for *cool* is tomorrow's word for *out-of-date*. However, no matter what the other signs say, remember the most important signs are the ones that say, "May I help you?" and "These items can be checked out."

When creating signs, follow these guidelines:

Think about all signs including directional, stack, promotional, and even spine labels.

Develop a signage planning and implementation strategy. Include a team of teens in the process.

When possible, work with professional sign systems (there are a lot of different price points out there) for a clean, polished look. Although not always necessary, for large-scale facilities projects a signage consultant may even be involved.

If you have limited funds, keep in mind that you don't have to spend a lot of money to get signs that look professional. Use a desktop publishing or word processing program and quality printer and paper.

For basic signs, pick a simple color scheme and font style. Make sure that the colors have enough contrast to be easily read.

Appropriately scale signs so they are easy to read from a distance and from up close.

Locate signs so they are easy to see, they get teens the information they need, and they get customers where they need to go.

Simplify your sign plan to reduce visual clutter and emphasize the important things, but don't let anyone tell you that signs aren't necessary.

Emphasize special collections, events, and other promotions by creatively incorporating color and simple graphics that complement products.

Be positive in your message.

Follow ADA guidelines when appropriate.

Ask teens for help with wording, design ideas, and location.

Avoid using library jargon and replace with user-oriented language. (Eliminate the YA acronym and other library jargon such as circ, AV, etc.)

In the Annex at the Palos Verdes (California) Public Library, a blackboard strip was painted on the wall so teens can easily create and change their own message or sign using

Signage example from the Orange County (Florida) Library System.

Entrance to the Teen Cave at the Cliff Cave Branch in St. Louis (Missouri) County Library (left). Promotional signage at the Daniel Boone Branch (right).

chalk. Colorful signs designate the popular fiction, graphic novels and magazine collections. They even had a design contest for the Annex logo, won by a thirteen-year-old girl. See photos of the Annex in chapter 5. Photos of the St. Louis (Missouri) County Library also illustrate some great signage examples. Go to the book's companion website for more signage examples.

NAMING YOUR TEEN SPACE

There has been much discussion about naming library spaces for young adults in public libraries. Libraries across the United States have chosen names based on teen input, and it works—The Loft, Teen Zone, ETC, the Best Cellar, The Corner, Teen Spot, Teen Zone, Teenation, Teen Pad, Teen Lounge, Club Q&A, the Bob, Teen Central, the Annex, the YELL (Youth Experimental Lounge Laboratory), and verbYL have all been successful. The Campbell County (Wyoming) Public Library System's young adult services manager Sue Knesel compromised with teens and decided that each year for Teen Read Week the teens would pick a new name. The winners make a sign for the entrance of the teen room. Knesel reports, "It has generated ownership and creativity." Louisville (Colorado) Public Library created a ballot and voted on the name of their teen area. See figure 4.3 for a copy of their ballot.

Over the past ten years, a consistent response from teens is that they dislike the "YA" acronym. Most often it is because they don't have a clue what "YA" means. When librarians refer to teens and their materials with a term they themselves do not understand and cannot relate to, this indicates to teenagers that adults don't really care about understanding or reaching them. Lesson number one in marketing: use terminology that your customer can relate to. To remedy this problem, teens tell us to get rid of YA and come up with something clearly identifiable, something universal, something *better*.

It's Your Place...
We Want You to Help Name It!
Select and rank <u>only</u> your top <u>three</u> choices, or give us your
own idea for the new library's teen area.

Suggested Name (select only 3)	Rank 1	Rank 2	Rank 3
☐ Teen Space	☐	☐	☐
☐ Teen Zone	☐	☐	☐
☐ Teen Scene	☐	☐	☐
☐ Teen View	☐	☐	☐
☐ Teen Place	☐	☐	☐
☐ Our Place	☐	☐	☐
☐ The Bubble	☐	☐	☐
☐ Teen Bubble	☐	☐	☐
☐ Teen World	☐	☐	☐
☐ The Loft	☐	☐	☐
☐ Teen Corner	☐	☐	☐
☐ Teen Central	☐	☐	☐
☐ Library Loft	☐	☐	☐
☐ Just Teens	☐	☐	☐
☐ Planet Teen	☐	☐	☐
☐ Club Teen	☐	☐	☐
☐ Teen Ramp	☐	☐	☐

Your Idea:

Optional

Name: _____

Age or Grade: _____

Figure 4.3
Teen Space Name Ballot

Areas labeled *young adult, YA,* and *teens* have all been criticized at one time or another. Some have suggested not naming the area at all, and others have broken out of naming the area for the age group and started working with teens to come up with creative names. The most important thing is not to worry about a *right* name and a *wrong* name, because there is no such thing. The best thing you can do is listen to what your teens have to say about what to call their area. Talk to teens, hold a contest, or vote on the name, but whatever you do, don't try to come up with something on your own—it will surely backfire. Many times adults assume a name is hip when, in actuality, it isn't. In general, teens say to avoid using names that sound too set up (e.g., The Hangout), are corny or childish (e.g., The Rad Bad Teen Center), are alliterative, or are intentionally misspelled (e.g., The Korner). The key here is not to waste time, effort, and money on a name that will turn teens away faster than you can get them in.

When designing a teen area or school library sign, remember that teen signs don't always have to be neon. Be creative—and if working with a trendy name, stay away from using materials that are expensive or difficult to modify. If a trendy name is chosen for your library, make sure that the sign can be changed easily when the name goes out of style; something painted on the wall would work well. An interchangeable sign where the letters slide in and out would also work well. More permanent options include

From top: Exterior sign at the Annex at the Palos Verdes (California) Public Library, a suspended sign depicting the Teen Zone at the Waukesha (Wisconsin) Public Library, and a custom LED sign and painted column denoting the Teen Lounge at the Santa Monica (California) Public Library. At right, the entrance to the Loft at the Louisville (Colorado) Public Library.

custom-made architectural, screen-printed, neon, and backlit signs or a programmable motion message display. See the photos for examples of attention-grabbing teen area signs.

NOTES

1. Taken in part from the American Society of Interior Designers, "How to Hire an Interior Designer," www.asid.org.
2. John Toppe, e-mail interview, November 16, 2006.
3. Sheri Thompson, "Color in Education," *School Planning and Management* (December 2003), www.peterli.com/archive/spm/551.shtm.
4. David Dalton and Kitty Bartholomew, "Make an Area Rug," HGTV: Kitty Bartholomew: You're Home, www.hgtv.com/hgtv/dc_floors_rugs_carpets/article/0,,HGTV_3414_1379523,00.html.
5. Wanda Higgins, "What Do Young Adults Want in Their School Library?" *Book Report* 18, no. 2 (September/October 1999): 25–27.
6. Rolf Erikson and Carolyn Markuson, *Designing a School Library Media Center for the Future* (Chicago: American Library Association, 2007), 46.
7. David Malman, "Lighting for Libraries" (Libris Design Project supported by the U.S. Institute of Museum and Library Services under the provisions of the Library Services and Technology Act, 2001, revised 2005), www.librisdesign.org.
8. Kimberly Bolan, comment posted on January 20, 2008, from "2006–2007 Teen Focus Group Summary," *Indie Librarian Blog*, http://indielibrarian.blogspot.com.

Chapter 5 | **Long-Term Promotion**

Now that you have figured out who your teen customers are and created the model teen space, how do you get teenagers to use the library? How do you connect teens with what the library is selling? Active and ongoing teen involvement throughout the planning, design, and implementation processes is an excellent start. Continuing this practice and carrying it into other facets of library service will only strengthen the success of the space and your relationship with your teens. Before you know it, more and more teens will be using the library and its services with little effort on your part. Long-term participation and promotion of your space and services are necessary to generate fresh ideas to keep teenagers interested long after the grand opening. Keep in mind, not even your regular users are always aware of the products and services you provide. Ask yourself, "Why would you invest time, energy, and money into something you're not going to tell people about and encourage them to use?"

Keeping a library filled with teenagers is not as difficult as one might think. The key is to let them know about the new space, materials, programs, and services available to them. Most important, let them know they are welcome. Strong and diverse collections and inventive and teen-inspired programming combined with up-to-date technology, excellent customer service, creative merchandising and advertising, strong public relations, user-friendly policies, and active teen involvement are all necessary elements for making a teen area thrive in the short term and in the long run.

THE COLLECTION

A winning young adult collection is a major asset of a teen space. The two elements that make a collection truly unbeatable are diversity of subject matter and formats, and overall appearance. The wider the variety of formats, the better. A strong, diverse collection filled with book and nonbook formats will

> attract existing and new users
>
> serve to bridge the haves and have-nots by supplying materials not readily available to many
>
> appeal to nonreaders and those with different learning styles
>
> boost circulation
>
> improve the library's image and relevancy to your customers

Fill your library with items that teens need and want such as

> paperback fiction and select hardcover fiction

an extensive magazine collection. Eight out of ten teens read magazines, so this is an affordable way to cover a wide variety of teen interests at a minimal cost. There are well over seventy titles relevant to a variety of ages and interests. See the companion website for details.[1]

a wide selection of audiovisual items: DVDs, audiobooks, music, downloadable items, and video games

graphic novels, manga, anime, and comic books

a strong nonfiction collection that includes a variety of topics that are curriculum-based as well as popular reading

e-resources such as educational and recreational databases and other online resources

well-defined special collections

a strong college collection including college catalogs, exam preparation guides, and college handbooks

a careers section that includes helpful resources for older teens such as job-search materials related to résumé writing and interview skills

a required reading or classics collection featuring curriculum-related items that students must read during the school year and during the summer

a board game collection

Including separate teen magazine and graphic novel/manga collections in your teen area is highly recommended. Avoid shelving them in your adult collections when at all possible. Even though in public libraries some of the previously described collections (audiovisual, careers, etc.) might not reside in your teen area, make sure that teens have easy access to the materials and that the shared collections are located near the teen area. In addition, make sure shared collections are prominently promoted in the teen area so teens know they are available to them. Melissa Jenvey, a young adult specialist at Donnell Library in midtown Manhattan (New York) reported that after redoing their teen section, circulation of young adult titles rose four hundred percent. "We just needed to have the merchandise that they wanted," she said. "It's like how they put the milk in the back of the supermarket to get you to buy all the other stuff."[2] For more tips on building your collection, see the "Collection Development Success" text box.

Creative merchandising at Hennepin County–Minneapolis Central (Minnesota) Library's Teen Central

A first-rate young adult collection also requires frequent and generous weeding. Materials must be current, and active weeding not only ensures an up-to-date collection, it creates space for new purchases as well as for merchandising new materials. Outdated content and cover art can be fatal to teen services. Items that are housed in a new teen space should be exciting and attractive.

Having teenage collection development assistants or creating a materials selection committee is an excellent way to give teens a sense of ownership while ensuring that the materials purchased for the library are what they want. (Not to mention, getting teen assistance will save you time.) This group could stem from a teen advisory board or exist as a separate entity. General guidelines include the following:

Involve as wide a variety of teens as possible, ages thirteen to eighteen, but keep the group to a manageable size.

Distribute lists and reviews of potential purchases to participants at the first meeting.

Meet once a month for approximately one to one and a half hours to review materials.

Choose a different media type each month to provide focus to the group and to prevent overwhelming participants. Consider creating a monthly schedule; for example, January, April, August for fiction books; February, May, September for movies/DVDs and music; March, July, October for graphic novels and manga; June, December for nonfiction; November for magazines and e-resources. (See appendix D for vendors.)

Create information packets for participants. At the end of each meeting, hand out a list of items to be considered for the following meeting. Consult relevant journals and publications to assist in the selection process.

At each meeting, ask teens to present their reviews and ideas, and have them vote on each item. The items with the most votes are the ones to purchase. As a reward, give the committee members first chance to check out new materials. Design special labels or bookmarks for the items so that other teens will know that the items were selected by their peers.

MERCHANDISING

Visual merchandising is the effort to make a library attractive and effective in its presentation of materials and services, as a means to increase use and circulation. A display is one form of visual merchandising and provides exposure to materials so that customers can see, handle and, ultimately, borrow the items. Effectively merchandising your collection will enhance the look and feel of the teen space, show teens you're listening to them and responding to their needs, promote browsing, and increase collection use and circulation. Twenty-first-century libraries understand the need to examine the layout of a facility through the eyes of their customers. Library customers must be able to easily shop, and the key is to create a dynamic, well merchandised, and well-laid-out environment that engages customers, encourages them to explore, stay a while, and, yes, take home materials.

Use merchandising techniques to help teens find what they didn't know they wanted; it's all about placing the right materials in the right formats in the right spots. Consider a variety of types of merchandising at various locations on a variety of fixtures in order to

COLLECTION DEVELOPMENT SUCCESS

- Get teen input—the Wilmington (Massachusetts) Public Library even has a link on their teen website where teens can submit requests for purchase for the collection.
- Don't rely solely on critical reviews—consider popular reviews and demand from teen customers.
- Utilize traditional review sources as well as nontraditional review sources such as blogs and podcasts.
- Collaborate with teenage collection development assistants.
- Regularly monitor collection activity and make adjustments in purchasing as needed.
- If a genre, format, etc., isn't circulating, find out why. Don't buy materials just because you've always bought them.
- Use circulation statistics to evaluate budget allotment.
- Split resources equally between traditional (books) and nontraditional collections (everything else).
- Weed regularly.
- Merchandise and publicize materials.

make the biggest impact. When merchandising, learn from others such as bookstores, retailers, and other libraries. When done correctly, merchandising serves two purposes: It makes the customer stop and look, and it assists in creating visual stimulus, functioning as part of the décor of the space. In fact, how the collection is presented and displayed will affect the entire look of the area. A library's ultimate merchandising goal is to effectively present materials as a means to increase circulation by getting the collection off the shelves and into a customer's hands. Merchandising is a great interactive, ongoing project for members of a teen advisory board or teen library pages. Schedule different teens or teams of teens to be in charge of promoting the collection each month. This is a terrific way to familiarize them with the collection while involving them in maintaining the space. Successful, attention-grabbing displays can be done at little to no cost, in a relatively small amount of time, and with very little effort. Add interest and visual stimulation by introducing exciting displays using new materials, audiovisual items, brochures, or whatever you think works. See figure 5.1 for a list of merchandising tips and tools.

Merchandising Techniques

One of the simplest and most effective ways to display materials is to highlight items using face-out merchandising in which the cover is showing. This can be done pretty much anywhere, but one of the most popular places is at the ends of shelves. Make sure each shelf has ample room for face-out display, and if it doesn't, rearrange the shelves or weed to make room. Never be skimpy with face-out merchandising; cover artwork is the key to circulation success, especially where books are concerned. Keep in mind that a cover with exciting artwork is always a better enticement than a boring spine.

Another resourceful way to create effective displays while adding interest to a teen space is to use nonstandard shelving that has built-in display potential. Products include mobile units, bookstore-style slant or zigzag shelves, slatwall, stackable wooden cubes, wall mounted grid racks, or other systems similar to those seen in a video store or retail space. Other types of displays would include end-of-the-range units and freestanding displays. Both can be created using readymade display racks or existing furniture such as tables or blocks. At the Pikes Peak (Colorado) Library District's East Library, three small portable shelves are used for display merchandising, and a two-level cube (small on top of large) sits by the entrance to the teen center with display materials, booklists, and other promotional materials. Above the cube at the entrance is a 36-inch flat-screen TV that

Figure 5.1   Merchandising Tips and Tools

Locations for Visual Merchandising

ends of shelves	end panels of shelving	walls
tops of shelves	service points	windows
ends of aisles	countertops	ceiling
window ledges	support columns	room dividers/partitions

Fixtures for Visual Merchandising

mobile showcases	slant shelves	shelf talkers
slatwall	wire book holders	book dumps and bins
grid shelving	periodical racks	baskets
zigzag shelving	kiosks	cubes
spinner racks	floor stands	plastic milk crates
subject signs	display racks	mobiles
gondolas	wall mount units	pedestals
literature racks	wall pockets	decorative props
easels or A-frames	display cases	signs and sign holders

Types of Merchandising

face-out	table displays	end-of-shelf displays
POP or point-of-purchase	island displays	floor stands
end-aisle displays	window presentations	step displays
cross-marketing	counter displays	

The entrance of ETC at Pikes Peak (Colorado) Library District's East Library includes display cubes and a 36-inch flat-screen TV that constantly advertises teen library programs.

More creative display in ETC features college materials in practical and artistic zigzag shelving.

Face-out slat shelving for popular paperbacks, graphic novels, and magazines at the Palos Verdes (California) Public Library's Annex.

Video game corner.

The Annex is an L-shaped room that incorporates slat shelving left over from a previous tenant, Herman Miller chairs salvaged from library storage, two couches (vinyl upholstery and on casters for easy mobility), beanbag chairs, and four round tables with chairs. Accessories include a bulletin board, two flat-screen TVs, and a white space on the wall that serves as a projection screen for gaming and showing movies.

constantly advertises teen library programs throughout the district. The Palos Verdes (California) Library's Annex effectively uses slatwall and face-out shelving for popular paperbacks, graphic novels, and magazines. The Mount Laurel (New Jersey) Public Library was the statewide demonstration site for a library merchandising program called Trading Spaces. Although this project wasn't exclusively teen-related, the $45,000 grant enabled the library to add a teen zone as well as an Internet café and a DVD collection for the entire library. Displays were improved with gondolas and slatwall end panels. Colorful and comfortable furniture was added throughout the library. The collection was reorganized into user-friendly categories.[3] See more about customer service in chapter 6.

When it comes to teen spaces, it's important to never waste space. The same holds true for displays. Look around at the spots that aren't being used but that have potential to make an impact. A few space-saving items to consider for purchase or in-house creation include end-of-the range shelving, mobile display units, freestanding shelving such as spinner racks and island displays, wall pockets for magazines and literature, window display units mounted with suction cups, and folding screens that can double as a room divider and a resourceful merchandising tool.

The key to success with freestanding displays is locating them in high traffic areas—anywhere they'll be noticed. Encourage POP (point-of-purchase) displays located near key service areas such as reference or circulation. If you're

QUICK TIP

An alternative location for a point-of-purchase display is near the front of the library, where it can grab the attention of those teens actively avoiding service areas.

Entrance into the William K. Sanford Town (Loudonville, New York) Library's Teen Room. Note the portable grid art panels located at the entrance.

View of inside of the room with decoupaged manga shelving and coffee table, comfortable seating, and series books with magnetic shelf labels.

in a multiple-story library, stock a display of new materials on the first floor to encourage teens to visit upstairs. In the business world, the POP advertising industry is a $12 billion a year business and still growing, so it must be doing something right. POP displays are great for highlighting hot items, encouraging impulse buying, and for showing teens something they might not have otherwise seen. Such displays can be created with counter display units, book dumps, or tabletop displays. Standard library counter units come in many sizes and are generally made of cardboard, wire, wood, or acrylic. Book dumps also come in a variety of sizes and styles and are extremely versatile. Simply throw materials in, pile them up, and let teens pick through them.

No matter what type of display you're creating or how and where you choose to build it, there are a few basic rules for ensuring display success:

> Use devices that get attention.
>
> Introduce visual variety by incorporating three-dimensional objects that complement the theme of the display.
>
> Present the materials with the covers face out.
>
> Incorporate signage that is eye-catching, easy to follow, and on target with the theme to direct teens to specific collections.
>
> Scan and replenish displays frequently (about once a week) to keep things looking fresh and exciting as well as to get an idea of what's moving and what's not.

Finally, remember that fabulous doesn't have to mean expensive. Inexpensive book easels are one of the best merchandising investments you could make, and they can be used almost anywhere to display materials or signs. Shelf talkers (a printed sign attached to a shelf to call attention to a particular product displayed on that shelf) are another great, low-cost way to quickly attract attention. Retail stores regularly use them to highlight items and provide information. Get creative with labels and signage because they too will go a long way for little money. The William K. Sanford Town Library (Loudonville, New York) highlighted their manga collection by decoupaging the shelving with pages from withdrawn manga books. The series book titles are kept on metal shelves and are labeled with magnetic labels so they can easily be moved as the series grow. See photos.

Bookstore Basics

Over the past several years there has been great interest in modeling libraries after bookstores. Bookstores are successful primarily because they know their customers, their products, and how to connect the two. They also know how to entice their customers with effective merchandising. As continually expressed in teen (and adult) focus groups, libraries are in competition with bookstores. Teens gravitate to bookstores because they can hang out, relax, wander, browse by familiar topics, freely eat and drink, and socialize. In a library teens are faced with the mystifying Dewey Decimal system, generally forbidden to eat and drink, and regularly reprimanded for socializing. Given that information, where would you choose to hang out?

The first thing we can learn from bookstores is the power of browsing. The way libraries organize materials can be intimidating to users, especially those with short attention spans or those unfamiliar with library classification rules. Featuring items by subject and highlighting teen-related materials are an essential part of making teens feel comfortable in a bookstore.

Bookstores are also good resources for signage and for labels in browsing areas. You can insert attractive, clearly labeled signage either projecting from or hanging above the nonfiction stacks. This is a simple and effective way to show customers where key subject areas begin.

Another great way to improve access to a library's teen fiction collection is to create genre lists. Generate recommended reading lists or viewing lists called *rave reviews* or *hot picks*. The American Library Association's Young Adult Library Services Association is a good resource for booklist and award information.

Including genre labels on materials is another easy way to improve access. Look through vendor catalogs to find labels that coordinate with the genre lists. (See appendix D for a list of suggested suppliers.) Video store catalogs are great resources for creative label ideas. Being able to find materials easily, as well as eat, talk, and listen to music, plays a large part in the comfort zone of teens. If teens feel more at home at the library, they are more likely to want to hang out there. Libraries should take a serious look at bookstores and other retailers providing service to teens. Even though bookstores do a good job, libraries *could* do it better.

QUICK TIP

If you don't like readymade genre labels or can't find all the categories you need, make them yourself. Create stickers using Microsoft Publisher, Print Shop, or even Microsoft Word, and print them on Avery Labels (size 5262). Enlarge the labels and print them as signs to advertise and as a handy resource for staff and teens.[4]

TECHNOLOGY

Technology is important to teens; it's part of their lives. Therefore it must play a part in any teen space. Consider a teen library filled with listening stations, a big screen TV, gaming equipment, and computers with access to the Internet, online catalog, games, research databases, and software necessary for school work (i.e., Microsoft Word, Excel, and PowerPoint). Having a strong balance of paper, electronic, and audiovisual resources is important, as is the technology that goes along with the resources—the machinery necessary to listen to music, watch movies, do homework, etc. Incorporating technology into a teen space does not have to be intimidating. From hardware and equipment to software, your website, and other online resources, follow this advice: start small, learn as you go, get teens involved, and add along the way.

Connecting to Teens

According to the Pew Internet and American Life Project, 87 percent of teens in the United States ages twelve to seventeen use the Internet, and 51 percent of them say they go online on a daily basis. At the same time, the scope of teens' online lives has also broadened. Wired teens are more frequent users of instant messaging; 75 percent of teenage Internet users use IM. And they are now more likely to play games online, make purchases, get news, and seek health information. Eighty-one percent of teen Internet users play games online; that represents about 17 million people and signifies growth of 52 percent in the number of online gamers since 2000. The report also says that 76 percent get news online and 31 percent use the Internet to access health information. In addition, 45 percent of teens have cell phones and 33 percent are texting. Teens who have cell phones are heavy users of online communication tools. One in four cell phone-owning teens have used their phone to connect to the Internet.[5] In addition, more than one-third of respondents ages twelve to nineteen listed MySpace as one of their two most-visited websites. Runner-up Yahoo collected 19 percent of teens' votes, while third-place Google claimed 14 percent.[6] As the data indicate, teens are immersed in technology; it's part of their culture.

Part of running a successful teen space or school library means keeping on top of data such as this in order to understand teens and technology and to deliver services that meet their needs. The Public Library of Charlotte and Mecklenburg County (PLCMC) (North Carolina) does an excellent job integrating technology into their services. Their Eye4You Alliance Island started as a partnership with the Alliance Library System and PLCMC in Charlotte. Teens were involved in building the island and are involved in leading and running events. The library continues to partner with organizations from around the world including the University of Kentucky, University of California–Davis, and NASA. These organizations provide programmatic and marketing support. Their representatives run programs on the library's island including college fairs, machinima (a form of filmmaking that uses computer game technology to shoot films in virtual reality) classes, and Science Friday programs in conjunction with NPR. All of this helps get the word out about PLCMC and the island. Kelly Czarnecki, technology education librarian, encourages libraries to "Just do it. Don't feel like you have to know everything to be able to start. [Technology] can be intimidating at times and that's okay. Trust the teens you work with. Build that trust so that they will want to work with you. Don't be afraid—just go with it."[7]

The following technologies for teens are popular—and regular—features in today's teen spaces:

> computers with access to the Internet, Microsoft Office software, online catalog, online databases, recreational software and games, video editing software, and photo editing software

flat-screen TVs

stereos with surround sound (play CDs, connect to MP3 players, etc.)

listening stations such as MP3 players, sound domes, etc.

DVD players

gaming stations (Wii, Xbox 360, PS2, and PS3)

projection units for projecting movies, gaming, etc.

If your library is small or medium-sized and the thought of setting up and maintaining technology of any kind is completely overwhelming, consider asking teens for assistance. Teenagers are a great resource for setting up computers, hooking up TVs, maintaining equipment once it's in place, and even conducting training sessions. It's always better to seek help rather than do without simply because you do not have the knowledge or the time to go about it. Contact the middle or high school technology specialist to get names of potential volunteers. You might even have a teenage page on staff who has a knack for computers and electronics.

In addition, look to outside sources for funding and assistance. Through three grants (one from the county and two from the state), the Taylor (Pennsylvania) Community Library went from one computer for all customers to five computers just for teens. The Baraboo (Wisconsin) Public Library solicited donations from local fitness centers and healthcare professionals to pay for new electronics (Wii system, Dance Dance Revolution, and Guitar Hero), explaining the physical fitness benefits of these games.

In-House Equipment

Another technology service that is quickly making inroads in libraries of all shapes and sizes is MP3 players, sound domes, circulating laptops, and gaming equipment for use in the library. The idea is that such equipment helps expand technology offerings as well as promotes and supports audiovisual collections. Circulating laptops is a great idea for those who want to maximize technology or for those with limited space. Be sure to incorporate appropriate furnishings and wiring throughout the facility to accommodate such services. Consideration should also be given to security issues. Will you hold identification at a service desk? Will equipment be tagged with security sensors?

The Pikes Peak (Colorado) Library District's East Library has MP3 players loaded with music that can be checked out for two hours. Their computer and video games check out for one hour and they can be used on the teen center's PCs and in their Media Pit (the pit includes a 40-inch flat-screen monitor for playing video games). They also have six laptop computers that can be checked out and taken anywhere in the teen center. Teens can check DVDs out of the regular collection to watch at home or on the TV in their teen area. The San Juan Island (Washington) Library, the Alden (New

Pikes Peak (Colorado) Library District's East Library's ETC has six desktop computers with Internet access, word processing, gaming, video editing and photo editing. They also have six laptop computers that can be checked out and taken anywhere in the teen center. Two public access catalogs, one customer management system for computer sign-up and printing, and one self-checkout station are also available in the teen center. ETC also has a Media Pit that includes a 40-inch flat-screen monitor for gaming.

York) High School Library, and the Port Jefferson (New York) Free Library are just three examples of libraries that circulate laptops. At San Juan Island Library, teen users must submit a special permission form signed by a parent; the form basically says that the parent is accepting responsibility for the minor's use of the laptop. Laptops are kept in a cupboard where they are charged, and customers sign them out on their library cards.[8] Staff members collaborated with the teen advisory board at the Blue Island (Illinois) Public Library to create the Tech Annex. Originally used to house historical community artifacts, the Tech Annex is paving the way for the future achievements of its residents. Intended to be a multipurpose, advanced technology space, the room provides

a safe place for young adults to be creative and hang out

an enclosed computer classroom

a recording studio

additional patron program and staff meeting and training space.

Some of the resources available in the Tech Annex include

3-D modeling and animation

audio sound recording

video and image editing

Web development station

10.1 megapixel SLR digital camera

Sony PlayStation 2

Yamaha keyboard, microphones, mixers, and headphones[9]

The Jerome (Idaho) Public Library's sound dome is hooked up to a receiver and a 300-CD changer and hangs over a café table and stools. Staff sign out the remote so teens can change CDs and listen to what they want while visiting or doing homework. The CD cases are numbered and are merchandised in a display unit bought from a music store that was going out of business. They are all face-forward and are easy to browse. Teens find their choice in the display and punch the number into the remote to listen.

Close-up of Jerome (Idaho) Public Library's sound dome, café table, and scooper stools.

VIRTUAL SPACE

A library's website is its virtual space, so it is critical that both the overall site and teen services site be attractive, up to date, interactive, and easy to use. Include everything from access to the online catalog and the collection, to an online suggestion box, to social networking, to information about new materials and programs, to online program registration, to online participation in programs such as summer reading. Visit successful library websites and teen web pages to see what actually attracts teens. (For a list of popular teen websites, refer to appendix C.)

WHAT TEENS WANT ONLINE

In Fall 2006 I was the dean of students at the Academy of the Sacred Heart in Bloomfield Hills, Michigan, an all-girls Catholic high school. (At this time I was also working toward my Master's of Library and Information Science at Wayne State University.) The high school was home to a unique laptop program, in which each student and faculty member was issued a laptop or tablet PC. Watching my students live most of their academic (and personal) lives online, I began to wonder, "What do they want their digital library space to look like?" and "Are current sites reaching them in a way that makes them *want* to access libraries through the Internet?"

I contacted Detroit Catholic Central High School, an all-boys high school, and conducted an informal study of both schools with the approval of Wayne State. I sent the students links to various search engines, online libraries, and brick-and-mortar libraries and museums. I then asked them to complete online surveys to tell me what they thought of the websites. Here are the results:

True to the independent nature of teenagers, students remarked they liked sites that provided a brief, five- to eight-word description. They noted that they were more likely to read about the resource because of the brevity of the explanation. They also maintained their pride because they felt they had navigated the site with little assistance. (See the "More Options" section of Google for their favorite example: www.google.com/intl/en/options/.)

Teens bemoaned websites that tried to be cool and use obnoxious colors and slang. In fact, one student even commented he was offended that the library site they were visiting only used slang as an attempt to reach out to them. Students rely on and expect librarians to be a professional and stable resource for them. As Kevin King of the Kalamazoo (Michigan) Public Library says, "If you're not cool, then don't try to be!"

Snap decisions were made about resources based on who created the resource. For example, after reviewing the Library of Congress' main page for mere seconds, students made assumptions that the site was historical. This happened for two reasons: they associated the Library of Congress with history and government and, at the time of the survey, historical references dominated the

site's main page. The students did not see how the website provided insight into culture, languages, music, poetry, and more.

Almost all of the students had Facebook and MySpace pages. They loved the sites that constantly changed. They also liked the interaction and involvement from their friends. In a library environment, wikis and blogs are great tools to add the elements of change and sharing. One note of warning: having a log-in to edit information deterred teens from making comments.

One important lesson that came out of this research is that, as librarians (and adults), we make the incorrect assumption that kids are web savvy and have the necessary skills to successfully use our websites. Many librarians teach information literacy—helping teens determine so-called bad information, while also assessing resources for high quality information. When working with teenagers in the virtual world, adults must continually focus on the assessment aspect of information literacy because it is consistently where teens fall short. This is especially true of Internet resources. Because they are making snap decisions and feel they know it all, they are missing great websites. This practice will also lead to building a generation of library users who can successfully find information both on the Internet and in our buildings.

At the end of the day, teens want the same things in their virtual world that they want in the real world:

They want to be guided toward information and good things, but they want to feel like they did it on their own.

They want to be treated as adults, but they want to be catered to as being slightly smarter and hipper than the rest of us.

They want good design. This doesn't necessarily mean neon colors and crazy graphics, but it does mean embracing fun web design that's clear and easy to understand and utilizing language that gently guides them to where they want to be.

By Christine Ayar, director, Adam Cardinal Maida Alumni Library (Orchard Lake, Michigan). Special thanks to the Academy of the Sacred Heart, Bloomfield Hills and Detroit Catholic Central High School, Wixom, Michigan.

There are also a number of excellent library websites out there, which are inspirational resources for ideas for your teen space. See appendix E for details. The rules for creating a successful teen area and a successful teen web page are the same: know your teen customers, get them involved, plan, address functionality, incorporate visual appeal, concentrate on interactivity, and keep it fresh and interesting. When designing a teen page consider these basic principles:

Include the most important information in the first half of the screen because most teens do not like to scroll.

Keep it clear, organized, and simple.

Use graphic design as a means of enhancing communication with teens as well as for decoration.

Consider reading patterns, because any design that works in opposition to the way a teen reads interrupts the flow.

Create a focal point for the page. Generally, this is one-third down the page and slightly to the right of center. This is the best place for important information.

Choose words appropriate for teens, and keep sentences simple and to the point.

Use contrast (dark versus light) to create visual excitement. Dark areas draw attention. Use tone and contrast sparingly for the greatest impact.

Invite teens to look at your page by using pictures. Pictures should supplement the text around them, not serve as barriers.

Focus on interactivity by including links to interactive web pages or creating polls or online surveys.

Involve teens in the planning, design, and maintenance of the web page.[10]

Miranda Doyle, author of *101+ Great Ideas for Teen Library Web Sites,* offers these additional tips:

Focus on function, not just appearance. Yes, cool graphics do attract teens, but research shows that they prefer a clean, easy-to-use website over a glitzy one that's slow and confusing.

Don't overload your site with text. When it comes to using the Web, teens are far less patient than adults. They also have less sophisticated reading and research skills, and don't like to wade through vast quantities of written information.

Make your site interactive, not just informative. Teens want to do something on a website—fill out a form, take a quiz, submit a book review, play a game, post a message, chat with a librarian, and so on.

Find out how your teens use technology. If they are obsessed with instant messaging, offer IM reference services. If they never go anywhere without their iPods, start a library podcast. If they're into blogging, get them to contribute to a library blog.

Teen participation is key. As you design your site, ask for input from teens along the way. Solicit book reviews, favorite links, creative writing and art, and other content. Better yet, put your student volunteers or teen advisory council in charge of web projects.

Be realistic about how much you can do. As you add new website features, those features will need to be monitored and updated regularly. Before you start and publicize a blog, online book club, or other service, think about the time commitment required and whether the benefits make it worthwhile.

Keep privacy and safety in mind. If you plan to post photos of teens online, or let them use their real names, be aware of any school or library policies on doing so. It's generally better to use first names only, and to avoid posting information such as phone numbers or e-mail addresses.

Decide how much risk you can tolerate. Teens will want to actively participate on your website by posting messages to discussion forums, commenting on the library blog, or contributing the library's wiki. You will need to weigh the risk of inappropriate postings against the benefits of an open exchange.

Don't be afraid to experiment. There are so many new and exciting opportunities for enhancing your library website. Stay current and try something cutting edge. Offer audio and video content on your site, start a library wiki, answer reference questions sent by cell phone, add an RSS feed, or come up with something no one has tried before![11]

See the text box in this chapter for Miranda's top six public and school websites.

The St. Louis (Missouri) Public Library involved more than twenty teens in developing a wiki for teens, by teens to highlight library resources. The project called MyTRACS (My Teens Research And Create Stories) is funded by a Library Services and Technology Act (LSTA) grant from the Missouri State Library. MyTRACS was designed to get teens involved and excited about learning, discovery, and knowledge. Teens discover what the library has to offer and record their discoveries on the Web to inspire other teens. It partners teens with library staff, educators, graphic artists, writers, photographers, and others. Weekly interactive sessions engage the imagination and help these teens develop research and writing skills, teamwork and networking skills, a sense of individual responsibility, and the ability to discern between good information and poor information. "The MyTRACS project offers teens an opportunity to participate in a meaningful project while gaining valuable job skills necessary to be successful in life," says Carrie Dietz, young adult librarian. "We recognize the importance of having teens involved in all aspects of library service, from space planning and design, to programming, to technology. When teens are involved they have a sense of ownership and responsibility for the space they helped create and the programming and services they helped develop. Teens view the library as an exciting place where their opinions are valued and their decisions are implemented."[12]

The Auckland City (New Zealand) Libraries include interactive features on their website including a "Readers React" review feature and an online "New Reads" e-newsletter. Several libraries are incorporating podcasts into their websites. All that's needed is a computer, a headset (such as a gamer's headset, which are available for around $20), and software such as Audacity for recording and editing and LAME to convert the MP3 files. (Both are free.) See appendix E for more information on these libraries.

CREATING AN ONLINE TEEN SPACE

Teens today are digital natives. They have never known life without the Internet, so it is not surprising that young people are seeking out information and connections online. Having an age-appropriate site that serves the needs of library patrons is a vital tool for customers and staff alike. Here are ten tips for creating an online space for teens:

1. Build a team.

    Choose people with a passion for services to young people and who are willing to respect and learn from each other. It also helps to have someone on your team who is involved with young people.

2. Ask for input.

    Have regular meetings with staff to show them what you're working on, or get input by sending out e-mail updates and asking for feedback. You could even start a blog where you post your progress and let staff comment. You want staff to feel like they have a say in your site. If they feel like they were part of it, they're more likely to promote it.

3. Brainstorm.

    Look at sites you admire for inspiration. Ask young people for their opinions; if you have a teen group, get them involved in the process. If you don't, create a survey to see what teens want out of a library site. Teens are the ones who will be using the site, so their input is important.

4. Create a vision.

    Ask yourself what your vision is for the site. Have that goal or vision in mind every step of the way. Respect for your user should be an important part of your vision.

5. Promote, provide, stimulate, and inspire.

    Promote your programs, collection, and services. Provide teens with easy access to library staff to help with all the things you promote. Provide a place for teens to express themselves. Stimulate with fun stuff like polls, contests, links, and featured library and local events. Inspire teens to grow by letting them discover things about themselves and the outside world with reliable links on a variety of subjects.

6. Be the experts.

    Librarians and other staff are experts, and one of the goals of the site should be to inform and inspire young people. Remember that reliable content is the most important part of a site. Don't worry about the design too much—if it's usable and reliable, it's great!

7. Appeal to teens

    Teens have a short attention span and want to be stimulated. They also want to be able to scan text quickly. They dislike jargon, dense blocks of text, and small font sizes. But, most important, teens want to connect and be heard. They want a voice. Teens are more likely to use a site if they are a part of it, so let them contribute art, writing, or book reviews. Take advantage of free tools like Flickr or Blogger to post images and writing and allow teens to comment on what you post.

8. Keep it fresh.

    Once the site is up, keep it fresh. People will be more likely to come back if there is something new every time. Using current events or holidays is a great way to highlight your collection. Find someone who is good at displays and ask them what they like to feature. A book display in your library can easily translate to something great online.

9. Use social networking.

    Teens are crazy about social networking sites. It's easy to use these sites to reach out to users and give them a new idea of what a library is and what it can do for them. Use it to promote your services and collections, blog, post photos, and more. And don't forget the networking element—if you're having trouble learning something, find a library that uses that tool and ask them for help!

10. Keep connected.

    Use the tools that work well for you and your customers and don't be afraid to try new things to stay connected with teens online. Being online is not just what teens today are about, it's who they are. Let's be there with them.

By Angela Sigg, web development librarian, Denver Public Library

TOP SIX PUBLIC AND SCHOOL WEBSITES

1. Central Rappahannock Regional Library, Virginia. http://teenspoint.org. Packed with teen creative work, this site offers teen reviews, poetry, writing, art, a photo scrapbook of library events, and plenty of well-designed booklists.

2. Greece Athena Media Center, Rochester, New York. www.greece.k12.ny.us/ath/library/. Colorful and exciting, this site offers great book blogs as well as teacher project pages, reading suggestions, databases, research help, Internet safety tips, and much more.

3. Hennepin County Library, Minneapolis, Minnesota. www.hclib.org/teens/. A discussion area, online polls, MySpace and Facebook sites, RSS feeds, a Flickr account, library search widgets, and other innovative features make this one of the most interactive, community-building teen library sites out there. Great booklists and informational resources are the icing on the cake.

4. New Trier Township High School, Illinois. www.newtrier.k12.il.us/library/. This site offers wonderful information literacy information, links to class research projects, a book blog, reading links, databases, and more.

5. Southeastern Massachusetts Library System. www.myowncafe.org. Active message boards, polls, information and entertainment centers, quizzes, and games make this site innovative and attractive, a place teens can go to interact with each other as well as get information about library resources.

6. Springfield Township High School, Erdenheim, Pennsylvania. www.sdst.org/shs/library/. Friendly artwork and tons of resources—pathfinders, teacher tools, online lessons, a virtual tour—make this an appealing and useful site.

By Miranda Doyle, author of *101+ Great Ideas for Teen Library Web Sites*

PROGRAMMING

Creative, appealing programs that are planned and implemented with the assistance of teens are a vital component of a successful teen space and service. Aside from the recreational and education functions, programs can also function as a promotional tool by providing a means of attracting teens to the library. Once teens are at the library, you can showcase what you have to offer them. Libraries with a solid programming plan, that involve teens in the process, and are dedicated to seeing it through are the ones that are the most successful in attracting teens to their libraries. When developing a programming plan, keep in mind that a variety of types and levels of activities for a variety of ages is necessary to meet the diverse needs and interests of adolescents.

Just as programming is critical to children's services, it is equally important to provide programmatic opportunities to teenagers. Throughout the marketing process for your teen space project, think about how the information applies to teen programming and activities. For public libraries, complete a quick analysis of your children's, adult, and teen programming budgets. How do they compare? Use all this information to develop your programming plan.

Find out directly from teens what types of programs they'd like to see at the library. Don't stop there. Have them assist in planning, implementation, and promotion. If they have a stake in it, they will be more likely to attend and encourage others to come. Following are some inventive program ideas to help spark creativity and assist in encouraging teens to come to the new teen area:

board game or video game tournament

gamers' group

movie screening and discussion

film festival

after-school study hall, homework help, or group study session

battle of the bands

art program (see figure 5.2 later in this chapter and the text box on the Phoenix Public Library)

poetry slam

writers' workshop

anime club

a zine project (see information on the Farmington Public Library)

online summer reading

anything with food, drink, and talking

The London (Ontario, Canada) Public Library developed programs around the idea of creative expression, including music, art, writing, and dance. One example is LOUD (London Ontario Underground Dimensions), a monthly, local indie band performance, held in the library during library hours. Young musicians are invited to apply to perform, learning at the same time about the music industry including public performance etiquette and protocol, showing up on time, being prepared, etc. Staff from mindyourmind .ca, a nonprofit youth website, partner with the library to interview and videotape the performers. The interviews are posted on the website. A video highlighting the first LOUD concert received over 1,000 views in just four months. Attendance at LOUD concerts ranges from fifty to one hundred and twenty people. The LOUD concerts also launched a new collection at the library: compact discs produced by local indie bands. Most of these CDs are not widely available.[13]

The Evanston (Illinois) Public Library has a Teen Reader's Theatre Troupe that performs adaptations of young adult literature in a performance space in their Loft. The teens of the Farmington (New Mexico) Public Library published *Blended: A Zine.* The mission of *Blended* is to showcase the uniquely blended, yet distinct cultures of San Juan County through the eyes of teens ages thirteen through nineteen. The zine project is an effort to reach those teens who are not traditional library users. *Blended* has a teen editorial board and the library's Teen Zone supervisor is their advisor. Not only did these teens write their own proposal for this project, they prepared a marketing plan and got their own money by presenting their idea directly to ConocoPhillips. They received a $17,000 grant as a result. The teen creators of this publication set their own deadlines, met goals, collected and reviewed over one hundred submissions, and compiled and laid out the publication on their own. A MySpace page was developed to promote the program. *Blended* is available in paper and web format.

Cover of the first issue of Farmington (New Mexico) Public Library's *Blended: A Zine* created for teens by teens

WHAT'S NEW AT PHOENIX PUBLIC LIBRARY?

Teen Central, which opened in 2001, was one of the teen space model sites in the first edition of *Teen Spaces*. Seven years later it serves more than three hundred teenagers per day, and library staff wanted to take the next step for their space. They decided to focus on after-school activities that would creatively engage their teen customers and involve staff in their teen customers' visits beyond day-to-day homework and computer questions. Innovative programs include

> *Hubcap Happening.* This event is about decorating something literally from the street: hubcaps. Staff member Chris Ruiz arranged for a donation of twenty-five hubcaps, solicited creative materials from staff, and encouraged teens to bring in things from their daily lives to decorate their hubcaps. The library provided puff paint, glitter, ribbons, colorful zip ties, etc. The response was terrific; teens actually got off of their computers to participate.

> *Graffiti Workshop.* Staff showed parts of a graffiti documentary to promote the idea of graffiti as art, and how to use it legally. The library provided markers and pieces of blank newsprint for teens to practice with. The goal was to have a large piece to hang in Teen Central. One of the teen regulars wrote *Teen Central* in a graffiti style on the center of two large pieces of poster board, and teens filled in around the words over the course of several weeks. The piece was mounted to foam board and hung above the art wall. The unexpected bonus was the teens continuing to gather after school to draw graffiti on newsprint and see it posted in the room. (No gang references are allowed.) The visual impact in the room is amazing.

> *Art in Motion.* This urban art program was inspired by Jackson Pollock. Staff draped everything in plastic sheets, provided large cardboard squares, paint, a variety of applicators from squeeze and spray bottles to shoes and tire pieces to make tread designs. A documentary about Jackson Pollock and his painting techniques was shown in the background. The teens were very enthusiastic, to the extent that staff broke down Baker and Taylor boxes for them to continue painting. Their creations were hung around both sides of their glass-walled conference areas.

> *Comic Collab.* An interactive, cumulative comic produced by teens and staff member Jeffrey Stoffer. Teens submit plot ideas in a drop box, turn in completed comic pages, or work directly with Stoffer to develop their drawings and ideas. Stoffer provides comic template pages that teens can take from the desk to facilitate their work. This program has been a great way to get teens to participate with staff at the desk. Many teens that had minimal staff interaction before are now regular faces at the desk.

The library has also partnered with the Phoenix Art Museum and a nearby comic store to provide some interesting events. Examples of all the urban art events were featured in their zine as well as exhibited in the @Central Gallery on the first floor of the Burton Barr Central Library. The urban art pieces and comics are also part of a rotating art collection that travels around all their library branches, all of which have a teen area.

Hubcap art is part of the urban art program in Teen Central at the Phoenix (Arizona) Public Library.

Libraries such as those in the King County (Washington) Library System have up-to-the-minute program listings with online registration for teen customers. For more information on teen programming and ideas to fuel your imagination, visit the teen web pages of the resource libraries (see appendix E) and refer to Amy Alessio and Kimberly Patton's *A Year of Programs for Teens,* the various editions of Mary K. Chelton's *Excellence in Library Services to Young Adults: The Nation's Top Programs* and Patrick Jones's *Connecting Young Adults and Libraries.* (See appendix C for additional details and additional resources.) Journals such as *Voice of Youth Advocates* and *Journal of Youth Services and Libraries,* youth-related discussion lists such as PUBYAC and YA-YAAC, and individual library web pages are also good resources for programming ideas.

ADVERTISING

One way to get the word out to teens about your new teen space and related services is through effective advertising. Advertisements come in the form of media types including television, magazines, radio, movie ads, posters, billboards, newspapers, mail, and the Internet, to name just a few. The common thread that links each of these media is *content.* To be successful in advertising, it is imperative that the content be exciting and appeal to its intended audiences. Ads geared toward teens must be created just for them—not for children under age twelve, parents, or any adults. According to teen marketing expert Elissa Moses, there is only one cardinal rule of advertising that is especially true when targeting teens: "Thou shalt not be boring!" Following are her top ten types of advertising that appeal to teens:

Make me laugh.

Be fun.

Use popular music.

Be realistic.

Use young actors.

Use contemporary colors and graphics.

Use special effects.

Show the product.

Tell an interesting story.

Show the company cares.[14]

Print Advertising

When dealing with print materials, keep in mind that people of all ages are bombarded with printed information every day—so much, in fact, that this type of advertising is generally ignored. Therefore, it is crucial that print advertising be creative and exciting. Teen-designed posters are great tools, as are advertisements in the school newspaper. Online and paper teen newsletters can also be quite popular. Bulk mailings of a teen newsletter are a great way to reach both library users and nonusers. See figure 5.2 for an example from the Farnsworth (Wisconsin) Public Library. Post fliers and posters in

Figure 5.2   Sample Newsletter

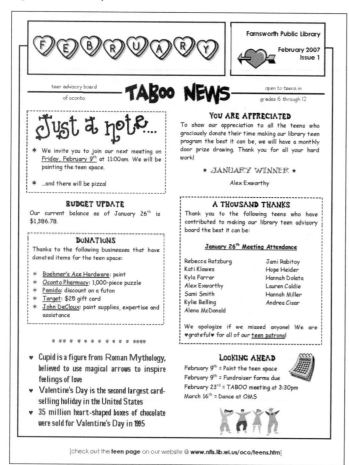

creative, attention-grabbing places including school, the school newspaper, and local teen hangouts such as movie theaters, community centers, arcades, and coffee shops. See figure 5.3 for an example of a teen space brochure. If you haven't already done so, this is the time to partner with local teen-related groups and businesses as well as to cultivate the valuable school-public library relationship.

Electronic Advertising

Alternative media such as TV, radio, and the Internet are also great ways to capture the attention of teens. Television advertising may seem prohibitive because of the cost, but check with your local television station to see if you can work out a deal. A less expensive and highly effective way to advertise is via your website, blog, and other online resources. Online newsletters can also be a great advertising and public relations tool as well as an excellent interactive, skill-building project for teen volunteers. Include photographs, drawings, stories, top ten lists, program information, teen reviews, editorials, an advice column, or whatever comes to mind. For examples of e-newsletters, see Orange County (Florida) Library System's "it" teen newsletter, Dorchester County (South Carolina) Library, Auckland City (New Zealand) Libraries, and St. Charles (Illinois) Public Library in appendix E. Orange County also does monthly podcasts that highlight some of their many great teen activities.

Following are twenty promotional and public relations ideas for marketing library services to teenagers. Many of these could be planned, designed, and implemented by teens themselves.

1. Create a dynamic, up-to-date, easy-to-use teen website. Enlist the help of teen volunteers to help design, choose content, and maintain the site.

2. Have teens help design and maintain displays throughout the library.

3. Call, e-mail, or text teens to invite them (and to remind them) about programs, committee work, etc. (See appendix D for various software solutions that have built-in, automatic e-mail and text capabilities.)

4. Send information about teen happenings to local teen-friendly radio and television stations.

5. Implement online registration and participation in everyday programs and summer reading programs. See the text box for an online program success story.

6. Start a teen blog with reviews of books, movies, music, and more. The State Library of Victoria in Australia created a service called "Inside a Dog," which became Australia's number one website about books for teenagers. The site

Figure 5.3 Sample Brochure

Please select the program suggestions and days / times that you are most interested in. If you have any more suggestions or comments, write them in!

Programs:

Writers' Group ___	Artists' Group ___
Game Night ___	Movie Night ___
Craft Club ___	Poetry Slam ___
Life Skills ___	Health/Fitness ___
Book Discussion ___	Anime Club ___

Other: _____
_____
_____
_____
_____

Day/Time:

Saturday	10-12 ___	12-2 ___
	2-4 ___	4-6 ___
Sunday	1-3 ___	3-5 ___
Monday	2-4 ___	4-6 ___ 6-8 ___
Tuesday	2-4 ___	4-6 ___ 6-8 ___
Wednesday	2-4 ___	4-6 ___ 6-8 ___
Thursday	2-4 ___	4-6 ___ 6-8 ___
Friday	2-4 ___	4-6 ___

CONTACT US:

The Loft Desk
303-335-4845

Kriska Daltonhurst
Teen Services Coordinator
303-335-4844
daltonk@ci.louisville.co.us

Sandra Richmond
Librarian
303-335-4824
richmos@ci.louisville.co.us

Louisville Public Library
951 Spruce St.
Louisville, CO 80027

Circulation: 303-335-4822
Renewals: 303-335-2665
Fax: 303-335-4833

Library Web Site:
http://www.ci.louisville.co.us/library/

OPEN:
Monday – Thursday 2p – 8p
Friday 2p - 6p
Saturday 10a - 6p
Sunday 1p – 5p

LOUISVILLE PUBLIC
L I B R A R Y
GO ANYWHERE FROM HERE

Welcome to The Loft!

The Loft is Louisville Public Library's new space just for teens. Created for library users aged 12-17, The Loft aims to create a dynamic environment where teens are inspired to live their dreams, express themselves and explore opportunities.

Only a few paces from the top of the expansive granite staircase, The Loft is a 1600-square-foot space made up of three distinct areas.

Step through the double doors and look around. You will see stacks and shelves displaying the Library's teen collection, 8 computer workstations, seating for 18, and a large plasma-screen TV. Continue through the space to the listening room—where a small group of teens can quietly enjoy their personal music or other audio media. Finally you will reach the homework center, with computers and enough room for 12 students to work independently or in small groups.

These areas also feature contemporary colors, exciting fabrics, and a variety of seating options including study tables, upholstered chairs, and even some bean bags. Surrounded by walls of tinted windows, The Loft offers abundant natural light and a wide-open view of the outdoors.

The Loft's collections include fiction and nonfiction books, graphic novels, and magazines of special interest to teens.

Internet connections allow access to the library's online resources and to the wealth of information on the Web. Office applications include Word, Excel, and Publisher.

Music CDs, recorded books, DVDs and videotapes are purchased with the teen group in mind.

Annual programs for teens include a writer's workshop in the spring, a summer reading program and Teen Read Week activities in October.

Teens are also invited to participate in a teen advisory group that will begin forming in September 2007. You may pick up an application at The Loft desk.

Your Opinion Counts!

Take an active part in making The Loft even better! Tear off this page of the brochure and turn it in at The Loft desk. Your feedback and suggestions will be taken into consideration for the next step in our program planning and collection purchases.

Favorite Bands:

1) _____
2) _____
3) _____
4) _____
5) _____

Favorite Movies:

1) _____
2) _____
3) _____
4) _____
5) _____

Cut or tear along this line

Source: From Louisville (Colorado) Public Library.

promotes young adult literature, highlighting Australian writers and their work, and includes the best of the international scene.

7. Create RSS feeds for lists of new teen programs and materials.

8. Have teens make public service announcements /or set up an interview for yourself and teen collaborators.

9. Provide online or instant message reference service.

10. Regularly hold promotional events. (See figure 5.4 for an example.)

11. For writing and other contests, display entries and winners at the library as well as on the library's website.

12. Hang and distribute teen-designed and -created posters and fliers about library happenings in the library, school, mall, and hangouts.

13. Keep up on what's hot in technology so you can utilize and promote these technologies to teens (e.g., MySpace, Facebook, and Tagged)

14. Stuff fliers into books and audiovisual materials.

15. Have teens create an online newsletter and regularly distribute it to teens, community youth groups, etc.

16. Send promotional articles to locally produced print publications such as the school newspaper, local recreation department's newsletter, and other publications teens would see and read.

17. Place a paid ad in the local paper or local teen magazine. Hint: make it look like a retail advertisement. The St. Louis (Missouri) Public Library placed an ad about their new teen spaces and new selection of teen magazines in *Louie: The Magazine for St. Louis Teens.* (See figure 5.5 for the full ad.)

18. Work with your local cable TV station to produce commercials advertising the library, the teen center and their services. Involve teens in making and filming commercials.

19. Have a booth at the community fair and ask teens to help run it.

20. Create online surveys to ask teens what they want. Incorporate questions so the survey functions as an informational tool, letting teens know all that the library has to offer and what they've been missing!

No matter what, make yourself and the library visible. Get out there so all the teenagers you're serving know your library and what it's about.

Figure 5.4   Deck the Walls Promo

DECK THE WALLS PROMO

Bring us a photograph we can display in the library—and receive a prize.

Selected photos will be displayed in the library during the month of June. **See a librarian or text us at 888-555-1212 for more details.**

Deadline: May 1

Figure 5.5   Advertising Example

Source: St. Louis (Missouri) Public Library teen lounge print advertisement.

Get the Word Out

Word-of-mouth is a fast and potentially effective way to promote and publicize teen services. Talk to teenage library users and nonusers about what the library has to offer and show them that it's a place with people who genuinely relate to them and care about their needs. Being proactive and talking to male and female teenagers of all ages and social groups is the best thing you can do. Once the word gets out, teenagers will positively talk to other teenagers about your library, its space, happenings, collections, and services. This is your most effective form of advertising.

Regular classroom visits are an excellent way for public and school librarians alike to get the word out about services. Michelle Deschene, young adult librarian at the Peabody Institute Library at Danvers (Massachusetts) says, "School visits are a great way to promote to teens. When engaged in something fun, they pick up on what the library has to offer." During school visits, Michelle has conducted mock teen advisory board meetings, created crafts, and held short story writing contests. As a result, teens come to the library for regular programs—and they bring friends.[15]

Keep in mind that appearance and personality are very important to teens. This is your one chance to make a good first impression. (A bad first impression might be your last impression.) Keep classroom visits brief and interesting. As with other advertising options, it always helps to incorporate an attention-grabber such as photos of cool teen areas across the world or photos of your library's teen area if a project is in the works. After teens get to know you, they will pass the word along to others. Again, there's no better publicity than positive peer-to-peer advertising. After all, teenagers are the primary source of information for teenagers, so get the word out and the rest will fall into place.

AN ONGOING PROCESS

Whether designing a new teen area or trying to figure out how to sustain interest after the space

ONLINE SUMMER READING SUCCESS

The Prince William (Virginia) Public Library System implemented online summer reading for the first time in 2006. Cathy Chang, assistant director, reports that teens are loving it and that review statistics are up. The number of reviews submitted in 2007 was up by 183 (3,609 this year as compared to 3,426 for 2006). Teens continued to submit reviews through the first ten days of September, past the last day of the summer reading program and into the first week of school. In 2007, the highest number of books read was 86. In 2006, the highest number read was 59. "Teens love it. Staff members love it. It's used all the time," says Chang. "I have to say I was thrilled when one of our young adult librarians brought a list to our top participating middle school of all the teens who participated. Needless to say, the PR was great and the school administration was proud," adds Chang.[16] The State of Massachusetts, San Diego (California) County Library, Farmington (New Mexico) Public Library, and Queens (New York) Public Library provide additional examples. For more information on these and other libraries, refer to appendix E. For details on online summer reading vendors and software, refer to appendix D.

TOP REASONS FOR TEENS TO VISIT THE WAUKESHA PUBLIC LIBRARY

The Waukesha (Wisconsin) Public Library created a flier that was distributed to area teens that listed the top reasons for teens to visit the Waukesha Public Library.

New Teen Zone—A special place just for teens

Computers—Internet, word processing, and PowerPoint available

DVDs and videos—Check out all your favorites

Books—Novels, graphic books, or informational, we have them all

CDs—From rock to classical

Magazines—For fun or facts

Homework support—A quiet place to study or get help finding the information you need

Group study rooms—Meet here to get that project completed

Special teen programs—Movies, game tournaments, performers and more

Teen summer reading program—Prizes, programs, and great books

Teen book club—Hang out with friends and discuss great books

Teen advisory group—Give us your input; make the library a better place for you and your friends

Looking into the Waukesha (Wisconsin) Public Library's Teen Zone and a view from the inside.

is finished, it's essential to constantly keep in touch with your teen customers. Never stop asking, "What do teens want, what do they need, and how do they use the library?" More important, never stop asking teens these questions directly. Continue to involve teenagers in as many aspects of service as possible, because the ideal teen space will need continual support. Teens are the best partners you could have. They will be the ones who will be faithful about helping out (if they have good adult leadership); they also will be the ones to draw in other teens. Simply remember the goal: to attract as many teenagers as possible and keep them coming back.

NOTES

1. Magazine Publishers of America, "Teen Market Profile," www.magazine.org/content/files/teenprofile04.pdf.

2. Lauren Mechling, "Come for the Xbox, Stay for the Books," *Boston Globe,* March 11, 2007.

3. "Merchandising the Library—Joan Bernstein," *Library Journal* 131, no. 5 (March 15, 2006), www.libraryjournal.com/article/CA6312504.html.

4. Idea taken in part from Laura Gruniger, young adult librarian at the Mercer County Public Library, Lawrenceville, NJ.

5. Amanda Lenhart, Mary Madden, and Paul Hitlin, *Teens and Technology: Youth Are Leading the Transition to a Fully Wired and Mobile Nation* (Washington, DC: Pew Internet and American Life Project, 2005), www.pewinternet.org/pdfs/PIP_Teens_Tech_July2005web.pdf.

6. "Teens' Space: MySpace Tops Teens' List of Online Destinations," TRU, www.tru-insight.com/PRview.cfm?edit_id=483.

7. Kelly Czarnecki, e-mail interview, November 5, 2007.

8. Shannan Sword, post to YALSA Young Adult Advisory Councils electronic discussion list (ya-yaac@ala.org), August 24, 2007.

9. Christina Stoll, "Library Invaded by Teens and Technology," Metropolitan Library System, June 6, 2007, www.mls.lib.il.us/announce/2007/01_10/blueislandteenstech.asp.

10. Taken in part from Gail Junion-Metz, "Planning and Designing a Website for Kids and Teens" (New York State Library Association Workshop, October 17, 2001, Albany).

11. Miranda Doyle, "Library Web Sites for Teens: Quick Tips" (handout developed for Kimberly Bolan), July 2007.

12. Carrie Dietz, e-mail interview, February 27, 2008.

13. Julie Brandl, e-mail interview, January 15, 2008.

14. Elissa Moses, *The $100 Billion Allowance: Accessing the Global Teen Market* (New York: Wiley, 2000), 182.

15. Michelle Deschene, e-mail interview, December 1, 2007.

16. Cathy Chang, e-mail interviews, August 17, 2006, and October 31, 2007.

Chapter 6 | **Policy and Practice**

The goal of creating teen space and related services is to have a long-term positive impact on your teenage customers. Also important is the impact that teen space and related services will have on the organization—its staff, policies, practices, and other customers. Understanding your teen customers, understanding the overall impact and affects of teen space and services on the organization, and applying that overall understanding to the development of policies and practice are critical to effectively serving teens. The objective is to make the experience positive for all your customers as well as to create positive public perceptions of your library. Positive public relations is essential. Keep in mind that once a teenager (or any customer) has a negative experience, it generally sticks with him or her and affects future interactions with and attitude toward the library; therefore, it is important to take a long, hard look at everything affecting interactions with teen customers. In order for a facility's project (or any of the methods described in this book) to be successful, adults must agree that teen services need to be a priority and that the type of relationship adults have with teenagers must evolve.

ADULT SUPPORT

Throughout the teen space process, administration and key staff members should be cognizant of how their organization functions, the personalities and mind-sets of staff, and the nature and opinions of the community and other library users. Getting buy-in from staff and at least a few adults in the community is vital. Staff and other key adult stakeholders should be actively involved and informed throughout the project (and beyond) to ensure support and avoid problems and miscommunications. Hold staff information sessions and get them involved in assisting with teen focus groups and other aspects of the process. See chapter 2 for more information.

Be aware that adults often have negative impressions of teenagers and are intimidated by them, so it is especially important to openly communicate, to promote teamwork and adult-teen collaborations, and to provide adequate training on adolescence. Having a proactive approach—understanding your staff, discussing issues and concerns before they arise, and actively training them—is a much better course of action than a reactive approach such as keeping staff uninformed and waiting until major problems present themselves. Project leaders and administrators should have a clear vision and openly share that with the entire staff. Specifics will vary based on the overall situation, the tasks at hand, and personalities involved.

Several of the resource libraries reported that they actively involved their entire staff during their teen space projects. Senior staff, administrators, teen and youth services staff, teachers, clerical staff—all were involved in everything from planning, to physically rearranging furniture, to recataloging collections, to promotional efforts, to relaying recommendations and information to the library, school boards, and the community. Pikes Peak (Colorado) Library District's East Library had active involvement from many teen staff members as well as adult services, the associate director, the entire IT department, the finance department, community relations, and facilities. The whole library staff was involved in the Wilmington (Massachusetts) Memorial Library's Teen Zone makeover from the very early stages. The teen librarian worked with the teens and created the proposal and plan; the library director assisted with budgeting and furniture vendor meetings; the children's librarian assisted with the design; and the head of adult services was involved in meetings and offered suggestions. (Going through the process assisted the adult department when they made over their space.) Robin Lettieri, director of the Port Chester Public Library (New York), reports that they involved everyone from the pages to the director. The pages helped shift the collection, and the entire staff knew their suggestions for the space were welcome.

The staff at the Terrazas Branch of the Austin (Texas) Public Library had a say in the design of their teen area as far as requesting the area to be visible from the circulation desk and not fully enclosed. This input led to a three-foot wall with mesh weaving that goes to the ceiling. This defines the space but is not soundproof. This feature allows front desk staff to see into the room easily, which makes it possible to keep the center open when there isn't a librarian staffing it.

POLICIES AND GUIDELINES

We say that we want teens to use the library, but we contradict ourselves by establishing rules that prohibit eating chips and drinking a soda.

Policies such as those addressing food in the library provide a point of reference or direction for staff, allowing for better decisions and consistency in service. They also serve as a source of support for personnel when there is a problem. Policies are not meant to rule over your teen customers. Instead, well-written and well-implemented policies provide a means for customers to know what to expect from the library. When creating policies related to service, the protection of library users' rights, or access to and use of library facilities, give thought to your teenage customers and treat them equally. Keep policies simple and review them annually to make sure they're up to date and relevant. Types of policies include, but aren't limited to

> customer service
>
> collection development or materials selection
>
> Internet and computer use (includes wireless access policies)
>
> confidentiality
>
> meeting room use
>
> equipment use
>
> patron behavior
>
> volunteer recruitment and responsibilities
>
> exhibit, bulletin board, and free materials distribution

Look at policy areas that relate to teens and ask questions such as

Are there age limits on computer use? Wireless use? Other equipment and technology use?

Are there restrictions on the use of the Internet (e.g., no chatting, no social networking, no downloading)?

If teens are only allowed to use computers in the children's area, why? How can this be changed?

Are all collections and services easily and readily accessible to teen customers?

Are library materials available in a variety of formats and subjects that are recreational, informational, and educational for those ages thirteen through eighteen? Basically, are teen collections comparable to adult and children's collections?

Are there age limits on the circulation of various material types, primarily audiovisual materials such as DVDs?

Is there equal access for teens related to meeting room use?

Are there noise regulations and other customer behavior guidelines?

Are there restrictions on cell phone use?

Do policies discriminate against teenagers when it comes to volunteering and exhibiting in showcases and posting information at the library?

Are there any restrictions on facilities and space use?

What is the policy on eating and drinking in the library?

Equally important, ask yourself, "Do the existing policies justifiably pertain to today's society and today's libraries?" Also ask, "Are all customers held to the same expectations? If policies are broken, are all customers held to the same penalties?" The suggestion here is not to change everything, nor is it to question a rule that has legitimate validity, or to let teens run wild in the library. The challenge is simply to take an honest look at some of the regulations libraries have been following for years and to see if they are appropriate for today's world and support a plan for excellent customer service. After all, it's not just teens who want to eat and drink in the library. The Jerome (Idaho) Public Library's digital native services coordinator Tina Cherry has worked hard getting her staff to appreciate teens' use of the library as a third place—cell phones are okay and it's definitely noisier after school. Jerome has also initiated student library cards for twelve- to seventeen-year-olds who are in good standing and aren't already on a family card. They don't need a parent to sign and they don't have to live in the library's service district as long as they go to school there.

One example of policy specifically related to the use of a teen area comes from the Orange County (Florida) Library System. Their policy states:

Club Central is a place on the first floor of the main library designed and reserved for use by teens from thirteen through eighteen. It is a comfortable, inviting place created for teens to study, socialize, and have fun. The use of the facility and resources, including the seating, computers and AV equipment, is limited to those from thirteen through eighteen years of age. Other library users wanting to use young adult materials will be assisted in retrieving materials by staff.[1]

GOT
YOUR
CARD?

A clever promotional tool from Orange County (Florida) Library System.

Orange County also has a knack for using simple things to make a big impact. For example, they use signage to send a positive message to teens. They post signage that says "Got Your Card?" to remind teen customers about having their library cards readily available. On another positive note, the Academy of Irving (Texas) ISD Library doesn't require students to have passes to come to the library. Instead they utilize an electronic sign-in process. Students are free to come and go as they wish as long as they are not creating disturbances. Librarian Gloria Willingham says, "Our goal is to always remember that our teens are our customers and that without them we would not be needed. Our policy is to keep it simple with as few rules as possible. We post our expectations on our website and let students know that if they follow those expectations, they will not be hassled by us." In addition, the academy was the only high school library in its area that didn't charge overdue fines. Now all the high schools in their region have done away with fines. Students are also allowed to listen to their MP3 players in the library.[2]

Guidelines are often confused with policies. Guidelines are a set of rules giving guidance on how to behave in a situation. When it comes to teen space, many libraries have developed use guidelines or rules for the space. This is a proactive way to prevent potential problems. The goal is to manage the space and set behavioral expectations, while also making teens feel comfortable with the library and the staff. If they are not at ease, they will not stay. Most guidelines reflect the overall behavior policy for *all* customers. When writing guidelines, follow these strategies:

Have teens assist in developing the guidelines.

Use positive language—avoid *no* signs and rules such as no food or drink, no talking, etc.

Don't insert your personal biases into guidelines. It is unacceptable to say that a teen area, or library for that matter, is only for readers or the good kids. Hanging out and talking are just as viable as reading and studying.

Clearly post guidelines so teens know the expectations.

Keep in mind that rules have a way of coming back to haunt you, so be careful of what rules you choose and how they are worded. The most important thing you can reflect in guidelines is *respect,* which applies to both teenagers and adults—respect for themselves, for each other, for other customers, staff, the facility, and its contents. In addition, if teens do not feel respected by the library and its staff, it won't matter what guidelines you post. Having a positive customer service approach will go a long way in supporting the guidelines. Organization-based issues and policies may also come into play here, including eating and drinking in the library, noise levels, cell phone use, and restricting teen areas to teen-only use.

You may eat and drink here. When it comes to food and drink, libraries such as the Calgary (Alberta, Canada) and Vancouver (British Columbia, Canada) Public Libraries have relaxed their rules around eating and drinking in the library because they want people to come in and stay, especially students who want to have a coffee or snack while studying. People were smuggling in food and drink anyway, so why not? "If we want to attract people, we have to kind of get over ourselves about eating and drinking," said Jean Ludlam, a library manager at Calgary.[3] Maureen DeLaughter at the William K. Sanford Town Library (Loudonville,

New York) says, "Definitely let them eat in the room. All they really want is to hang out with friends and eat. If you give teens food, they will be happy." See the "Healthy Vending" text box for additional food and drink guidelines.

Talking welcomed. Quiet libraries are more an exception than a rule these days. More libraries are relaxing their no talking rules to entice more customers. It is expected that teens will talk and make noise (within reason, of course). Creating flexible library spaces that allow teens to study as well as to socialize and hold noisy programs is fundamental.

Cell phone use is OK. Allow teens to communicate, but set guidelines for cell phone etiquette. For example, please set cell phones to vibrate or silent and keep a low voice when speaking.

Teen-Only Areas

In medium-sized and large public libraries, there is the consideration of designating teen space for teen-only use. Your decision will ultimately be determined by your customer service plan, staffing situation, space size, use patterns, and security issues. When considering a teen-only area, ask yourself the following questions:

Can teens adequately use the library facilities during key times or are other customers impeding on teen service?

Is there regular conflict between teens and adults related to seating, technology, etc.?

Is the teen area a safe place for teenagers? Are there security issues?

Are other customers being disturbed by teen activities?

QUICK TIP

Having trouble with library staff's attitude toward teens? Ask each staff member to practice these simple customer service essentials: smile, greet teens in a positive manner, and talk to them rather than at them.

Other considerations include

Will the age limit in the teen area be enforced all day, every day or will it be enforced only while teens are out of school?

How will the limit be enforced? By staff, signage, physical barrier, or combination?

If the space is teen-only all day, every day, how do adults access the space and the collection? Do they need to be accompanied by a teenager? Do they need to get assistance from a staff member?

If adults are allowed in when teens are in school, how will you handle getting adults out during teen-only hours?

Handling adults using the teen area has been an issue for years. Five to ten years ago, it was a common occurrence in most public libraries to see adults sitting in the teen area. Generally, this was due to lack of attention to teen services and lack of use of libraries by teen customers. Now, it is more common to see adults in teen space because it is the area with the comfortable seating and new technology. Nevertheless, if a teen area is empty, no matter how new it is, adults will eventually find their way there because, to them, an empty area, no matter whom it's designated for, is a quiet place to think and read. When

QUICK TIP

Share this tip with your general library staff: The majority of adult library users report they want the same things teens want—comfortable furnishings, the latest technology, food and drink in the library. What can you do to make the nonteen spaces in your facility welcoming and pleasant?

considering guidelines for facility use, it's equally critical to examine the options for adult customers. Having amenities for adults that are equally exciting and appropriately meet their needs and wants will allow great buy-in and acceptance of teen space. There are a few questions to consider here:

How comfortable is the rest of your library for your adult customers?

Do you have quiet spaces for adult users?

Is the technology up to date throughout the library? Are there enough computers and other technologies for adult users?

What other elements in the teen area attract adults? How can these be incorporated into the rest of the library?

By creating a twenty-first-century library facility for all ages, you will surely be able to meet all users' needs and have a more positive impact on teen services.

GENERAL TEEN AREA GUIDELINES

1. Respect yourself
2. Respect others
3. Respect the space

An Example from Campbell County (Wyoming) Public Library System

Welcome to the Young Adult Area!

You may hang out in the teen room and enjoy all it has to offer IF YOU

- are in junior high or high school
- respect library property *and* the property of the other teens here
- keep your hands to yourself
- use clean language
- remember that public displays of affection are not appropriate here
- pick up after yourself
- use your indoor voice

Please keep the above guidelines or you will be asked to leave the library.

These guidelines were developed by the Teen Advisory Board and library staff.

Guidelines by Teens, for Teens

Hennepin County (Minnesota) Library Minneapolis Central Library opened its Teen Central in 2006 with a Meeting Zone, a popular room with silver metallic wallpaper that teens can write on, similar to a dry erase board. Teens can jot down poetry, math problems, messages, and more. Unfortunately, after the space opened, they had some difficulties with the room, but came up with a creative way to solve their problem. Here are the guidelines (created with teen input) that are currently posted:

Express Yourself—Write on the Walls—But Please Respect Library Property

Writing on the walls of the Teen Meeting Zone is limited to the silver wallpaper.

Please do not write on the carpet, the floor, the doors or other areas not covered with the silver wallpaper.

In September 2007, writing on these areas forced us to close this room for cleaning. That cleaning cost the library more than a thousand dollars.

What would that have bought Teen Central?

One more laptop
150 more CDs
25 video games
125 books

The Teen Central Teen Advisory Group asks that you please respect this space and the rules we've set for it. Thanks!

"Having teens involved in the design of the process—right down to setting the rules of the space and being a welcoming presence on opening day—has laid the foundation for success in Teen Central," says Christy Mulligan, Teen Central librarian. "That, combined with our positive staff who focus on serving all teens regardless of their reason for being in the library, has made this a top spot for youth during out-of-school time and on weekends."[4] Look to the Web and various resource libraries (see appendix E) for additional sample policies and guidelines. Post yours online to share with others.

HEALTHY VENDING GUIDELINES

The Cleveland Heights–University Heights (Ohio) Public Library has developed healthy vending guidelines. Here's an overview:

Objectives

1. We will refine our dedication to customer service.

2. We will increase the library's value to the community.

With the introduction of vending areas at the Lee Road Library and, thereafter, in our other buildings, we acknowledge a shared, social responsibility to be supportive of positive nutritional and healthy lifestyle choices.

In 2004, Congress addressed this issue with schools by passing the Federal Child Nutrition Act. To improve the overall health of the nation's children, this act requires all schools participating in federal lunch programs to enact a Wellness Policy by the start of the coming school year. The act does not spell out specific requirements but, instead, encourages an approach that promotes healthy learning, activity, and nutrition.

For our customers, staff members have been working towards creating our own "Healthy Vending" guidelines that would support recommended nutritional choices.

When considering contents for our machines, we will make selections based on the following recommendations from the U.S. Department of Health and Human Services and the U.S. Department of Agriculture's *Dietary Guidelines for Americans 2005*.

With these guidelines in mind, staff will work with providers to negotiate vending arrangements, with all profits going to the Friends of the Library.[5]

BEST PRACTICES

Best practices in teen space are all about new ways of thinking about library facilities design and customer service. A large part of establishing best practices for teen space means excellent service. To be successful with a facilities plan, a library must establish high-quality practices including garnering support from adults in the community, creating fair, well-thought-out policies and guidelines, and developing a first-rate customer service model.

Cape Central (Missouri) High School provides a wonderful example of forward-thinking, collaborative, teen-centered practices that apply to both school and public libraries. Principal Mike Cowan says, "A good public high school is a microcosm of the community it serves and we meet this standard well. It is our mission to provide a comfortable atmosphere so that upon graduation, students will feel comfortable in any library they may encounter."

Cape Central's library and practices are a must-see as librarians, educators, and design teams investigate best practices for libraries and library spaces. Here are some details of their space and program:

Entrance. The library was designed to have space between the hallway and the physical collection of books. In a high school, hallways are a source of romance, conflict, and heartbreak; staff felt the need for breathing space between all of that and the collection. They refer to the entrance as their front porch with overhead flying books, comfortable seating, a sculpture, and of course, displays featuring books.

Comfortable seating. At the entrance of the library, rather than being greeted by the circulation desk, their teen customers find plum leather love seats and over-stuffed chairs around a coffee table and fountain. "This is a popular spot to sit and read and everyone who enters the library comments on the comfortable ambiance that this establishes," relays Jorgensen. "This was our intent, of course. We did not want to appear stuffy or childish, but rather sought to find a balance between public or college libraries and elementary libraries." Jorgensen says she never expected to have leather love seats and over-stuffed chairs in her school library, but that's what the kids liked, so that's what they got. Selecting the furnishings provided both an educational opportunity and gave them ownership in the space. Incidentally, the furniture was donated by a local furniture store whose owners represent five generations of Central graduates.

The Bookend. Students can purchase cappuccino and popcorn to enjoy while in the library. Again, it was their intent to design and provide a space that was comfortable and inviting and, when your customers are teenagers, food is a major draw. They have had only a few accidental spills and rarely do they have to pick up trash. The students are aware that this is a unique feature and rise to the occasion, utilizing self-serve and paying on the honor system. They adopted a high school library in Mississippi and proceeds from the sale of cappuccino and popcorn were donated after Katrina. Financial support for projects varies depending on need and students' interest.

The front porch-style entrance provides a welcoming atmosphere with comfortable seating, a fountain, and plants.

The Bookend, with laptops and self-serve cappuccino and popcorn.

Circulation desk. The circular circulation desk is in the center of the library. The computer monitors are sunk into the counter because desk staff wanted to see and be seen by their customers rather than viewing them through wires or over plastic boxes. Both staff members who work at the desk enjoy teenagers and exude a friendly, upbeat attitude. This is a crucial requirement for dealing with teen angst. Their teen customers find adults with genuine warmth and smiling faces when they check out books or ask for assistance, a feature that is a key component of their mission.

Collection and display. Acknowledging that their customers are in a hurry to get on with their lives, they have made a conscious effort to create a user-friendly library with effortless browsing so students can quickly find materials. They encourage their students to be independent. Favorite authors have a shelf label, and authors of the classics have a small Lucite holder by their works that include a photo on one side and a brief biographical sketch on the other. Far from the traditional biography, these have little-known facts that librarians think their teen readers would find amusing, intriguing, or interesting. On the shelf by John Grisham's *A Painted House,* for example, the observant customer will find a child's toy tractor from the 1950s. Typically, they have twenty-five to thirty titles on the *USA Today* best-seller list, which are highlighted and updated each Thursday. Graphic novels and audiobooks are also prominently displayed. The advantage of having shelving spread around the room in a variety of shapes and sizes is that it allows for flexible displays that break up the monotony of a large space, thereby creating a cozy environment for casual browsing and investigating. Staff members feel that it is important to pay attention to details. Their displays are unique and unexpected, yet focused on student learning and academics.

Other. It is the school's philosophy that the arts should be an integral component of the facility. A sound system provides classical music for customers to enjoy Monday through Thursday, and students hear the sounds of their favorites on Fridays. Tables are designated as chess tables during lunch and before and after school. With grant funding, the library is able to provide tutoring to students. The facility opens at six o'clock each morning with subject-specific tutoring provided by a member of the teaching staff. After-school tutoring and transportation home is also available because of grants. In addition, students are learning to knit, crochet, and make jewelry in the library as part of the library after-hours program. During the school day and extended school hours, technology instruction is also available with individual help sessions. A computer lab adjacent to the library, in addition to the lab within the library, has increased popularity and workload. A voter registration center is also provided close to elections. County officials bring a voting booth and speak with students.

Looking into the library.

BEST PRACTICE—QUEENS BOROUGH (NEW YORK) PUBLIC LIBRARY

In 2007, the Queens Borough (New York) Public Library planned, designed, and opened its first facility solely dedicated to teens—the Far Rockaway Teen Library. The new 3,200-square-foot facility does not reside in the Far Rockaway branch, but instead is located a block away in a leased corner retail space with an open floor plan and huge windows. The library started having trouble with overcrowding after school and disruptive teen behavior at the branch, so it applied for and received a federal 21st Century Community Learning Center grant in 2003. The grant focused on academic, social, and behavioral issues for middle school students. The program was more successful than the library anticipated, and the lack of space became an increasingly problematic issue. Library staff knew they needed to do something and they wanted to promote the concept of community and service to its customers. Their solution: a unique teen library filled with forty computers, seventy magazine titles, loads of multifunctional soft seating and configurable tables and chairs, homework assistance, and interactive programming.

The bright, energetic, colorful reimagined teen library was a collaborative effort between Queens Library staff, a library consultant who designed the space based on input from Queens' teens, and a library design and furnishings company. (See floor plan below.) Part of the project's success stems from library administration starting with clearly defined goals and scope. All parties took ownership in designing and creating a space to meet the end goal—a community-centered, innovative, flexible space to accommodate a variety of activities including individual and collaborative study, socializing, computing, gaming, and more. The space is also distinctive in that it is staffed by youth counselors rather than librarians and is only open during after-school hours. A tutor/licensed teacher and social worker are also available to assist teens. There are multiple mobile service points in the space so staff are more accessible.

Everyone worked together to keep the project on schedule (with only three months from start to finish), on budget ($100,000 for minor construction, electric and data, flooring, furniture, and décor), and within design parameters.

Teens, parents, library staff, and the community are thrilled with the library. "There has been very positive feedback and results," says Maureen O'Connor, director of library services, "Positive programming is occurring, there's an increase in use, and parents are telling staff they are more comfortable sending their kids to the library." Several teens are in awe of the space that was created just for them and have commented to staff that the space is so nice they "feel like they're in Manhattan." The new teen space has also reduced overcrowding issues at the Far Rockaway Branch down the street, so the library is better able to serve the public, including the teens who visit both locations. Phase two of the project, to begin in 2008, will include purchase of textbooks, exam preparation and reference materials, and a portable recording studio.

A positive solution to an initially negative situation, the Far Rockaway Teen Library encourages learning, positive adult-teen interaction, and community building. According to Denise Clark, Queens Library's government grants manager, "This is a very attractive project to donors and government funders who find this a unique avenue to address the needs of teens." The library has already received a juvenile justice award from the New York State Division of Criminal Justice Services.

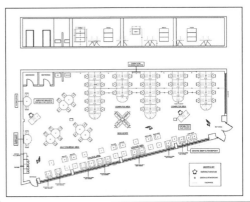

Far Rockaway Teen Library (New York) designed by Kimberly Bolan, Kimberly Bolan and Associates, and DEMCO Library Interiors. Photo courtesy of Queens Library and DEMCO, Inc.

Source: Far Rockaway Teen Library planned by Kimberly Bolan of Kimberly Bolan and Associates and DEMCO Library Interiors (DLI). Floor plan courtesy of DLI and Queens (New York) Public Library.

Events. In an effort to create an environment that is high-energy and exciting, the library frequently hosts events for students and the greater Cape Girardeau community. As the only public high school in the city, they feel it is important to encourage the community to come into the building so that they can see their tax dollars at work. Programs range from fund-raisers and promotions for clubs and athletics, to authors' and writers' workshops, to book clubs and discussions, to special program such as the September Project, which opens the library to the community on September 11 with an original program featuring the talent of students and staff.

Staff and more. A monthly newsletter is published by the library for school staff and can be read online by parents and the community. Effectively communicating with the 125 adults that work with the school's teenagers is imperative. A Professional Reading Room in the front of the library was designed to be a sanctuary from students and noise but close to the collection. A local furniture store donated the furnishings for the room, making it a comfortable place to spend some time catching up on professional journals and recent trends or enjoying a cup of hot tea or coffee. Teachers like to be nurtured too![6]

CUSTOMER SERVICE

Customer service plays a huge role in teen services best practices. First-rate customer service for all ages should be part of a library's mission, vision, and planning process. San Jose (California) Public Library has the motto "Everyone Services Youth." This is a reminder that no matter what age the customer is, they are valued and their use of the library is just as important as anyone else's. Rather than shushing teens, staff at the Evansville Vanderburgh (Indiana) Public Library welcome teens and chat with them. Movable chairs that can be easily rearranged are a big hit as they can rearrange the seating into clusters for socializing. The Seward (Nebraska) Memorial Library has after-hours for ninth- through twelfth-graders on Thursday evenings from eight to nine-thirty. No registration is required for the evenings, which offer twenty-five-cent cans of soda, free food once a month, and various activities. Teens can also be the first to see new books added to the collection. From positive staff interaction with teens, to incorporating simple tools such as an online suggestion box for gathering teen input on collections, programs, and facilities, strong customer service is fundamental in making teen space successful.

Changing Attitudes

How many times have teens been treated poorly just because they're teenagers? We want teens to help libraries increase our statistics and be future library supporters, yet we continue to treat them badly. Quite clearly, this attitude tells teens that we don't want their business. Many library workers admit that they want teens to use the library but that teen behavior and attention level drives them crazy; consequently, these workers are turned off to helping teens. Others struggle with being liked versus letting teens walk all over them. No doubt these are tough issues, but they're not as hopeless as you might think. Staff members who are trained to understand the developmental needs and behaviors of teens are better able to cope and respond positively to difficult situations. Everyone needs to clearly understand that customer service means consistently treating all customers equally and with respect. Teens can recognize good service as quickly as anyone else, and it's this good service (and an occasional smile) that will keep them coming back.

When the Peabody Institute Library at Peabody (Massachusetts) had behavioral issues with teens, instead of banning them, they started a young adult drop-in program. By providing teens with computer access, a place to hang out, casual homework assistance, after-school snacks, daily crafts, games, and other activities, they changed the atmosphere of the entire library. When teens were asked to comment on the newly redesigned YA Drop-In space and the program as a whole, teens responded, "I love the YA Drop-In" and "YA Drop-In rocks!" Because this program is one of the only free after-school programs in the city and due to its great success, the Peabody City Council now provides the library with additional funds for extra programs and new computers each year as part of their effort to prevent teen drug use.[7] The Campbell County (Wyoming) Public Library System has a window which allows staff to see into the bathroom and water fountain areas without leaving the teen room. That was an afterthought when they had problems in the hallway and there was concern about noise and behavior problems. The window solved their problem fast and opened up the feel of the room too—without impacting customer service.

First and foremost, dedicated, enthusiastic, and open-minded employees are key to good customer service; all staff members (not just youth staff) are important. Providing great customer service consists of knowing the customer and applying the golden rule—treat others as you would like to be treated. To begin the process of evaluating and developing a customer service plan, have all staff rate themselves from one to five on the following points, with one as the lowest score. Staff should ask themselves how the last three teen customers they worked would have rated them.[8]

> I like what I do.
>
> I believe the library is a great asset to teenagers.
>
> I like people.
>
> I like working with *all the users* of the library.
>
> I'm a great person to work with.
>
> I have a good sense of humor.
>
> I am patient.
>
> I really listen when others are talking.

Scores

> 8–23 might indicate a need to work a bit on self-image and learn more about the value of the library.
>
> 24–31 would indicate that you are above average. Keep smiling and do your best.
>
> 32 and above reflects a great attitude.
>
> 40 would indicate that you are perfect (and therefore probably very annoying!).

Use these questions and the results as a point of discussion to further discuss customer service practices and goals.

Customer Service Training

Regular, ongoing customer service evaluation and training are essential. For more customer service information and a sample training program, visit the Houston (Texas) Area Library System's online training site. See appendix C for details. Modules include a basic practices and skills overview, overcoming barriers in difficult situations, cultural diversity, basic skills of frontline public services, working with teens, Web and e-mail, telephone, and challenging situations.

As part of a library merchandising initiative in 2004 called Trading Spaces, the Mount Laurel (New Jersey) Public Library staff members were trained in new merchandising and customer service techniques. Even though this project was library-wide (not solely a teen project), the general idea behind the process is essential. Staff were involved throughout the entire project, which promoted buy-in to making the project work. As with teen services, there were uncertainties and unfamiliarity with what, at the time, were new techniques and practices. With perseverance and teamwork, the project was a success. Now every staff member is a marketer, a passionate public speaker, and knowledgeable about big-picture policies and procedures.[9] See more about this project in chapter 5.

Beginning in 2004 with the support of the Wallace Foundation, the New York Public Library, in cooperation with the Brooklyn Public Library and Queens Library, has offered a workshop titled "Everyone Serves Youth" which encourages staff to reach out to children and teenagers as library customers. Teen librarians are encouraged to participate on community youth councils to increase public awareness of the library and services to teenagers. As a result, service is booming at New York's Bronx Library Center for Teens, which opened in January 2006. A statistical comparison between July 2005 through June 2006 and July 2006 through June 2007 showed that teen circulation increased 56 percent, attendance at programs increased 41 percent, and the number of teen-related information requests increased 128 percent.[10] See appendix E for additional information on these model libraries.

STAFFING THE SPACE

There is no doubt that excellent customer service and well-trained, welcoming personnel play a major role in teen space success. The bigger questions for many libraries are

---

CUSTOMER SERVICE TIPS

Here are a few customer service tips for adults working with teens:

Smile.

Be proactive—go to them, don't wait for them to come to you.

Don't try to be one of them—be friendly and be yourself.

Show leadership and supervision, but don't be dictatorial and condescending.

Greet teen customers, even if it's brief.

Don't stare or give the evil eye.

Don't have Velcro butt—come out from behind the desk.

Make eye contact and use positive body language when speaking to teens.

Really listen—show interest in what teens are saying.

Don't interrupt.

Be approachable and nonjudgmental.

Encourage teens to come to you if they have questions.

Be aware of teens' different learning styles and cultural differences, if possible. This is very helpful when working directly with them, creating signage, instruction, and more.

Get customer service training as well as training on adolescent development and teen needs and behaviors.

Treat all patrons the same—no double standards.

Work to change negative librarian stereotypes.

Remember to smile!

Should the area be constantly monitored?

Should your teen space have a separate service desk?

Who should be responsible for monitoring the space?

To answer these questions effectively, consideration should be given to the size of your space, its location, the amount and type of activities that are taking place or expected to take place, and security issues. Obviously a 400-square-foot area will be treated differently from a 3,000-square-foot area, or a space that is more secluded from sight lines may be treated differently than one visible from service points, and so on.

Take into consideration the items previously discussed under the "Teen-only Areas" section. It is more than reasonable to staff a teen space during certain hours such as after school and weekends. For example, hours might be: Monday through Thursday from two to eight o'clock, Fridays from two to six o'clock, Saturdays from ten to five o'clock, and Sundays from one to four o'clock. Some school libraries might also vary hours from regular school hours, opening early in the morning and staying open after school.

It is also reasonable for medium-sized and large facilities to include one or more service points for staff assisting teens. The East Brunswick (New Jersey) Public Library has one portable service desk inside their 1,500-square-foot teen space. It is staffed after school and on evenings and weekends from one to nine o'clock at night. They don't always have a librarian in the teen space; sometimes they staff it with a customer service representative. The Cleveland Heights–University Heights' (Ohio) Lee Road Library has a teen services office that resides in the teen area (see figure 6.1), while the Melton (Indiana) Public Library gives teens the power to police their own space and discovered that many step up to the plate. The Orange County (Florida) Library System's Club Central is not separately staffed; instead, they utilize a mobile reference model, which means that staff are not stationed in one specific area, but move around the building assisting customers where and when needed. There is a small service point next to Club Central with staff computer, scrap paper, pencils, pens, etc. Staff use the service point when they need a computer to access customers' accounts or to work with reservations for public computers with Internet access. Customers also come to this service point when they need assistance. Staff members regularly check the area and can easily spot a customer who needs assistance. The area is staffed at all hours the library is open. During the school days, there is increased after-school traffic from the nearby middle school. If staffing permits, they will place an extra staff member in the area during after-school hours. There are three different levels of staffing:

Figure 6.1   Cleveland Heights–University Heights (Ohio) Lee Road Branch Teen Area floor plan. Floor plan complete with a computer area, homework/gaming counter, lounge with healthy vending, a quiet study room, stack and study area, and a staff office.

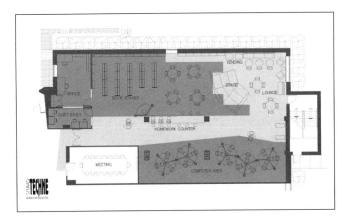

Source: Courtesy of Studio Techne Architects and Cleveland Heights–University Heights Public Library.

1. Two storytellers, two youth services librarians, three youth program assistants, and one youth programs coordinator. They don't work exclusively in the teen area, but cover the entire first floor where children's and teen services are located.

East Brunswick (New Jersey) Public Library's teen area with portable service point. The space is staffed after school and on weekends. Teen area designed by Kimberly Bolan, Kimberly Bolan and Associates, DEMCO Library Interiors, and local teens. Photos courtesy of DEMCO, Inc.

2. Librarians from other departments of the library are scheduled to cover the teen area.

3. Reference clerks from the youth services department and other library reference departments are scheduled to work on the first floor.

VerbYL in Yeppoon, Queensland, Australia, is the result of a community collaborative: it's not a library with a youth worker, nor is it a youth center with a library in the corner—rather it is a truly equal partnership of the two. The center has a full-time youth librarian responsible for all library programs and library-based resources. VerbYL also has a full-time qualified youth worker who guides young people toward positive activities, conflict management, confidential information and referrals for issues such as drugs, alcohol, pregnancy, and employment. The two employees work in a complementary fashion to deliver quality services to their young adult customers. See chapter 1 and appendix E for more information on verbYL.

Having friendly, knowledgeable staff that teens can relate to and talk to is a high priority for many teenagers. Teens are more likely to visit the library and use its services if they like and feel comfortable with the people working

QUICK TIP

One answer to flexible staffing is to fill in gaps with well-trained volunteers. Several of the resource libraries rely on volunteer hours to make their teen services successful.

VerbYL in Queensland, Australia, combines library services with a teen hangout.

there. It's essential that teens see the new image of librarians. Regarding this image, Tyrone Ward, a manager at a west side branch of the Chicago Public Library, was quoted as saying, "The schoolmarmish librarian with the reading glasses and the long dress and the bun in her hair was a wonderful lady, very loving and very devoted to her work, but her day is gone. The stereotype has more life than she does."[11] Even in the age of computers, there is no substitute for the human touch—a touch that comes from someone who is friendly, smart, and helpful.

Just as it's important to have staff who specialize in children's services, it is equally important to have staff who specialize in teen services. Libraries such as the Southfield (Michigan) Public Library created a teen specialist position when they opened their new teen area. The Missouri River (Missouri) Regional Library increased the teen staff by two part-time staff (giving them a total of three) so they could increase the hours their teen space was open. Even libraries such as the Wilmington (Massachusetts) Memorial Library, with less than 25,000 people in their communities, have dedicated full-time teen service personnel. This person doesn't necessarily have to be a librarian and certainly doesn't have to be right out of library school or the youngest person on staff; some of the best teen specialists are over forty! Decisions should be based on the person's ability to work with teens, not on their age or degree. For example, the Queens (New York) Library's Far Rockaway Teen Library is supervised by youth counselors, which is an excellent option for urban libraries (and even small environments with a lot of activity). See the text box earlier in this chapter for more information.

NOTES

1. Vera Gubnitskaia, e-mail interview, September 25, 2007.
2. Gloria Willingham, e-mail interview, December 4, 2007.
3. Allison Jones, "Not Your Mother's Library: Institutions Shedding Stodgy Image to Attract Teens," *Canadian Press,* March 2, 2007.
4. Christy Mulligan, e-mail interview, February 29, 2008.
5. Cathy Hakala-Ausperk, e-mail interview, February 19, 2008.
6. Julia Jorgensen, e-mail interviews, October 3, 2005, and February 15, 2008.
7. Melissa Rauseo, interview, November 29, 2007.
8. Taken in part from Deana Noack, "Customer Service 123," Houston Area Library System (2004–2007), www.hals.lib.tx.us/cust123/1staff.htm.
9. "Merchandising the Library—Joan Bernstein," *Library Journal* 131, no. 5 (March 15, 2006), www.libraryjournal.com/article/CA6312504.html.
10. Christopher Shoemaker, e-mail interview, January 17, 2008.
11. John W. Fountain, "Librarians Adjust Image in an Effort to Fill Jobs," *New York Times,* August 23, 2001.

Appendix A | **Templates**

[Insert Library Name]

TELL US WHAT YOU WANT IN YOUR NEW TEEN AREA

An Online Survey

The [insert library name] is in the planning stages of creating a **new teen area**. We would like your input on the library and the new teen space, so if you are between the ages of thirteen and eighteen, please take a few moments to fill out this survey. You'll help us better serve you and get a chance to win a [**enter name/type of prize**].

1. Where do you like to hang out? Select as many as you like.

    Answer format: radio buttons or check boxes so they can select multiple answers. Potential answers:

    - The mall
    - My bedroom/My house
    - Friends' houses
    - Other _____ [*short text box for inputting information*]
    - Online
    - School events
    - Bookstores

2. How do you communicate with your friends? Select as many as you like.

    Answer format: radio buttons or check boxes so they can select multiple answers. Potential answers:

    - IM
    - Text messaging
    - E-mail
    - Other _____ [*short text box for inputting information*]
    - Phone
    - MySpace, YouTube, Facebook, etc.

3. How often do you come to the public library?

    Answer format: radio buttons or check boxes. They may select only one answer here. Potential answers:

    - every day
    - once a week
    - once a month
    - a few times a year
    - once a year
    - never

4. What do you like about the public library?

    Answer format: text box so they can type their answer

5. What do you dislike about the public library?

    Answer format: text box so they can type their answer

6. Why do you use the library?

    Answer format: radio buttons or check boxes so they can select multiple answers. Potential answers:

    - to use the Internet
    - to do homework/research
    - to hang out with friends
    - to read magazines
    - to borrow materials (books, music CDs, videos/DVDs, magazines/newspapers, etc.)

- to read
- to find information of personal interest
- to get help from a librarian
- to attend library programs and events
- other _____ [*short text box for inputting information*]

7. What would make you want to use the library more?

Answer format: radio buttons or check boxes so they can select multiple answers. Potential answers:

- having a space just for teens that is comfortable and welcoming where I can hang out
- adding more computers
- bringing in more technologies such as listening stations, big-screen TV, etc.
- adding more magazines
- adding more books
- adding more music CDs and videos/DVDs
- friendlier library workers
- having a café, vending machines, etc.
- more interesting library programs and events
- other _____ [*short text box for inputting information*]

Additional comments or suggestions [*Include a text box here so they can type in additional comments.*]

8. What kind of "look and feel" would you like the library's teen/young adult area to have? Please think about your favorite places to hang out. What makes them so wonderful? How can the library create a space that is warm and welcoming to teenagers? What colors, furnishings, etc., appeal to you and others you know? Describe your ideas below.

Answer format: text box so they can type their answer

9. Would you be willing to serve on a teen space planning committee and or a teen advisory board to help plan the new teen area?

Answer format: radio buttons or check boxes. They may select only one answer here. Potential answers:

☐ Yes   ☐ No   ☐ Maybe—I'd like more information

If you answered Yes or Maybe, please provide your name and a way to contact you.

Answer format: text box so they can type their answer

10. Optional: If you would like a chance to win a [**enter name/type of prize**] please complete the following information.

Name: _____ Age: _____ Grade level: _____

Phone number: _____ E-mail address: _____

Gender: ☐ Male ☐ Female

Thank you for helping us.

Stay tuned for more information on your new space!

BYLAWS FOR THE ROARING SPRING COMMUNITY LIBRARY

Teen Advisory Board

Adopted December 2005

ARTICLE I: NAME

This organization shall be called "The Teen Advisory Board of the Roaring Spring Community Library" and abbreviated as "TAB."

ARTICLE II: MISSION

The mission of TAB is to promote the Roaring Spring Community Library's services to teens by

- planning and implementing teen programs
- creating an inviting atmosphere at the library by maintaining a safe, attractive teen area
- promoting ideas regarding the young adult collection
- promoting and encouraging reading by teens
- advocating the rights of teens

The existence of TAB does not preclude the development of other teen programs by library staff.

ARTICLE III: MEMBERSHIP

Section 1

TAB shall be coordinated by an adult library staff member who will serve as TAB advisor and supervise all TAB meetings, activities, and special projects. The TAB advisor will provide guidance in planning TAB activities and reserves the right to reject and/or revise an idea due to space or budget constraints.

Section 2

TAB shall maintain an open membership, with no limit on the number of members.

Section 3

TAB membership is open to students in grades six through twelve.

Section 4

Members may continue to serve on TAB until they graduate from high school or reach nineteen years of age, whichever is later.

Section 5

A member shall be held accountable for absences and become inactive after six consecutive, unexcused absences. Inactive members will not be informed of meetings. They will be taken off the mailing list and will no longer be eligible to vote. An absence shall be considered unexcused when a member is absent from an official TAB meeting and makes no effort to inform the TAB advisor. It is solely up to the TAB advisor to decide if an absence is excused or unexcused.

ARTICLE IV: OFFICERS

Section 1

The officers shall be a president, a vice-president, and a secretary, elected from the members of TAB. All officers should make a special effort to attend all meetings, programs, and special events sponsored by TAB.

Section 2

The president of TAB will work closely with the TAB advisor to organize TAB meetings. The president will assist the TAB advisor in creating the meeting agenda and will preside over TAB meetings. The president will act as a contact person for other TAB members who want items added to the meeting agenda.

Section 3

The vice-president will serve as the president in his or her absence. The vice-president will serve as membership coordinator, keeping track of active and inactive members and new applications. The vice-president will inform and remind all members of upcoming meetings, programs, and special events.

Section 4

The secretary will keep minutes of TAB meetings and keep them on file in a notebook in the YA area. The secretary will be responsible for the attendance sheets at all meetings and inform the vice-president of absent members at meetings. The secretary will read the highlights of the previous meeting's minutes at the beginning of each regular meeting. The secretary will see to the upkeep of the master file of minutes to be kept in the YA area. The secretary will keep track of all votes taken at each meeting. The secretary will serve as the president in the absence of the presiding president and vice-president.

Section 5

Officers will serve a term of one year, from June to the following June.

Section 6

Each June a new election will be held. Officers may serve in the same office for unlimited terms.

ARTICLE V: MEETINGS

Section 1

The regular meetings will be held every other Monday at 4:00 p.m. during the months of September through June.

Section 2

Special meetings may be called by the TAB advisor to complete tasks as needed.

ARTICLE VI: CODE OF ETHICS

Section 1

TAB members will keep the TAB mission at the forefront of all TAB activities.

Section 2

During all TAB meetings, activities, and library functions, TAB members will act in a way that reflects positively on the Roaring Spring Community Library.

Section 3

TAB members will show respect for other TAB members, library staff, and library patrons. Members will demonstrate respect for others by listening attentively when someone else is speaking, asking questions when clarification is needed, and by refraining from negative comments when responding to other people's ideas.

Section 4

TAB members will show respect for library materials and property by taking care to leave meeting spaces neat and orderly.

Section 5

TAB members will strive to make use of their time during meetings and while working on projects by staying on task.

Section 6

TAB members will respect the privacy of other TAB members.

ARTICLE VII: REMOVAL OF MEMBERS FROM TAB

In the extremely rare case that a member of TAB is consistently disruptive to the mission of TAB, it is the responsibility of the TAB advisor to remove that person from the membership. The TAB advisor will make every attempt to resolve the situation before removing the member from the board.

TEEN ADVISORY BOARD APPLICATION

Roaring Spring Community Library

Please fill out the following information and return it to the Roaring Spring Community Library.

Name _____

Address _____

Phone_____   **E-mail** _____

School _____   **Grade** _____

Please help us get to know you by answering the following questions. Use the back if necessary.

What are some of your hobbies and interests, and extracurricular school activities?

What is your favorite book of all time, and why do you love it?

What are some good books you have read lately?

I am aware my teen is applying for a position on the Roaring Spring Community Library's Teen Advisory Board.

Signature of parent or guardian_____

SAMPLE TEEN ADVISORY BOARD AGENDAS

Sample Agenda 1

Date: December 28, 2:00 p.m.

1. Board purpose and introductions/icebreaker
2. Name for the board
3. Board officers and their roles
4. Ground rules
5. Teen space
6. Ideas for January
7. Fund-raising ideas
8. Handouts
9. Establish monthly meeting dates

Sample Agenda 2

Date: January 12, 3:30 p.m.

1. Icebreaker
2. National Hobby Month: Origami project
3. February ideas; contest/drawing/prizes

   Presidents' Day: match presidents with their pets

   Valentine's Day: match love songs with singers

   Black History Month: match photos and names with accomplishments

   Chinese New Year: Chinese horoscopes or haiku contest
4. Name and rules for teen space
5. Painting and decorating
6. Calendar/next meeting

Sample Agenda 3

Date: May 11, 3:30 p.m.

1. Budget update
2. Teen space additions (TV/DVD player)

3. Fund-raisers/activities:

   Donation drive for the humane society

   Summer fund-raisers (ideas: booth at Thompson's, car wash, bake sale)
4. Teen Summer Program/other incentives
5. Mother's Day craft

Sample Agenda 4

Date: October 25, 3:30 p.m.

1. Welcome and introductions/select next chairs
2. Budget ($878.18)
3. Fund-raisers/activities:

   Holiday fund-raiser—cookie mixes in a jar

   Assign ingredients: who can bring an ingredient?

   Begin assembling November 16th (no school)

   Begin selling December 1st

   Activities up to next meeting

   Read & Feed (10/30)

   Popcorn and movie (11/16) NO SCHOOL

   TABOO meeting (11/29)
4. Volunteer opportunities

   We need people to help assemble the cookie mix in the jars on November 16th

   Thanks to those who helped with the book sale setup and to those who are helping Mrs. Spice with the Halloween party tomorrow
5. New business

   Leadership and responsibility
6. Other business
7. Next meeting (November 29th at 3:30 p.m.)

Courtesy of the Farnsworth (Wisconsin) Public Library's TABOO group

DESIGN FEEDBACK SHEET

Rate the Room_____   Your Name:_____

Number	Rating (1–5)	Comments
1		
2		
3		
4		
5		
6		
7		
8		
9		
10		
11		
12		
13		
14		
15		
16		
17		
18		

Number	Rating (1–5)	Comments
19		
20		
21		
22		
23		
24		
25		
26		
27		

Instructions: First rate the room overall on how much you like it, where 1 = "Ugly, I would never want to be in this room" and 5 = "My dream room, the best I could imagine." Under comments, list things you like or don't like about the room. Think about color, furniture, arrangement of the room, overall atmosphere, warm vs. cool, specific aspects of the room you do or don't like.

We are going to go through them very quickly, so just put down your first impressions now, and then we will go back and talk about all of them and you can add to what you wrote down.

Courtesy of the Park Ridge (Illinois) Public Library

DESIGN QUESTIONNAIRE FOR TEENS

Name _____ Date _____

Store or place visited_____

Please record your responses or answers to all items that apply for this visit.

1. How did the space make you feel? _____
_____

2. Did you like the

   Walls?   ☐ yes   ☐ no   Why or why not? _____
   _____

   Floors?   ☐ yes   ☐ no   Why or why not? _____
   _____

   Ceiling?   ☐ yes   ☐ no   Why or why not? _____
   _____

   Lighting?   ☐ yes   ☐ no   Why or why not? _____
   _____

   Layout?   ☐ yes   ☐ no   Why or why not? _____
   _____

   Colors?   ☐ yes   ☐ no   Why or why not? _____
   _____

3. Was the atmosphere warm and inviting?   ☐ yes   ☐ no   What made it that way? _____
_____

4. What did you *like* most about this space (or place)? _____
_____

5. What did you most *dislike* about the space (or place)? _____
_____

6. What three paint colors did you like best? (Record their names and numbers. If possible, attach samples.)
_____

7. What four pieces of furniture (couches, chairs, tables, etc.) did you like best? Complete the following information for each.

Name	Style	Order number
_____	_____	_____
_____	_____	_____
_____	_____	_____
_____	_____	_____

8. What were your favorite items? (Draw a quick sketch of each or attach a photo.)

Sample Teen Shopping Order Form

Library: _____

Quantity	Color (circle)	Item	Vendor (URL)	Cost

Item Name:

Item Descripton:

<Insert image of item here>

Item Name:

Item Descripton:

<Insert image of item here>

Item Name:

Item Descripton:

<Insert image of item here>

Courtesy of the Kent District (Michigan) Library

Appendix B | **Worksheets**

BRAINSTORMING IDEAS WORKSHEET

Service	Where have we been? (What are the library's current and past attitudes toward teens and young adult services?)	Where should we be? (How do young adult services relate to the library's mission, service priorities, long-range plan?)	Where are we headed? (Where would we like to see the library headed in regard to teens and young adult services?)
Target age range (grades 6–12 or grades 7–12)			
Scope of service (programs and special services)			
Collection (formats and budget)			
Technology (PCs, Internet, etc.)			
Staff and teens (customer service, staff time, teen stereotypes, behavior problems, etc.)			
Physical Space	Where have we been? (What are the library's current and past attitudes toward teens and young adult services?)	Where should we be? (How do young adult services relate to the library's mission, service priorities, long-range plan?)	Where are we headed? (Where would we like to see the library headed in regard to teens and young adult services?)
Location			
Function			
Content			
Layout			
Staffing			
Design			
Overall "feel" or "image"			

ACTION STEP BUDGET WORKSHEET

Action Step	Current Budget	Proposed Project Budget	Difference	% of Project Budget (Difference/ Total)	Notes
TOTAL					

CATEGORIZED BUDGET WORKSHEET

Action Step	Current Budget	Proposed Project Budget	Difference	% of Project Budget (Difference/ Total)	Notes
Architect/designer and consultant fees					
Furniture and fixtures					
Labor (remodeling, moving, etc.)					
Supplies (attach list)					
Rental equipment					
Technology					
Collection development					
Misc. long-term expenses (e.g., additional staffing, telecommunications cost for Internet access)					
Publicity					
TOTAL					

TEEN SPACE PLANNING WORKSHEET

Goal(s):

Action Step	Value	RESOURCES		
		People	Money	Time

PUBLIC LIBRARY COMPARISON WORKSHEET

Library name _____ Date of comparison _____

	Entire Library Statistics	Children's Statistics	Adult Statistics	Teen Statistics	Proposed Teen Statistics
Service population					
Budget (include miscellaneous)					
Number of volumes					
Circulation					
Percentage of total circulation					
Books					
Magazines					
Audiovisual materials					
Online resources					
Other materials (attach list)					
Number of staff					
Program attendance (annual)					
Square footage					

INVENTORY CHECKLIST

	Yes	No	N/A	Comments

A. Layout

1. Is the teen area/school library a separate area? If so, what is the size of the room? ☐ ☐ ☐ _____ × _____ square feet

2. Is the building entrance nearby? Describe. ☐ ☐ ☐

3. Is there some level of privacy? Can teens socialize without disturbing others? ☐ ☐ ☐

4. Is the teen area near or in the children's area? If so, how far is it? Describe the situation. ☐ ☐ ☐

5. Is the teen area near key service points? Computers? Audiovisual materials? Restrooms? Describe where the teen area is in relationship to other departments in the library or school. ☐ ☐ ☐

6. Is there sufficient floor space? Explain, describing how it relates to the demographics and entire square footage of the library or school, other departments, etc. ☐ ☐ ☐

7. Is everything handicapped accessible? Describe. ☐ ☐ ☐

8. Is there a smooth traffic flow? Describe. ☐ ☐ ☐

9. Is everything logically arranged? Are collections, equipment, etc., easy to locate by teens? Easily monitored by staff? ☐ ☐ ☐

10. Other ☐ ☐ ☐

B. Furniture

(Compile and attach a complete list of furnishings.)

1. Is there lounge-style, comfortable seating? Describe and include seating count, condition, and any other notes. ☐ ☐ ☐

2. Are furnishings flexible and portable to accommodate variations in usage? Describe. ☐ ☐ ☐

3. Is there furniture for group seating? Are these furnishings comfortable? Do they take into account ergonomics? Describe and include seating count, condition, and any other notes. ☐ ☐ ☐

	Yes	No	N/A	Comments
4. Are there furnishings available to the individual browser or studier? Are these furnishings comfortable? Do they take into account ergonomics? Describe seating count, condition, and any other notes.	☐	☐	☐	
5. Do the overall style and color scheme of the furnishings correspond to the space? Describe.	☐	☐	☐	
6. How many people can be simultaneously seated in the area?	☐	☐	☐	No. of people:
7. Will furnishings accommodate a variety of programs and activities? Describe.	☐	☐	☐	
8. Other	☐	☐	☐	

C. Shelving and Display

No. of shelves:

Dimensions:

(Compile and attach a complete list of shelving and display items. Include a complete shelving count and dimensions of shelving here.)

	Yes	No	N/A	
1. Does the area have adequate shelving for:				
hardcover books?	☐	☐	☐	
paperback books?	☐	☐	☐	
graphic novels?	☐	☐	☐	
audiovisual materials?	☐	☐	☐	
magazines?	☐	☐	☐	
2. Are shelves empty or jam-packed? Is there enough room for display and face-out merchandising at the ends of shelves?	☐	☐	☐	
3. Are there display fixtures? If so, how many and what are they, and what are they used for?	☐	☐	☐	No. of display fixtures: Dimensions:
4. Are shelving and display fixtures truly functional? Do they adequately accommodate the various formats? Do the items stand up properly or do they fall over? Can they be easily browsed by teens?	☐	☐	☐	
5. Are collections presented in an eye-catching manner?	☐	☐	☐	
6. Are new and high-interest materials highlighted?	☐	☐	☐	

	Yes	No	N/A	Comments

C. Shelving and Display (cont.)

7. Are walls, pillars, ceilings, etc., used to their maximum display potential? ☐ ☐ ☐

8. Are materials that are not physically present in the teen area marketed in the teen area? ☐ ☐ ☐

9. Other ☐ ☐ ☐

D. The Collection

(Compile a list of collections available to teens, noting if they're located within the teen space or outside the teen space.)

1. Is the teen collection strong and up to date? ☐ ☐ ☐

2. Is the teen collection diverse? Is there a good selection of materials? Does it include a variety of genres and multiple formats (e.g., graphic novels, etc.)? ☐ ☐ ☐

3. Does the collection need weeding? ☐ ☐ ☐

4. Does the library offer alternative formats (graphic novels, videos, DVDs, music, audiobooks, video games) for teens? If so, are there any restrictions on audiovisual materials? Can teens check out these materials? ☐ ☐ ☐

5. Are materials attractive? Describe. ☐ ☐ ☐

6. How are materials arranged? Are materials grouped by genre or designated by a spine label (e.g., horror, science fiction)? Are they easy to find? ☐ ☐ ☐

7. Are there teen materials in the children's collection? Describe. ☐ ☐ ☐

8. Are there children's materials in the teen collection? Describe. ☐ ☐ ☐

9. Other ☐ ☐ ☐

E. Technology

1. Are there any computers designated just for teens? If so, how many? If not, where are the closest computers? ☐ ☐ ☐

	Yes	No	N/A	Comments

2. Do computers have access to

      an online catalog? □ □ □

      the Internet? □ □ □

      research databases? □ □ □

      games? □ □ □

      Microsoft Word, Excel, PowerPoint? □ □ □

3. Are there age restrictions on use of the Internet? Describe. □ □ □

4. Is Internet access filtered for teens? If so, what is the cutoff age? □ □ □

5. Is there restricted use of the Internet (e.g., no e-mail, no chatting, no downloading, no social networking)? Describe. □ □ □

6. Are electrical and data outlets adequate throughout the space? How many wall-mounted outlets are there? Floor outlets? Data outlets? Are there any phone jacks? □ □ □

7. Is there wireless access? Describe. □ □ □

8. Are there laptop computers or other equipment (e.g., MP3 players) that can be checked out? Describe. □ □ □

9. Are listening stations, sound domes, or other sound systems available for teens to listen to music or audiobooks? Describe. □ □ □

10. Are viewing stations and/or a television available for teens to play games on or to watch television or movies? Describe. □ □ □

11. Other □ □ □

F. Staff

1. Is there staff directly or indirectly assigned to teen services? If so, how many staff? Part-time or full-time? □ □ □   No. of staff:

2. Does your library utilize adult volunteers to work with teens? If so, how many? How many hours per week? □ □ □   No. of volunteers:

    Hours per week:

3. Is there currently a service desk(s) within the area? If so, how many? What are the dimensions? Describe. If not, is a service desk nearby? □ □ □   No. of service desks in space:

    No. of service desks nearby:

	Yes	No	N/A	Comments

F. Staff (cont.)

4. Is it easy to discern where a teen can find assistance? Describe. ☐ ☐ ☐

5. Are staff members friendly, approachable, and knowledgeable? Describe. ☐ ☐ ☐

6. Other ☐ ☐ ☐

G. Additional Items for Consideration

(Compile and attach a complete list of miscellaneous elements including lighting and flooring information, vending machines, signage, decorative elements, etc.)

1. Is there adequate artificial lighting? What type of lighting (e.g., fluorescent overhead, table lamps)? Is lighting functional? Is it conducive to reading or studying? Does the lighting support the atmosphere and décor of the space? ☐ ☐ ☐   No. lights:

   Types:

2. Is there adequate natural light? How many windows are in the space? What are their dimensions? ☐ ☐ ☐   No. windows:

   Dimensions:

3. Are there doors? How many are there? What size are they? ☐ ☐ ☐   No. of doors:

   Dimensions:

4. Is there adequate storage? Describe. ☐ ☐ ☐

5. Is flooring appropriate for the activities in the space? What kind of flooring is it (carpet, laminate, area rugs, etc.)? Is it in good shape? Is it single surface or multiple surfaces? Does it support the atmosphere and décor of the space? ☐ ☐ ☐

6. Are there any special elements or architectural extras in the space such as a cathedral ceiling, multiple levels/loft, or window seats? If so, describe and include counts and measurements. ☐ ☐ ☐   No. and type:

   Dimensions:

7. Are there food services available in or near the area (e.g., vending machines, café, drinking fountains, etc.)? Describe. Include information about the eating and drinking policy in the teen area or library. ☐ ☐ ☐

	Yes	No	N/A	Comments
8. Are heating and cooling adequate for the space? Is there adequate ventilation? Describe.	☐	☐	☐	
9. Are there any safety hazards in the space? Describe.	☐	☐	☐	
10. Is the space accessible and usable to people with disabilities? Is it physically compliant? Technologically compliant?	☐	☐	☐	
11. Is signage attractive and functional? (Include all signage, such as stack signs and labels, directional signs, and promotional signs.) Do signs get you to where you want to go? Are digital/electronic signs available and well utilized? Describe.	☐	☐	☐	
12. Are there any artworks, accessories, knickknacks, display areas, and other decorative items? Do they support and enhance the atmosphere and functionality of the space?	☐	☐	☐	
13. Other	☐	☐	☐	

Appendix C | **Resources**

Chapter 1: Understanding Teens and Their Space

"American Library Association Youth and Library Use Study." Harris Interactive, 2007. www.ala.org/ala/yalsa/HarrisYouthPoll.pdf.

A survey of young people's use and impressions of their local libraries.

Bolan, Kimberly. "Bridging the Gap: Proactive Approaches for Adults Working with Teens." *Young Adult Library Services* 4, no. 4 (Summer 2006): 32–34, 46.

Discusses ways to more effectively relate to teens and how to use staff training to build a bridge between generations.

Bolan, Kimberly. "Why Teen Space?" Young Adult Library Services Association, 2008. www.ala.org/ala/yalsa/profdev/whitepapers/teenspaces.cfm.

White paper discussing why teen space is important in libraries.

Burek Pierce, Jennifer. *Sex, Brains, and Video Games: A Librarian's Guide to Teens in the Twenty-First Century.* Chicago: American Library Association, 2007.

A look at today's teen through the lens of neurological, psychological, and educational research. Putting this research in the context of library services, the author challenges librarians to question their assumptions about teen patrons and provides new answers based on research.

Carter, Betty, ed. *Best Books for Young Adults.* 2nd ed. Chicago: American Library Association, 2000.

An update to the 1994 release, this book is an essential resource for all teen librarians. It includes twenty-five bibliographies of best books as well as author-by-author, year-by-year, and topic-by-topic lists of exceptional books. For additional lists of best books, check out the YALSA website at www.ala.org/yalsa/booklists/.

Chelton, Mary K., ed. *Excellence in Library Services to Young Adults,* eds. 1–3. Chicago: American Library Association, various dates.

All three editions present prize-winning programs that show teens as volunteers, employees, and mentors. Terrific resource for those interested in getting teens involved

Cox, Robin Overby. "Do Not Let the Library Be Cool." *Voice of Youth Advocates* 23, no. 4 (October 2000): 240–241.

Presents a tongue-in-cheek analysis of how to improve young adult services in libraries. Highlights include funding; providing technology that includes Internet access; comfortable furniture; food; longer evening hours; research needs; staff attitudes; job and volunteer service opportunities; restrictive rules and fees; and better books and media.

Drusch, Andrea. "Give Me a Reason to Go to the Library." *Dallas Morning News Online,* September 27, 2007. www.dallasnews.com/sharedcontent/dws/dn/opinion/viewpoints/stories/DN-drusch_29edi.ART.State.Edition1.4229cbf.html#.

Andrea Drusch considers why high school media centers are not student-friendly, why they need to be, and how they might reach that goal.

Fox, Bette-Lee. "Betwixt and Be Teen." *Library Journal* 131, no. 20 (December 2006): 42–56.

A summary of public and academic library building projects and renovations. Cost, square footage, and architect information are listed. Of the projects listed, more than 60 percent include the addition or renovation of a teen space.

Goodstein, Anastasia. *Totally Wired: What Teens and Tweens Are Really Doing Online.* New York: St. Martin's Griffin, 2007.

Discusses the negative behavior teens and tweens engage in using the Internet and cell phones. Topics range from cyber-bullying to purchasing illegal drugs online.

Howe, N. "Harnessing the Power of Millennials." *School Administrator* 62, no. 8 (September 2005): 18–22.

An article with tips on how educators should approach the Millennial generation. Focuses on the neo-traditionalism and positive nature of this generation. Also discusses the need for parents and educators to collaborate because faculty and administration can no longer "pull rank" when it comes to issues in school. This can be reflected in the library . . . through library outreach, space development, and getting parent support for library events.

Kelsey, Candice. *Generation MySpace: Helping Your Teen Survive Online Adolescence.* New York: Avalon, 2007.

Discusses the lifestyles of teens involved in social networking. Relates real-life stories from teens in how they use MySpace and similar sites in their daily lives, for both positive and negative activities.

Lippincott, Joan K. *Net Generation Students and Libraries.* Boulder: Educause, 2006. www.educause.edu/NetGenerationStudentsandLibraries/6067.

This Educause e-book discusses the enmeshment of technology in teenagers' lives, how they use information, and information literacy training techniques that effectively reach them.

Mind Your Mind. http://mindyourmind.ca.

Award-winning site for youth by youth. This is a place where teens can get information, resources, and the tools to help manage stress, crisis, and mental health problems.

Myers, J. "Tweens and Cool." *Admap Magazine,* March 2004, 37–39.

Savvy generation of kids. They know what is cool and do not appreciate those who try to be cool and are not. As the article says, those who try to be cool and fail are doomed. The playground of tweens is the ultimate viral marketing area and companies (i.e., libraries) can get a bad name quickly.

National Youth Development Information Center. www.nydic.org/nydic/.

> NYDIC provides practice-related information about youth development to national and local youth-serving organizations at low cost or no cost.

Oblinger, Diana G., and James L. Oblinger, eds. *Educating the Net Generation.* Boulder: Educause, 2005. www.educause.edu/content.asp?PAGE_ID=5989&bhcp=1.

> A collection of essays studying teenage use of technology. Insightful reading that touches on many aspects of the Net Generation, from their perspective on technology in everyday life to how to best integrate new technology in learning settings and a specific chapter on how libraries can best serve this generation.

The Pew Research Center for the People and the Press. "A Portrait of 'Generation Next': How Young People View Their Lives, Futures and Politics." http://people-press.org/reports/display.php3?ReportID=300.

> A report on the social beliefs of Millennials and how they compare to previous generations.

Pink, Daniel. *A Whole New Mind: Moving from the Information Age to the Conceptual Age.* New York: Riverhead, 2005.

> Lays the groundwork for the author's premise that the Information Age of the past couple of decades, built on the superiority of left-brain skills, is now giving over to the Conceptual Age, in which a holistic or whole-brained approach will be essential.

Pletka, Bob. *Educating the Net Generation: How to Engage Students in the 21st Century.* Santa Monica: Santa Monica Press, 2007.

> Discusses how teens can be engaged in learning and living through technology.

Public Agenda. *Long Overdue: A Fresh Look at Public and Leadership Attitudes about Libraries in the 21st Century.* New York: Public Agenda, 2006. Also available online at www.publicagenda.org/research/research_reports_details.cfm?list=99.

> A research study that shows how highly communities value their libraries—but how unaware most people are of the difficult financial problems libraries face.

Reynolds, Leah. "Who Are the Millennials?" Deloitte Consulting, 2005. www.deloitte.com/dtt/cda/doc/content/us_consulting_millennialfactsheet_080606.pdf.

> A brief summary of the Millennial generation: how they are defined, ways they use technology, what they do for fun, and what work environments they excel in.

Sanchez Gibau, Gina, Silvia Bigatti, Khadija Khaja, Kathleen Grove, Edgar Huang. "Beyond a Basic Definition of Generation." Presentation at Indiana University Faculty Colloquium on Excellence in Teaching Retreat, Bloomington, IN, May 19, 2007. www.facet.iupui.edu/events/Retreat/2007%20Presentations/Gibau.ppt.

> Focuses on how generations are alike and different and how this affects teaching and learning. This has significant impact on library design.

Scales, Peter C., Peter L. Benson, and Eugene C. Roehlkepartain. "Grading Grown-ups." Search Institute, 2000. www.search-institute.org/grading-grown-ups-2000.

> A nationwide study from Lutheran Brotherhood and Search Institute assessing American parents' relationships with their children and teens.

Search Institute. www.search-institute.org.

> An independent, nonprofit organization whose mission is to advance the well-being of adolescents and children by generating knowledge and promoting its application. The website is a great place for gathering information on teen needs and teen development.

Sullivan, Edward T. "Teenagers Are Not Luggage." *Public Libraries* 40, no. 2 (April 2001): 75–77.

> Commentary on "what can be done for teens instead of what can be done about them." Includes a helpful list of additional resources for those serving young adults.

Teen Ink. www.teenink.com.

> Teen Ink is a website, a monthly print magazine, and a book series. In particular, the website includes photos, teen issues, favorites lists, a teen art gallery, and reviews of music, movies, and books. Everything here is written by teens for teens.

"Teen Market Profile." New York: Magazine Publishers of America, 2004. www.magazine.org/content/files/teenprofile04.pdf.

> Designed to help marketers understand and effectively connect with teenagers. It includes a teen market overview, an examination of the media habits of teenagers, and evidence about how magazines reach, connect, and influence teens and their purchase decisions.

Urban Libraries Council. www.urbanlibraries.org/showcase/plpyd.html.

> The Urban Libraries Council (ULC) is an association of large public libraries in the United States and Canada and the corporations that serve them. Includes a variety of useful information, including information on youth and youth development.

Walter, Virginia A., and Elaine Meyers. *Teens and Libraries: Getting It Right.* Chicago: American Library Association, 2003.

> The authors share an inspiring narrative of young adult history, and also offer a plethora of new voices and stories that advocate the power of technology and teen spaces. These story lines are melded to highlight practical tools to involve teens at the library and make a bright future possible.

Whelan, Debra Lau. "HS Senior Explains Why She Doesn't Use the School Library." *School Library Journal's Extra Helping,* October 30, 2007. www.schoollibraryjournal.com/article/CA6495685.html.

> One teenager's criticisms of her school library got a lot of media attention. In this interview, read her views and learn how librarians reacted.

Chapter 2: Ask and Analyze

Asis, Susan. "Types of Youth Participation Programs in Public Libraries: A Webliography." *Young Adult Library Services* 4, no. 4 (Summer 2006): 26–30.

> Describes various youth participation models and cites examples of successful programs across the United States.

At the Table. http://atthetable.org.

> Provides resources and information about how to involve young people in decision making.

Bryan, Cheryl. *Managing Facilities for Results: Optimizing Space for Services.* Chicago: American Library Association, 2007.

> A comprehensive guide to planning projects, analyzing space and space needs, and preparing reports. Includes extensive tools and worksheets, including space analysis, sign and furniture evaluation, expense estimates, and an ADA compliance guide. The assessment tools are particularly helpful. (See Toolkits section.)

Dahlgren, Anders C. *Public Library Space Needs: A Planning Outline.* Madison: Wisconsin Department of Public Instruction, 1998. Also available online at http://dpi.wi.gov/pld/plspace.html.

> Space planning guide with ready-to-use worksheets.

Freeman, Geoffrey. *Library as Place: Rethinking Roles, Rethinking Space.* Washington, DC: Council on Library and Information Resources, 2005.

> Discusses changes in library trends, from technology and digital librarianship to joint-use libraries and user environments.

Friends of Libraries USA. www.folusa.com.

> Everything you need to know to help you start a Teen Friends group.

Hughes-Hassell, Sandra, and Kay Bishop. "Using Focus Group Interviews to Improve Library Services for Youth." *Teacher Librarian* 32 no. 1 (October 2004): 8–13.

> Looking for input from teenagers? This practical guide to involving teens in focus groups is a good place to start.

The Innovation Center for Community and Youth Development. www.theinnovation center.org.

> Connects thinkers and leaders of all ages to develop fresh ideas, forge new partnerships, and design strategies that engage young people and their communities.

Rubin, Rhea Joyce. *Demonstrating Results: Using Outcome Management in Your Library.* Chicago: American Library Association, 2006.

> A complete guide to measuring goal-based initiatives. Includes tips on developing questionnaires and data sampling.

State Library of Iowa. "Online Library Survey Examples." http://ia.webjunction.org/home/articles/content/1113020.

> Examples of web-based surveys used at libraries across the country, including surveys for youth.

Tucillo, Diane. *Library Teen Advisory Groups.* Landham, MD: VOYA Books, 2005.

> How to make teen advisory committees work, from membership and fund-raising to projects and perks.

Youth Activism Project. www.youthactivism.com.

> Nonpartisan organization encouraging young people to speak up and pursue lasting solutions to problems they care deeply about. Source of publications, support, and how-to advice.

Youth on Board. www.youthonboard.org.

> Helps young people and adults think differently about each other so that they can work together to change society. Offers community and institutional training, publications, and other resources.

Chapter 3: Plan and Propose

American Association of School Librarians. www.ala.org/aasl/.

> A wide variety of resources from AASL are available on their website, including advocacy and issues information and professional tools.

American Libraries. www.ala.org/ala/alonline/index.cfm.

> Devotes their April issue each year to new and renovated library facilities.

Americans with Disabilities Act (ADA). www.usdoj.gov/crt/ada/adahom1.htm.

> *ADA Standards for Accessible Design,* as published in the Code of Federal Regulations, is available on the ADA website in both HTML and PDF formats and with graphics, links to figures, and cross-referenced sections. A free CD-ROM containing a complete collection of ADA materials including architectural design standards, regulations, etc., is also available.

Bolan, Kimberly. "Library Design Tips for the 21st Century." *WebJunction,* March 2006. http://webjunction.org/do/DisplayContent?id=13018.

> Practical and simple tips are presented that consistently lead to the most successful projects, whether planning a new building, an expansion, renovation, or a simple revamp.

Bolan, Kimberly. "Looks Like Teen Spirit." *School Library Journal* 52, no. 11 (November 2006): 44–48. Also available online without photos at www.schoollibraryjournal.com/article/CA6386669.html.

> Outlines the major elements of successful teen space in school and public libraries. Information on getting teen input, layout 101, finding teen style, furniture, and design is presented as well as a "Take the Teen Space Challenge" quiz.

Bolan, Kimberly, and Janet Nelson. "Just for Them." *Library Journal's Library by Design* (Fall 2008): 11–13.

> Overview of the planning and design process behind the innovative Queens Library for Teens in Far Rockaway, New York. Also available at www.libraryjournal.com/article/CA6593537.html?g=bolan+nelson.

Burger, Leslie, and Nicholas Garrison. "Construction Funding 101." *American Libraries* 37, no. 4 (April 2006): 63–65.

> Successful fund-raising strategies from the New Jersey Public Libraries.

Chelton, Mary. "Perspectives on YA Practice: Common YA Models of Service in Public Libraries; Advantages and Disadvantages." *Young Adult Library Services* 3, no. 4 (Summer 2005): 4–6, 11.

Covers staffing, space, and service models that should be considered in library plans.

Connecticut State Library. www.cslib.org.

Library space planning resource. Includes guides and worksheets on a variety of topics.

Council of Educational Facility Planners International (CEFPI). www.cefpi.org.

Professional association whose sole mission is improving the places where children learn. They are actively involved in planning, designing, building, equipping, and maintaining schools and colleges.

Demmers, Lisa. "Focus on Space Planning for Libraries." *WebJunction,* January 2006. www.webjunction.org/do/DisplayContent?id=12748.

Whether planning a new building or renovating an old one, this guide provides excellent tools and resources for library space planning. Includes space planning terms, guides, and more.

Dempsey, Beth. "Power Users: Designing Buildings and Services from the End User's Viewpoint Transforms Access for Everyone." *Library Journal* 130, no. 20 (December 2005): 72–75.

How to use information architecture techniques to increase your library's usability.

Erikson, Rolf, and Carolyn Markuson. *Designing a School Library Media Center for the Future.* 2nd ed. Chicago: American Library Association, 2007.

Sharing their experiences of working on more than 100 school building projects, two expert school library media specialists draw a road map for becoming building-savvy, avoiding renovation pitfalls, and creating a school library media center for the future. Highly recommended for school and public libraries.

Foundation Center. http://foundationcenter.org.

Maintains database on U.S. grantmakers and their grants. It also operates research, education, and training programs designed to advance philanthropy at every level. Free resources available in its five regional library/learning centers and its network of more than 340 Cooperating Collections.

George Lucas Educational Foundation (GLEF), Edutopia. www.edutopia.org/index.php.

Nonprofit foundation celebrating and encouraging innovation in schools. Provides information including research, tips, tools, information on grants, etc. for providing exemplary programs in K–12 public schools.

Grantsmanship Center. www.tgci.com.

Training and resources for nonprofit grant seekers.

Harish, Chandra. "Planning, Design and Construction of the Central Library Building." International Federation of Library Associations and Institutions 2006 Conference, Seoul, South Korea, August 2006. www.ifla.org/IV/ifla72/papers/124-Chandra-en.pdf.

> Discusses building of a central library at a university in Madras, India. Images and facilities description are paired with lists related to facility needs ranging from shelving to offices to book storage.

International Federation of Library Associations and Institutions, Libraries for Children and Young Adults Section. www.ifla.org/VII/s10/index.htm.

> IFLA is the leading international body representing the interests of library and information services and their users. Their "Libraries for Children and Young Adults" section features best practices.

Johnson, Doug. "Jolt of Java @ Your Library." *Blue Skunk Blog,* October 13, 2005. http://doug-johnson.squarespace.com/blue-skunk-blog/2005/10/13/a-jolt-of-java-your-library.html.

> This blog entry summarizes electronic discussion list responses to questions about incorporating coffeehouses into libraries.

Klima, John. "Creating a Place for Teens to Hang Out." *Pop Goes the Library: A Weblog,* October 20, 2006. www.popgoesthelibrary.com/2006/10/creating-place-for-teens-to-hang-out_20.html.

> A reflection on the purposes and uses for teen spaces, with links to a few successful programs.

LibraryConsultants.org. www.libraryconsultants.org.

> Online directory for libraries and library consultants. Includes consultant information as well as a place for libraries to post requests for proposal (RFPs).

LibraryJournal.com. "Building and Facilities." www.libraryjournal.com/community/Building+%26+Facilities/47090.html.

> The website of *Library Journal* includes a buildings and facilities page, and the December issue features an array of new library buildings, an annual buyer's guide, and a website directory of vendors.

Libris Design Planning Documentation. www.librisdesign.org/docs/index.html.

> Helpful planning tools provided by Libris Design, a facility-planning database that assists with the planning of public library buildings in California. It includes a website with recent information on facility planning topics, a database of recently constructed California public libraries, an area for users to communicate with each other, user help documentation, and a trial version of the Libris Design database.

Lushington, Nolan. *Libraries Designed for Users: A 21st Century Guide.* New York: Neal-Schuman, 2002.

> A practical, comprehensive guide of solutions to design questions, including background, planning, function, and resources.

Massachusetts Board of Library Commissioners. http://mblc.state.ma.us/grants/construction/planning/index.php.

This resource for Massachusetts public libraries has checklists, planning guides, and resources related to procurement and construction.

Mid-Hudson Library System's Library Space Planning, Children's and Teen Areas. http://midhudson.org/department/youth/space_planningys.htm.

A comprehensive site with resources and ideas related to signage, furnishings, and more. The site is divided between best resources for children's areas and teen areas.

Murphy, Tish. *Library Furnishings: A Planning Guide.* Jefferson, NC: McFarland, 2007.

Checklists and information about furnishings: from terminology and measurement conventions to user-friendly arrangements and technological issues.

National Clearinghouse for Educational Facilities. www.edfacilities.org/ir/libraries.cfm.

An excellent resource list of links, books, and journal articles on the design of K–12 school libraries, including sample city and state guidelines and technology requirements.

New York Library Association. Youth Services Section. www.nyla.org/index.php?page_id=54.

Includes revised minimum standards for youth services in public libraries of New York and "The Basic Young Adult Services Handbook," among other youth-related resources.

NMRLS YA Web Resources. www.nmrls.org/youth/yaweb/.

Blog, forum, and resources for teen librarians on a variety of topics. Includes indexes of young adult spaces, web pages, and blogs.

Nunan, Kaye. "One Small Room." Youth Arts Queensland and the State Library of Queensland Australia, 2004. http://publib.slq.qld.gov.au/onesmall/index.htm.

An arts-based research project that explores the creation of dedicated youth spaces in public libraries.

Project Kaleidoscope. www.pkal.org/collections/FacilitiesHandbook.cfm.

Project Kaleidoscope (PKAL) is one of the leading advocates in the United States for what works in building and sustaining strong undergraduate programs in the fields of science, technology, engineering, and mathematics (STEM). This section of the website offers guidelines and strategies for building facilities not only related to science, but also technology and education. Includes information on project management, determining project scope, and the overall process for new facility development.

Ramos, Theresa. "From the Outside In: Library Renovations from the Perspectives of a Project Manager, an Architect/Designer, and a Technology Consultant." *Journal of Youth Services in Libraries* 14, no. 2 (Winter 2001): 9.

Get tips for working with outside consultants in renovation and new construction library projects.

Sannwald, William W. *Checklist of Library Building Design Considerations.* 4th ed. Chicago: American Library Association, 2001.

How to evaluate your current space, analyze various design elements, and make purchasing decisions. Includes information about technology, teen space, eco-friendly design, and more.

Sannwald, William W. "Designing Libraries for Customers." *Library Administration and Management* 21, no. 3 (2007): 131–138.

Describes the way design is changing to meet the needs of library users. It highlights design trends including youth spaces, joint-use libraries, and technology-friendly and sustainable design.

School Planning and Management. www2.peterli.com/spm/index.shtm.

A monthly magazine for architects, facility managers, and others who work in school facilities management.

Subel, Sue. "Facility Design as an Agent of Learning." *Knowledge Quest* 35, no. 3 (January–February 2007): 38–41.

Facilities planning resource. Examines the facility design of the new Kenston High School Library Media Center in Chagrin Falls, OH, including floor plan.

Survey of Library Cafés. New York: Primary Research Group, 2007.

Extensive data on library café sales volume, best-selling products, impact on library maintenance costs, reasons for starting a café, effect on library traffic, and many other issues regarding the decision to start and manage a library café.

Tanner, Kenneth, and Jeffery Lackney. *Educational Facilities Planning: Leadership, Architecture, and Management.* Boston: Pearson Allyn and Bacon, 2006.

Focuses on the development of educational spaces, with particular attention to high school and university spaces. Innovative concepts of space, flow, and community are discussed. Throughout the book, *premises* are listed that indicate the key components of success in a new facility. These include not only issues related to the facility itself, but also the community and leaders of the facility. Includes formulas that help calculate the costs that might accrue after a facility is built (Example: how long does it take to clean a certain amount of square feet, and how much does that cost in terms of personnel and products?).

University of British Columbia. Planning and Building Libraries. www.slais.ubc.ca/resources/architecture/index.htm.

This site was created for architects, librarians, and design consultants. Its primary purpose is to provide its users with an outline of design-related resources. Includes general planning guidelines for specific types of libraries, sample plans, and more.

Utah State Library Space Planning Resources. http://library.utah.gov/librarian_resources/toolkit/spaceplanning.htm.

An annotated bibliography from the state of Utah of library planning books, articles, and websites.

Vandermark, Sondra. "Using Teen Patrons as a Resource in Planning Young Adult Library Space in Public Libraries." *Planning the Modern Public Library Building.* Englewood, CO: Libraries Unlimited, 2003.

How to solicit and integrate teen input into your building or remodeling plans.

Voice of Youth Advocates. www.voya.com.

Published bimonthly. Starting in June 1999, each issue includes a "YA Spaces of Your Dreams" article featuring teen spaces from libraries across the United States. Helpful for both planning and designing, these articles outline the communities and planning processes along with descriptions and photos of teen areas. Also includes helpful information on teen programming, collection development, and more.

Weitzner, Wendy. "5 Facilities Planning Mistakes and How to Avoid Them." *Healthcare Financial Management* (May 2006). www.allbusiness.com/health-care-social -assistance/1173327-1.html.

This article is addressed to the health care field but offers a strong analysis of mistakes that planners make, including solving symptoms rather than problems, starting with perceived space needs rather than population needs, focusing on precision rather than accuracy, focusing on size rather than quantity, and planning based on preference rather than function.

Young Adult Library Services Association (YALSA). www.ala.org/yalsa/.

Helpful resources for all things young adult—collection development, state and local news, grants and awards, space design, and much more.

Chapter 4: Design and Decorate

American Institute of Architects. www.aia.org.

Excellent resource for finding and learning about architects and architectural standards.

American Society of Interior Designers. www.asid.org.

Professional designer and design-related information.

Benya, James, and Mark Karlen. *Lighting Design Basics.* Hoboken, NJ: Wiley, 2004.

A concise, visual introduction to lighting design. Includes planning and construction guidelines.

Better Homes and Gardens Online. www.bhglive.com.

A good general decorating and ideas website that includes articles, plans, and useful tools. Supplement the online resource with the print magazine for additional helpful tips and inspiration.

Block, Marylaine. "How to Become a Great Public Space." *American Libraries* 34, no. 4 (April 2003): 72–76.

Author interviews Fred Kent and Phil Myrick of the Project for Public Spaces, with tips and advice for collaborating with the community, especially teens, in library design projects.

Cohen, Sacha, and Maggie Philo. *The Practical Encyclopedia of Paint Effects.* London: Hermes House, 2006.

Chock-full of photos and fresh ideas, this book includes comprehensive instructions for over 150 projects and painting techniques.

Design*Sponge. www.designspongeonline.com.

Launched in August 2004, this blog dedicated to home and product design is run by Brooklyn-based writer Grace Bonney. Features store and product reviews, sale and contest announcements, new designer profiles, trend forecasting, project ideas, and more.

Doityourself.com. www.doityourself.com.

Jam-packed with decorating information such as finding a contractor, obtaining free estimates, and much more.

Flickr: Library Signage. www.flickr.com/groups/79623799@N00/.

A collection of signs from around the country ranging from creative displays to signs to help users navigate library collections. Use this site to find teen-friendly signage ideas.

Freecycle. www.freecyle.org.

A network for giving away and finding free used stuff in local communities.

Harmon, Sharon, and Katherine Kennon. *The Codes Guidebook for Interiors.* Hoboken, NJ: Wiley, 2005.

Explains codes, standards, and federal regulations for interior design.

Home and Garden TV. www.hgtv.com.

An excellent general resource for design and decorating tips, ideas, and suggested vendors.

Ingham, Vicki, and Shelley Stewart. *Color Schemes Made Easy.* Des Moines, IA: Better Homes and Gardens, 2004.

With advice and how-to basics, this book offers color scheme advice from interior decorators and color experts. Includes suggestions for paints, fabrics, and accessories.

Lanthier, Yves. *The Art of Trompe L'oeil Murals.* Cincinnati, OH: North Light Books, 2004.

Written by a master muralist, this book explores visual illusions in murals and the basic techniques that create them.

Libris Design. www.librisdesign.org/docs/index.html.

Documents that help guide the details of library design and planning including cost estimating, furniture, interior finishing materials, and sustainable library design.

"Millennials Make Their Mark." *360 Steelcase,* 2006. www.360steelcase.com/e_article000526534.cfm?x=b11,0,w.

This article explores how Millennials perceive, shape, and use work spaces. Steelcase designers offer suggestions for creating effective spaces within offices where Millennials can thrive.

National Institute of Building Sciences. "Libraries." *Whole Building Design Guide* (August 1, 2005). www.wbdg.org/design/libraries.php.

Links specify public, academic, and school libraries provide insight into calculating square footage, seating needs, and more.

Nielson, Karla, and David Taylor. *Interiors: An Introduction.* Boston: McGraw-Hill, 2007.

Introduces the basic concepts of interior design, including materials, furnishings, and aesthetics for both commercial and noncommercial spaces.

PaintIdeas.com. http://paintideas.com.

A forum and resource portal in which experts and do-it-yourselfers share ideas, techniques, and tips.

Rippel, Chris. "What Libraries Can Learn from Bookstores." Presentation for the Kansas Library Association, Hesston, KS, September 11, 2003. www.ckls.org/~crippel/marketing/bookstore.html.

Discusses the ways in which bookstores excel at design and layout and how libraries can follow the same trends. Hints on colors, lighting, and even scents that can make the library a more comfortable place.

Schmidt, Philip, and Jessie Walker. *Decorating with Architectural Details.* Upper Saddle River, NJ: Creative Homeowner, 2004.

A guide to making an impression with trim, molding, doorways, ceilings, stairways, and other details.

Starmer, Anna. *The Color Scheme Bible.* New York: Firefly, 2005.

Featuring two hundred color combinations, tips for finding design inspiration, and basic information about color theory, this book is a truly comprehensive handbook of primary, accent, and contrasting color.

Stephens, Michael. "Ten Signs I Hope I Never See Again." *Tame the Web: Libraries and Technology,* July 7, 2006. http://tametheweb.com/2006/07/ten_signs_i_hope_i_never_see_i.html.

This blog post features signs from libraries that are not necessarily welcoming to students. It highlights important things to think about when determining signage and other marketing pieces that reach out to (or turn away) students.

Chapter 5: Long-Term Promotion

Abram, Stephen. "Advocating for Teens' Technological Needs." *Young Adult Library Services* 4, no. 4 (Summer 2006): 35–37.

A discussion of services and standards for reaching teens in libraries, as well as advice about becoming a helpful "Librarian 2.0."

ALA Techsource Gaming, Learning and Libraries Symposium Wiki. ALA Techsource. http://gaming.techsource.ala.org/index.php/Main_Page.

A wiki containing videos, notes, and blog posts from the Gaming, Learning and Libraries Symposium held in Chicago on July 22–24, 2007.

Alessio, Amy, and Kimberly A. Patton. *A Year of Programs for Teens.* Chicago: American Library Association, 2007.

Practical program suggestions and strategies for public libraries, school libraries, and anyone serving teens. Programs are scalable, geared at older and younger teens. Includes program-specific details about supplies, preparation time, setup, marketing tactics, and more.

Alternative Teen Services. http://yalibrarian.com.

A grassroots blog that covers teen library services from program ideas to service philosophy. The collaborative blog provides an ongoing discussion about the issues that librarians face when serving teens in addition to support for overcoming these obstacles. Includes information on marketing, programming, materials, technology, and more.

Bolan, Kimberly, Meg Canada, and Rob Cullin. "Web, Library, and Teen Services 2.0." *Young Adult Library Services* 5, no. 2 (Winter 2007): 40–43.

Information about Web 2.0, Library 2.0, and teen services in the twenty-first-century library. Focuses on teen involvement and participation, and on designing a program that fits teen needs.

Bolan, Kimberly, and Robert Cullin. *Technology Made Simple: An Improvement Guide for Small and Medium Libraries.* Chicago: American Library Association, 2007.

A primer about how librarians can meet the growing need for electronic information and services, from how technology affects libraries to troubleshooting software and more.

Developing Educational Standards. "Computers, Libraries and Information Literacy." http://edstandards.org/StSu/InfoLit.html.

Links to state-specific official documents related to standards for technology and learning.

Display and Design Ideas. www.ddimagazine.com.

Product news and design solutions for store planning and visual merchandising.

Doyle, Miranda. *101+ Great Ideas for Teen Library Web Sites.* New York: Neal-Schuman, 2007.

Teens want their own space online. This book assists in creating teen library sites that are cutting-edge, engaging, and effective in connecting young adults to libraries. Includes examples and ideas from groundbreaking teen librarians across the United States.

Edublogs Awards. http://edublogawards.com.

Portal to the best education blogs on the Web, as decided by user votes.

Farrelly, M. G. "YA Services in a Post-Harry Potter World." *Public Libraries* 46, no. 5 (September/October 2007): 48–49.

Harry Potter captured the attention of generations of readers: this article suggests ways to mimic the mania in your own library marketing and programs.

Fisch, Karl. "Did You Know?/Shift Happens." *The Fischbowl,* August 15, 2006. http://thefischbowl.blogspot.com/2006/08/did-you-know.html.

A PowerPoint presentation that summarizes how technology is changing the world, including the way in which teens use technology.

Friedenwald-Fishman, Eric, and Laura K. Lee Dellinger. "Building Public Will." *Library Journal* 131, no. 2 (February 2006): 44–47.

Sets out a five-phase strategy for building public will that goes beyond marketing to foster ongoing community support for libraries.

"Gaming." *Library Success: A Best Practices Wiki.* www.libsuccess.org/index.php?title=Gaming.

A wiki containing news and information on gaming in libraries. Books, websites, blogs, resources, success stories, and more are listed. Every link is full of great ideas and inspiration.

Goodstein, Anastasia. *Ypulse.* Modern Media. http://ypulse.com.

Anastasia Goodstein provides daily news and commentary about Generation Y for media and marketing professionals. Great source of additional marketing resources. Sign up for their newsletter.

Hannold, RoseMary. *See YA Around: Library Programming for Teens.* www.cplrmh.com.

Book information and resource links from RoseMary Hannold.

Helmrich, Erin. "What Teens Want: What Libraries Can Learn from MTV." *Young Adult Library Services* 2, no. 2 (Spring 2004): 11–13.

Reports on a conference about marketing to teenagers and discusses ways to implement business marketing strategies in modern libraries. Includes statistical and categorical information about teenagers in the twenty-first century.

Infoisland. http://infoisland.org.

A blog documenting the Second Life Library Project from the Alliance Library System.

Information Age Consultants. www.iage.com.

Consulting resource for designing websites for teens.

International Federation of Library Associations and Institutions. "Internet and Networking Standards and Organizations." www.ifla.org/II/standard.htm.

An online bibliography of various national and international technology standards.

Johnson, Lisa. *Mind Your X's and Y's: Satisfying the 10 Cravings of a New Generation of Consumers.* New York: Free Press, 2006.

Highlights the wants and needs of the eighteen- to forty-year-old age range—a group of consumers unlike any other. Covers ten key needs of the X and Y Generations and discusses unconventional but effective tactics for marketing to them.

Krug, Steve. *Don't Make Me Think.* Berkeley: New Riders, 2006.

A humorous and easy-to-understand guide to web design. A common sense approach to usability that goes beyond the Internet and into the physical world.

McCormick, Aislinn. "Tap into Teen Spirit with Wicked Websites." *Children's Bookseller,* supplemental (August 2006): 16–17.

Aimed at publishers and booksellers, this article addresses website design, dos and don'ts of online marketing to teenagers, and issues of security, design, functionality, and cost.

Michelli, Joseph. *The Starbucks Experience: 5 Principles for Turning Ordinary into Extraordinary.* Columbus, OH: McGraw-Hill, 2006.

Draws on five key elements that have led to the success of Starbucks. The tips are simple and clear but provide great inspiration on how to create a library that reaches out to teens and library users of all ages.

Moses, Elissa. *The $100 Billion Allowance: Assessing the Global Teen Market.* New York: Wiley, 2000.

Helpful marketing and advertising tool for professionals targeting teens. Provides information for understanding their similarities and differences, as well as the results of a survey revealing teens' attitudes, values, and views.

MySpace and Teens. www.libsuccess.org/index.php?title=MySpace_%26_Teens.

A wiki that indexes library MySpace profiles oriented toward teen patrons.

Neiburger, Eli. *Gamers . . . in the Library?! The Why, What, and How of Videogame Tournaments for All Ages.* Chicago: American Library Association, 2007.

A guide to planning, setting up, and running video game tournaments in a public library. Written by an avid gamer, the book explores software and hardware options, audiences, program benefits, and other variables that can lead to a successful event.

Nichols, Mary Anne. *Merchandising Library Materials to Young Adults.* Greenwood Village, CO: Libraries Unlimited, 2002.

Discusses basic marketing and merchandising concepts that can be applied to a library setting. The author argues that libraries, in marketing their collections and services to teenagers, need to be just as aggressive as the brand-name advertisers that target adolescents.

Nicholson, L. "Technology and Teens: Helping Rural Libraries Grow." *Bookmobile and Outreach Services* 8, no. 2 (2005): 21–44.

Exploring the impact of technology on the life of teenagers today, Nicholson considers the possibilities of library expansion through e-books.

Nielson, Jakob. "Usability of Websites for Teenagers." *Alertbox: Current Issues in Web Usability,* January 2005. www.useit.com/alertbox/teenagers.html.

A concise overview of teenager web use studies. Addresses misconceptions about teenage users and ways to tailor a website for a given demographic.

North Dakota Standards and Benchmarks for Library and Technology Literacy. www .dpi.state.nd.us/standard/content/tech.pdf.

Standards for library and information literacy in North Dakota public schools. Broken down by grade range with technology and library skills requirements for high school students.

Ohio Library Council. "Marketing the Library." www.olc.org/marketing/.

Six self-paced modules with links to marketing resources and tools.

Oleck, Joan. "Libraries Use MySpace to Attract Teens." *School Library Journal* 53, no. 7 (July 2007): 16.

This short article describes how one library uses MySpace to reach local teens.

Pew Internet and American Life Project. www.pewinternet.org.

Terrific resource for learning about the impact of the Internet on children, families, communities, schools, and more. An authoritative source for timely information on the Internet's growth and societal impact.

Pfeil, Angela. *Going Places with Youth Outreach: Smart Marketing.* Chicago: American Library Association, 2005.

Corporations know that marketing to kids is big business, with children influencing more than $500 billion in family purchases each year. This hands-on guide shows librarians how to apply marketing concepts to expand their outreach and nurture these new audiences.

Schmidt, Aaron. "The Young and the Wireless." *School Library Journal* 51, no. 10 (October 2005): 44–46.

We know that teens are wired. This article gives hard data about just how wired—and wireless—Millennials can be, and what that should mean for youth services in libraries.

School Libraries on the Web. www.sldirectory.com.

This site indexes K–12 school library web pages. You can quickly see how school library media centers are promoting themselves on the Web.

Technology Leadership Network. "Creating and Connecting: Research and Guidelines on Online Social and Educational Networking." National School Boards Association, July 2007. www.nsba.org/SecondaryMenu/TLN/CreatingandConnecting.aspx.

A fascinating report about teen demographics and Internet use, with an emphasis on social networking, Internet safety, and policymaking.

Virtual YA Index. http://yahelp.suffolk.lib.ny.us/virtual.html.

This A-to-Z index of public library web pages provides a simple way to check out how public libraries are marketing to teens on the Web.

Whelan, Debra Lau. "Generation Tech: Today's Teens View Technology Not Only as a Part of Life, but as a Way of Life." *School Library Journal* 50, no. 3 (March 2004): 48–50.

An overview of the key findings from recent research on how teenagers view technology.

Woodward, Jeannette. *Creating the Customer-Driven Library: Building on the Bookstore Model.* Chicago: American Library Association, 2005.

With the goal of helping libraries market their services using low-cost or no-cost techniques, the author shares practical lessons for any library's revitalization inspired by the success of bookstores.

Young Adult Library Services Association. "Teen Tech Week." www.ala.org/ala/yalsa/
teentechweek/.

> Valuable resources for integrating technology into library services. Includes tech
> guides, activity ideas, and more. The linked wiki is a helpful gateway for related
> resources and promotional ideas.

Zollo, Peter. *Getting Wiser to Teens: More Insights into Marketing to Teenagers.* Ithaca,
NY: New Strategist Publications, 2003.

> This new and expanded update of Zollo's popular *Wise Up to Teens* gives readers a
> thorough understanding of what teens think, feel, and need as well as what they do,
> what they buy, and how marketers should (and shouldn't) reach them. Packed with
> invaluable insights and information.

Chapter 6: Policy and Practice

Anderson, Sheila. "How to Dazzle Maslow: Preparing Your Library, Staff, and Teens to
Reach Self-Actualization." *Public Library Quarterly* 23 no. 3/4 (2004): 49–58.

> Uses Maslow's Hierarchy of Needs to examine ways in which library staff can better
> serve teens.

Anderson, Sheila, ed. *Serving Young Teens and Tweens.* Westport, CT: Libraries
Unlimited, 2006.

> Includes programming ideas for working with young adolescents, as well as resources,
> booklists, and book talk ideas.

Conway, Susan. "Young Adult Public Library Services: An Overview." *Rural Libraries*
25, no. 2 (2005): 37–58.

> Provides an overview of the objectives, practical methods, values, and research studies
> that are pertinent to effective teen library services.

Heeger, Paula. "Better Late Than Never." *School Library Journal* 53, no. 2 (February
2007): 30.

> Suggests alternatives to traditional fines for teenagers who return books late, in an
> effort to make libraries more teen-friendly.

Hubert, Jennifer. "Ten Tips for Taming Teens in the Library." *Voice of Youth Advocates*
25, no. 6 (February 2003): 444–445.

> Excellent advice for taking on the challenges of teen librarianship.

Jones, Patrick, Michele Gorman, and Tricia Suellentrop. *Connecting Young Adults and
Libraries.* New York: Neal-Schuman, 2004.

> Includes chapters about teen spaces and youth involvement, as well as an annotated
> list of various space elements that should be considered.

Jones, Patrick, and Joel Shoemaker. *Do It Right! Best Practices for Serving Young Adults in
School and Public Libraries.* New York: Neal-Schuman, 2001.

> Guide for both public and school librarians that takes a customer service approach to
> serving young adults. Includes discussion of space needs, planning redesign projects,
> youth involvement, and adult-youth interaction.

King, Danielle. "Tame the Beasts: Try a Little TLC with Your Teens." *Florida Libraries* 50, no. 1 (Spring 2007): 8–9.

Describes the Teen Library Corps (TLC) initiated by one Florida library to integrate teens into library leadership.

Noack, Deana. "Customer Service 123." Houston Area Library *System*, 2004–2007. www.hals.lib.tx.us/cust123/.

Houston Area Library System's customer service training for public libraries.

Young Adult Library Services Association. "Young Adults Deserve the Best: Competencies for Librarians Serving Youth." www.ala.org/ala/yalsa/profdev/yacompetencies/competencies.cfm.

YALSA's complete list of the knowledge and skills needed in working with youth in a library.

Appendix D | **Vendor List**

The following is a list of select vendors related to the various subject areas presented in this book. Please note that many of these companies provide products or services beyond the category under which they are listed. For a thorough search for teen space items or services, a full review of this list is recommended.

Design Services

Beacon Architectural Associates
www.beaconarch.com
> Responsible for the 2005–2007 renovation of the Leominster (Massachusetts) Public Library

BiblioTECH Associates
Contact: Rolf Erikson, erikson@tiac.net
> Library consultant specializing in school library facilities design

Brodart Creative
www.brodartcreative.com
> Collaborative between Brodart Furniture and Creative Arts Unlimited, Inc.

DEMCO Library Interiors (DLI)
www.demcoservices.com
> Part of DEMCO, Inc., DLI offers consulting and design services for libraries of all shapes, sizes, and budgets.

DesignGroup
www.dgcolumbus.com
Contact: Jack Hedge
> This AIA Ohio Gold Medal firm provides expertise in planning, architecture, interior design, graphics, and sustainable design.

DSGN Associates
www.dsgn.com
Contact: Robert Meckfessel
> Dallas-based architecture firm

Frye Gillan Molinaro Architects
www.fgmarch.com
> Chicago-based architects specializing in academic and community libraries throughout the country

Gifford Spurck Associates
www.giffordspurck.com
    Denver-based architecture firm

HGA Architects and Engineers
www.hga.com
    Hammel, Green and Abrahamson Inc. architectural
    firm has offices in Los Angeles, Milwaukee (WI),
    Minneapolis (MN), Rochester (MN), Sacramento
    (CA), and San Francisco. Created the teen area at
    the Maplewood Branch of Ramsey County (MN)
    Library

HKS Inc.
www.hksinc.com
    Headquartered in Dallas with offices in Fort Worth,
    Orlando, Atlanta, Richmond, Los Angeles, Mexico
    City, London, New Castle, Tampa, and Salt Lake
    City

Integrated Design Group
http://idgarchitects.com
    New York-based architecture, interior design,
    strategic planning, graphic design, equipment
    planning, and multimedia firm

Janko Rasic Architect
www.jankorasic.com
    New York-based full-service architects

Kimberly Bolan and Associates
http://indielibrarian.blogspot.com
Contact: Kimberly Bolan, bolan_kimberly@yahoo.com
    Library consultant specializing in strategic planning,
    facilities planning for public and school library
    facilities, customer service, and marketing

Library Consultant's Online Directory
www.libraryconsultants.org
    A listing of library consultants, searchable by name,
    state, and expertise

Longo Libraries: Complete Library Planning
www.longolibraries.com
    Consultation, space planning, budgeting, project
    management, construction, and installation services,
    along with specialized library furnishings

Lucas Stefura Interiors
    Assisted in the creation of the Bob (or Robert
    Cormier Center for Young Adults) at the Leominster
    (Massachusetts) Public Library

Meehan Architects, Inc.
www.meehanarchitects.net
Contact: Dan Meehan and Catherine Grey
    Cleveland-based architects specializing in library
    planning and design

Prince/Alexander Partners, Inc.
www.princealexander.com
Contact: Steve Alexander
    Indianapolis-based full-service architecture,
    engineering, project management, and land
    planning firm

Studio Techne Architects
www.technearchitects.com
Contact: Marc Ciccarelli and Heather Schmucker
    Cleveland-based full-service architecture firm

Toppe Consultants, Inc.
www.toppearchitects.com
Contact: John Toppe, john@toppearchitects.com
    St. Petersburg (Florida)-based architecture firm

Furniture

AGATI
www.agati.com
    Designs, engineers, and manufactures furniture for
    educational spaces, including a library division

Arcadia
http://arcadiacontract.com
    Innovative product design, quality manufacturing,
    and excellent value for seating and tables

ATD American Co. and High Point Furniture
www.atdgsa.com
    Furniture resource that specializes in government
    contracts

August Incorporated
www.augustinc.com
    A furniture company that specializes in seating,
    including forms to fit special architectural space

BFI
www.bfionline.com
> Innovative and creative commercial interiors

Bola by Ron Kemnitzer
www.fixturesfurniture.com/products/bola.asp
> A line of chairs with distinctive, funky ball gliders

Brandrud
www.brandrud.com
> Furniture retailer with designs for a variety of environments

Brayton International
www.brayton.com
> Furniture manufacturer that specializes in European and custom design

Bretford
www.bretford.com
> Resource for library furniture and equipment from circulation desks to privacy screens with "a higher form of function"

Community Furniture
www.communityfurniture.com
> Chairs, tables, and lounge seating for institutions. This company specializes in wood.

Cranberry Clouds
www.cranberryclouds.com
> Beanbag + Stylish Chair Design = Omnipod, the feature product of Cranberry Clouds

Danko Design
www.peterdanko.com
> Seating and tables made from eco-friendly ply-bent wood, in lots of fun designs

David Edward
www.davidedward.com
> Tables and chairs in sophisticated styles, with custom product development available

Design Public
www.designpublic.com
> Their mission is to sell fresh and inspiring design. It equates to functional, aesthetic-driven, modern furniture at a good value.

Design Within Reach
www.dwr.com
> Sells new furniture with classic designs from the mid-1900s

Diner Booths
www.dinerbooths.com
> Restaurant booths, diner booths, kitchen booths, circle booths, l-shaped booths, and office booths—classy, durable, and fun!

Embury Ltd.
www.emburyltd.com
> Specialists in library furniture design, sales, and service

Emeco
www.emeco.net
> Aluminum chairs, made out of 80 percent post-consumer and post-industrial metal, with an estimated lifespan of 150 years

Febland Group Ltd.
www.febland.co.uk
> Beautiful and original furniture, ceramics, lighting, and chairs, including a large selection of contract furnishings

Fixtures Furniture
www.fixturesfurniture.com
> Chairs and tables by a company with a long-standing reputation for durable products targeted at institutional customers

The Foof Store
www.thefoofstore.com
> Giant comfier-than-beanbag chairs, including rockers, ottomans, and themed cushions

Funky Sofa
www.funkysofa.com
> Stylish and unique sofas, loveseats, chairs, sectionals, ottomans, and chaises at good prices

Furniture Lab
www.furniturelab.com
> Inventive, extremely customizable tables, seating, booths, and outdoor furniture

Haworth
www.haworth-europe.com
> One of the world's leading office furnishing companies, Haworth features a product line for creating "great spaces."

Herman Miller, Inc.
www.hermanmiller.com
> Award-winning furniture designer, manufacturer, and distributor that uses problem-solving research and design to develop educational and business solutions

IKEA
www.ikea.com
> Inexpensive, stylish furniture and accessories from one of the world's most popular retailers

ISA International
www.havaseat.com
> Seating and tables in classic, innovative, or custom designs

izzydesign
www.izzydesign.com
> Seating and other furniture with a focus on practicality and flexibility

Keilhauer
www.keilhauer.com
> Manufacturer of high quality commercial seating

KI
www.ki-inc.com
> A contract furniture manufacturer with an educational and governmental focus

Klein Design
www.kleindesign.com
> Innovative, high-quality, ergonomic chairs, sofas, and seating accessories

KronUSA
www.kronusa.com
> Seating and tables for heavy-use environments by award-winning designers

Loewenstein
www.loewensteininc.com
> European-style furnishings by a company committed to innovation and environmentalism

LoveSac
www.lovesac.com
> A beanbag-sofa-pillow hybrid; comfortable, unique seating in a variety of sizes and colors

LumiSource, Inc.
www.lumisource.com
> Stylish furniture, accessories, contemporary lighting, and novelty lighting

Martin Brattrud, Inc.
www.martinbrattrud.com
> A furniture manufacturer with stylish and comfortable ideas

Meblo Expo
www.mebloexpo.pl
> Funky and unique lounge seating, tables, chairs, and accessories

Metro
www.metrofurniture.com
> A furniture designer and manufacturer specializing in comfort, style, and ingenuity

Modus Furniture
www.modusfurniture.co.uk
> Seating, tables, storage, and accessories with contemporary, international design

Nienkämper
http://nienkamperlibrary.com *or* http://nienkamper.com
> International furniture company providing office seating, lounge seating, shelving, and more

Plymold
www.foldcraft.com
> Restaurant and cafeteria-style seating, tables, and accessories

RS (Restaurant-Services.com)
www.restaurant-services.com
> An international equipment and furniture guide

Stylex
www.stylexseating.com
> Swivel, multi-use, and lounge seating in modern styles

Turnstone
www.turnstonefurniture.com
> Sleek, modern, and simple business-style furniture

Vecta
www.vecta.com
> Furniture with clean lines and modern style, including foldable tables and stackable chairs

Versteel
www.versteel.com
> Tables, chairs, seating, personal workstations, and auxiliary products

Vitro Seating Products
www.vitroseating.com
> Specializes in fifties-style chairs, stools, booths, and tables

VS Furniture
www.vs-furniture.com
> High quality furniture. Based in Germany

Wesnic
www.wesnic.com
> Furniture for public places: excellent design, quality, and durability

Worden
http://wordencompany.com
> Furnishings for libraries, from seating and tables to circulation and technical furniture. Custom designs available

Fabric

Architex
www.architex-ljh.com
> Innovative small scale, solids, textures and coordinate upholstery

Carnegie
www.carnegiefabrics.com
> Fabric and upholstery for furniture, walls, windows, and more

CF Stinson
www.cfstinson.com
> Commercial fabrics, including upholstery, panels, leather, and vinyl

Crypton
www.cryptonfabric.com
> "Super fabrics" that protect against stains, spills, mildew, odors, mold, and bacteria

Maharam
www.maharam.com
> Stylish textiles for commercial spaces

Mayer Fabrics
www.mayerfabrics.com
> A company that prides itself on exceptional fabrics and great customer service

Momentum Group
www.themomgroup.com
> Woven fabrics, vinyl, panel, and cubicle cloth, as well as extensive custom services

Robert Allen
www.robertallendesign.com
> Fine fabrics with innovative design and construction

Shelving

Corman and Associates, Inc.
www.cormans.com
> Custom-manufactured fixtures, displays, props, and exhibits. A catalog with thousands of items—an excellent design and idea resource—is available through the website.

DisplayCase Depot
www.displaycasedepot.com
> Standard and customized display cases, kiosks, showcases, and exhibit booths with European designs are all available at this site.

Facements
www.facements.com
> File coverings, cushions, and tackboards that add color and coordination and provide a look that can be easily updated as tastes and fashions change

Franklin Fixtures
www.franklinfixtures.com
> Standard, modified, and custom display fixtures with a unique design system for coordinating an entire project

JD Pacific Rim Inc.
www.jdstore.com
> Various custom-capable shelving, fixtures, showcases, signage, accessories, and more

Library Display Shelving
www.librarydisplayshelving.com
  Modular, clear, acrylic display shelving

MJ Industries
www.mjshelving.com
  Shelves and shelving accessories for libraries

Opto International, Inc.
www.optosystem.com
  Supplier of fixtures and display systems

Siegel Display Products
www.siegeldisplay.com
  Floor displays, plastic frames, tabletop displays,
  sign holders, wall displays, kiosks, office storage,
  reception furniture, and more

Specialty Store Services
www.specialtystoreservices.com
  Creative shelving and display ideas including mini
  grid cubes, various natural wood displays, creative
  lighting alternatives, and more. The company's
  signage products include motion message displays,
  neon-like illuminated signs, backlit signs, custom-
  designed signs and banners. Visit online or request a
  free catalog.

This Into That
www.thisintothat.com
  Makes functional shelves (and other art) out of old
  books!

The Video Store Shopper
www.shopperinc.com
  Shelving (grid, slatwall, etc.) and display ideas,
  including a wide variety of media products and
  accessories. Send for a catalog to see creative
  alternatives for labels, lighting, and poster frames.
  You can even purchase celebrity stand-ups.

Flooring and Ceilings

Acoustical Solutions, Inc.
www.acousticalsolutions.com
  Supplier of soundproofing and noise control
  products

All Noise Control
www.allnoisecontrol.com
  Manufacturer of noise barrier and absorption
  materials

Armstrong
www.armstrong.com
  Acoustical and design products for floors and
  ceilings

Centiva
www.centiva.com
  Standard and custom flooring designs with colors,
  textures, and finishes for any space

Decorative and Area Rugs.com
www.decorativeandarearugs.com
  Rugs in contemporary, classic, modern, kid's, shaped,
  and shag styles

Eco Friendly Flooring
www.ecofriendlyflooring.com
  A one-stop source for eco-friendly wall and flooring
  options, including recycled metal tiles, bamboo,
  cork, recycled glass tiles, linoleum, stones, and
  reclaimed or sustainable wood

EcoFlooring.com
www.ecoflooring.com
  Wood flooring from recycled, reclaimed, and salvage
  sources, as well as sustainably managed forests. Also
  offer bamboo and palm floors

ECOsurfaces
www.ecosurfaces.com
  Offers recycled rubber flooring—a customizable,
  colorful, versatile, durable, and eco-friendly option

Forbo
www.forboflooringna.com
  Floor coverings and surface solutions for
  sophisticated, versatile, and even branded looks

InterfaceFLOR
www.interfaceflooring.com
  Environmentally responsible modular flooring

Joy Carpets
www.joycarpets.com
  Carpet, modular carpet, and area rugs in fun
  patterns and customizable designs

Milliken Floor Covering
www.millikencarpet.com
>Carpet construction and design options for any library space

nora Rubber Flooring
www.norarubber.com
>Rubber floor coverings in traditional, innovative, and customizable styles

RugsRugs.com
www.rugsrugs.com
>Modern, contemporary, classic, and unique area rugs

USG
www.usg.com
>Manufacturer of construction and remodeling building materials provides technical information geared toward the professional designer, but if you can get past that, you'll find some very interesting ideas for ceilings and flooring.

Miscellaneous Décor

AllPosters.com
www.allposters.com
>The world's largest poster and print store

Architectural Products by Outwater, LLC
www.outwater.com
>Extensive catalog of building and remodeling ideas and products

art.com
www.art.com
>Retailer of art prints, including movie, music, and sports-themed posters

AS Hanging Systems
www.ashanging.com
>Producers of hardware for mounting artwork on walls

Blik Surface Graphics
www.whatisblik.com
>Oversize, self-adhesive, removable wall decals for quick and creative decoration

Creative Arts Unlimited, Inc.
www.creativeartsinc.com
>Ideas for design, lighting, flooring, and more. Click on the libraries page for a gallery of pictures chock-full of creativity.

E-Z Decorator
www.ezdecorator.com
>Interior design tools for creating drawings, room plans, and interior design presentations

Home Decorators Collection
www.homedecorators.com
>High-quality furniture and home décor merchandise at reasonable prices

Kling Magnetics
www.kling.com/magneticpaintindex.html
>Custom magnets and magnetic products, including paint

Lifesize Celebrity Cutouts
www.cardboardcutouts.com
>Cardboard stand-ups of celebrities, popular icons, and animated characters

Magnetic Poetry
www.magneticpoetry.com
>The original poetry kit, plus related kits and word-themed products

RetroPlanet.com
www.retroplanet.com
>Provider of cool retro products

Sherwin-Williams
www.sherwin-williams.com
>Click on professional services, then architects and designers to access the paint company's color tools and resources, as well as product specifications.

StretchWall
www.stretchwall.com
>A unique finishing solution that uses stretched fabric as décor

Ten Speed Press
www.tenspeed.com/books/posters.htm
>Entertaining, thematic posters from a publisher we know and love

Technology

Advanced Communication Design
www.acdstar.com
> Developer and manufacturer of interactive digital audio and video delivery systems

Apple, Inc.
www.apple.com/itunes/
> Music downloads and equipment

Audacity
http://audacity.sourceforge.net
> Free, open-source software for recording and editing sounds. Can be used for podcasting

Bebo
www.bebo.com
> A social media network

Brown Innovations, Inc.
www.browninnovations.com
> Directional speakers for playing audio exactly where you want it—and nowhere else

The Cell Zone
www.salemiindustries.com
> A phone booth for cell-phone users! These pods provide callers with privacy while reducing the noise pollution of mobile phone conversations.

DBI International
www.dbiint.com
> Listening station, viewing station, and interactive display vendor

Evanced Solutions, Inc.
www.evancedsolutions.com
> Leading provider of software and services for online summer reading, library program and event management, and meeting room management

EventKeeper
www.eventkeeper.com
> Provider of online calendar, museum pass, and meeting room software

Facebook
www.facebook.com
> An increasingly popular social networking site, great for publicizing events, organizing groups, and more

Gaia
www.gaiaonline.com
> An anime-style social hangout online, with everything from art contests to poetry forums and fully customizable profiles and digital characters

Game Asylum
http://gameasylum.us
> Online vendor of video games and accessories, with an extensive collection at reasonable prices

iLike
www.ilike.com
> A "social music discovery" site that lets users recommend and share music. The main music application for Facebook, iLike is a great tool for tracking trends.

Interface Electronics
www.interface.com
> Digital signage solutions, directed speakers, and more

LAME
http://lame.sourceforge.net/index.php
> Free MP3 encoder

LibraryInsight
http://libraryinsight.com
> Online summer reading software and other web-based management solutions

LimeSurvey
www.limesurvey.org
> Open source software to help manage surveys of all kinds

Movie Licensing USA
www.movlic.com
> Provides public performance site licensing to K–12 schools and public libraries on behalf of the major Hollywood motion picture studios, ensuring that showings are legal

MP3.com
www.mp3.com
> Digital music downloads, along with artist fan pages, forums, podcasts, and charts

MySpace

www.myspace.com

> The most popular social networking site—a great resource for learning about and reaching teenagers

NextReads

www.nextreads.com

> A product of EBSCO Publishing, this newsletter subscription service provides reading suggestions for adults, teens, and children.

NoodleTools

www.noodletools.com

> Software that supports research from initial searching to compiling style-guide perfect bibliographies

Playaway

http://store.playawaydigital.com

> Self-contained audiobooks—just plug in headphones!

SoundDomes.com

www.sounddomes.com

> High fidelity, directed audio equipment for sound that stays put

SoundTube Entertainment

www.soundtube.com

> Specialized speakers for customized sound design

Turnitin

www.turnitin.com

> Many teens are now required to submit their work through this website, which monitors for plagiarism, allows for peer reviewing, and provides a paperless grading system for teachers.

YouTube

www.youtube.com

> The leader in online video, and the premier destination to watch and share original videos on the Web

Promotional

4imprint

www.4imprint.com

> Excellent promotional product website, offering free samples and free art service

Archie McPhee

www.mcphee.com

> Fun and crazy products for giveaways and promotions

ASI-Modulex

www.asimodulex.com

> Architectural signage solutions

BookLetters

www.bookletters.com

> Provides a toolkit for creating web pages, e-newsletters, and RSS feeds that integrate your library's style and branding with Bookletters' marketing content: reviews, promotions, discussion guides, and more

Branders.com

www.branders.com

> Hundreds of promotional products perfect for giveaways and marketing

CoolStuffCheap.com

www.coolstuffcheap.com

> The name says it all: funky, fun products from lava lamps and lighting to clocks and gadgets

CreateSurvey

www.createsurvey.com

> Web-based software that lets you build and run online surveys, as well as access a powerful survey management system

Hasbro

www.hasbro.com

> The leisure-time and entertainment products website offers special promotions as well as information about "Playathon," a unique fund-raising alternative.

iContact

www.icontact.com

> E-mail marketing service for sending and tracking e-mails. Great for newsletter distribution, surveys, and more

IncredibleGifts.com

www.incrediblegifts.com

> Novelty products from life-size cardboard stand-ups to board games, wall stickers, art, electronic toys, and T-shirts

Mannequinland

www.mannequinland.com

> Mannequins and display forms of all kinds

Northern Sun

www.northernsun.com

> Specializing in message-oriented stickers, posters, buttons, T-shirts, magnets, and more

QuestionPro

www.questionpro.com

> The QuestionPro website hosts online surveys; check out their free pages about survey design and analysis.

Raymond Geddes and Company, Inc.

www.raymondgeddes.com

> School supplies galore! Be sure to check out the toys and novelties section, as well as the seasonal decorations.

Rhode Island Novelty

www.rinovelty.com

> A wide variety of novelty items with various themes

SUDANCO, Inc.

http://affalt.bizland.com

> Alternative company for classification and genre labels. Their "no-res" labels are fantastic, and their specialties are customization and problem solving.

SurveyMonkey

www.surveymonkey.com

> Hosts online surveys. Includes tools for survey design, response collection, and analysis

U.S. Toy Company

www.ustoy.com

> Great selection of novelty items, including party and holiday-themed products

Zoomerang

www.zoomerang.com

> Software for web-based and SMS (mobile phone text messaging) surveys, with online panels, marketing research, and survey consultation available

Collection Development

Alliance Entertainment

www.aent.com

> Information on music, movies, games, and more

Audible, Inc.

www.audible.com

> Provider of digital audio editions of books, newspapers and magazines, original programming, and TV and radio subscriptions

Baker and Taylor Entertainment

www.btol.com

> Collection development resource for school and public libraries

Barnes and Noble

www.barnesandnoble.com

Brodart Co.

www.brodart.com

> Collection development resource for school and public libraries

CDNow

www.cdnow.com

> Search by artist, album title, song title, record label, and soundtrack. Sound clips are available. Includes top 100, news, interviews; they also have video and DVD information.

Critics' Choice Video

www.ccvideo.com

> Classic as well as popular movie titles

Ingram Book Company

www.ingrambook.com

> Wholesale distributor of book product

Instructional Video

www.insvideo.com

iTunes

www.apple.com/itunes/store/

> Listen to tunes and albums before purchase

Library Video Company

www.libraryvideo.com

Midwest Tape

www.midwesttapes.com

Full-service DVD and music vendor. Great online database, helpful catalogs, and excellent resource lists. Music standing order and cataloging programs available

NetLibrary

www.netlibrary.com

Provider of e-content and collection development resources

OverDrive

www.overdrive.com

Distributor of digital content including e-books, audiobooks, music, and video

Playaway

http://store.playawaydigital.com

Music and audiobook products that combine the audio with an easy-to-use player in one small unit

Recorded Books, LLC

www.recordedbooks.com

Publisher of audio and video products and downloadable services for the K–12 and public library markets

Multiproduct Vendors

Amazon.com

www.amazon.com

Retailer of books, audiovisual materials, electronics, furniture, décor, and more

BCI and Eurobib

http://bci.dk *and* www.eurobib.com/Default.aspx?ID =3154

Shelving, counters, carrels, computer stations, display furniture, tables, chairs, signage, and more

BJ's Wholesale Club

www.bjs.com

Various wholesale products available at discounted prices, including furniture

Brodart

www.brodart.com

A familiar library vendor with progressive ideas for teens. Check out its website under Library Supplies

and Furnishings to find products for young adult areas, including an entire page dedicated to teen furniture and lounge-style seating. Also a great resource for library supplies, equipment, and display fixtures

Costco

www.costco.com

Another wholesaler with a huge variety of product at discounted prices

DEMCO, Inc.

www.demco.com

Offers teen-friendly ideas for furniture, shelving, display, teen decor, supplies, audiovisual equipment, and signage

Eurway

www.eurway.com

Cool, contemporary furniture, storage, lighting, and accessories at great prices

Gaylord

www.gaylordmart.com

Library shelving, display fixtures, supplies, and furnishings

Gifts In Kind International

www.giftsinkind.org

A charitable organization that provides products, goods, and services from the private sector to the nonprofit sector. There are more than 350 Gifts In Kind affiliates worldwide. Free goods include, but are not limited to, furniture, computer equipment, paint, lighting fixtures, household goods, and office supplies and equipment.

Highsmith, Inc.

www.highsmith.com

Includes a variety of library-related products including shelving, furnishings, sign solutions, supplies, and design services

The Home Depot

www.homedepot.com

Planning and decorating resource. Includes tools and information for calculating carpeting, drywall, paint, wallpaper, and more

J. S. McHugh, Inc.
www.jsmchugh.com/home.html
    Architectural and institutional furnishings

Library Interiors Inc.
www.libraryinteriorsinc.com
    Library products from shelving and furniture to
    signage and acoustic panels, as well as evaluation,
    planning, consulting, customization, and
    installation services for all kinds of libraries and
    departments

LIFT
www.liftonline.com
    Listening and viewing stations as well as display
    options for multimedia formats

Lowe's
www.lowes.com
    Resource for all kinds of remodeling project needs,
    including hardware, building products, and basic
    project consulting

Menards
www.menards.com
    Another hardware store for project supplies,
    equipment, and consultation

Nu-Tech Products
www.nu-techonline.com
    Library and media center specialists offering
    furniture including Brodart Contract Furniture and
    services such as facilities assessment, space planning
    and more

Overstock.com
www.overstock.com
    Vendor of furniture, electronics, design accessories,
    and more

PBTeen
www.pbteen.com
    Pottery Barn's fun twists on furniture and storage
    solutions. Great accessories section includes items
    like easy-to-hang wall murals with fun sports and
    nature images.

Sam's Club
www.samsclub.com
    Another wholesaler with deep discounts on a variety
    of products

Steelcase Inc.
www.steelcase.com
    An "everything" vendor: architectural design and
    consultation, planning, financing, building, and
    project management services, and products from
    lighting and seating to technology and work tools

Target Corporation
www.target.com
    Alternative resource to traditional library furniture
    vendors with affordable furnishings, accessories,
    gaming and computer equipment, and electronics

Vernon Library Supplies, Inc.
www.vernonlibrarysupplies.com
    All kinds of library essentials: protection, repair, and
    storage products, processing supplies, circulation
    technology, presentation equipment, furniture,
    shelving, accessories, and more

Appendix E | Resource Libraries

Disclaimer: The information presented here was submitted by each resource library. This is for informational use only. The author disclaims any liability for any content error or omissions. The intent is to simply make readers aware of potentially helpful resources related to teen space.

Library	Location (City, State)	Type (public, school, other)	Website	Estimated Population Served by Library / Library System	Estimated Teen / Student Population Served	Estimated Teen Vols.	Estimated Teen Area (Sq. Ft.)	Notes
Abington Community Library	Clarks Summit, PA	public	http://www.lclshome.org/abington/Teen_Wiki.php	24,246	n/a	n/a	n/a	Collaborations with teens and community support.
Academy of Irving ISD Library, The	Irving, TX	school	http://www.irvingisd.net/academylibrary/	n/a	1,401	14,564	5,568	Progressive policies and practices and student-designed website.
Aiken County Public Library	Aiken, SC	public	http://www.abbe-lib.org/teens and http://www.myspace.com/aikenlibrary	28,829	3,499	3,634	300	Good example of doing more on a tight budget. Opened in April 2005.
Alden High School	Alden, NY	school	http://aldenschools.org/	n/a	680	10,729	3,826	Colorful, warm space that opened in October 2005. Includes circulating laptops.
Allen County Public Library	Fort Wayne, IN	public	http://acplteens.wordpress.com and http://www.flickr.com/photos/acplinfo/2120830209/	300,836	4,500	45,000	4,450	One of the original model libraries from the first edition. See what they've done since 2003.
Ames Public Library	Ames, IA	public	http://www.amespubliclibrary.org/teens/youthHome.asp	51,557	8,833	7,733	575	Gives warmth to white walls with colorful furnishings and accessories.
Ann Arbor District Library	Ann Arbor, MI	public	http://www.aadl.org/axis	155,611	n/a	n/a	n/a	Great program ideas and integration of technology. See their Axis program publication in print and online.
Arapahoe Library District	Englewood, CO	public	http://teens.arapahoelibraries.org/go2.cfm?pid=9385&aldredirect	202,609	n/a	n/a	n/a	Good online presence including an online teen newsletter.
Arlington School at McLean Hospital	Belmont, MA	school	http://www.mclean.harvard.edu/patient/child/as.php	n/a	48	3,000	500	Small school library designed by Rolf Erikson and Demco Library Interiors. Not run-of-the-mill.
Atlanta-Fulton Public Library System, Central Library	Atlanta, GA	public	http://www.afplweb.com/cms/index.php?option=com_content&task=view&id=169	786,727	n/a	n/a	n/a	Computer lab, study rooms, lounge, collections, programming, and more.
Auckland City Libraries, Central City Library	Auckland, New Zealand	public	http://www.aucklancitylibraries.com/teens and http://anyquestions.co.nz/en/anyQuestions.html and http://www.bebo.com/Profile.jsp?MemberId=4428799413	401,500	37,700	14,991	484	Good physical and virtual teen space. Check out their "Readers React" page on the Web. They have online real-time homework help too.
Austin Public Library, St. John Branch and Terrazas Branch	Austin, TX	public	http://www.wiredforyouth.com/	656,562	85,917	43,367	96 (St. John); 286 (Terrazas)	Good branch examples. Success with accessorizing and creative solutions for small spaces. Since 2000 they have provided Wired for Youth technology centers.
Baraboo Public Library	Baraboo, WI	public	http://teens.baraboopubliclibrary.org/	19,739	1,720	1,598	126	Small space example that includes a variety of activities, programming, and technology.

Library	Location (City, State)	Type (public, school, other)	Website	Estimated Population Served by Library / Library System	Estimated Teen / Student Population Served	Estimated Teen Vols.	Estimated Teen Area (Sq. Ft.)	Notes
Bedford Free Public Library	Bedford, MA	public	http://www.bedfordlibrary.net/youngadult.htm	12,519	n/a	6,000	1,200	Reevaluated shifts in reference service to reduce paper collection to allow for a larger teen area.
Belgrade Middle School	Belgrade, MT	school	http://www.belgrade.k12.mt.us/	n/a	457	8,460	1,980	Low-budget solutions.
Bloomingdale Public Library	Bloomingdale, IL	public	http://www.mybpl.org/bpl/index.php?q=node/42 and http://democoservices.com/html/promoi_prt_makewin05.htm	21,625	1,621	2,946	400	Winner of DEMCO makeover contest.
Blue Island Public Library	Blue Island, IL	public	http://www.blueislandlibrary.org/library/6a.htm and http://www.myspace.com/122318522	23,463	n/a	n/a	n/a	Their Tech Annex includes 3-D modeling and animation, audio sound recording, and video and image editing equipment, as well as a web development station, a digital camera, a Sony PlayStation 2, a Yamaha keyboard, microphones, mixers, and headphones.
Bookworm, The	Beijing, Chengdu, and Suzhou, China	public	http://www.chinabookworm.com/	n/a	n/a	n/a	n/a	Third Place model including three Bookworm sites in Beijing, Chengdu, and Suzhou.
Bronx Library Center, The New York Public Library	Bronx, NY	public	http://www.nypl.org/branch/local/bx/fdc.cfm and http://teenlink.nypl.org/index.html	80,461	24,000	17,948	1,600	Model for teens being contributors to the Teen Center, rather than just participants. Good space and programming example.
Brookfield Library	Brookfield, CT	public	http://brookfieldteensrock.wordpress.com/	16,000	2,000	1,900	200	
Brookline, The Public Library of	Brookline, MA	public	http://www.brooklinelibrary.org/teen-blog/	57,107	5,408	7,129	1,550	Teen space coming soon. Check out their blog.
Buckingham Browne and Nichols Middle School Library	Cambridge, MA	school	http://www.bbns.org/ac_middleschool.htm	n/a	170	6,600	640 (plus outdoor reading terrace)	The library has an outside terrace. Great furniture. The kids just love the space. Rolf Erikson project.
Calgary Public Library	Calgary, AB, Canada	public	http://calgarypubliclibrary.com/teens/welcome.htm	991,759	70,000	88,202 (all locations)	400–600 (depending on location)	Nine of their seventeen locations have Teen Zones. Good web design, which included teen input.
Campbell County Public Library System	Gillette, WY	public	http://www.ccpls.org/html/teens.html	33,689	3,400	13,819	2,000	A model site from the first edition. Very active teen participation. Their new and improved space opened in December 2005.

203

Library	Location (City, State)	Type (public, school, other)	Website	Estimated Population Served by Library / Library System	Estimated Teen / Student Population Served	Estimated Teen Vols.	Estimated Teen Area (Sq. Ft.)	Notes
Canandaigua Middle School	Canandaigua, NY	school	http://www.canandaiguaschools.org/district.cfm?subpage=11618	n/a	977	n/a	5,500	Teen input in design process. Space is divided into function areas.
Canton Public Library	Canton, MI	public	http://www.cantonpl.org/ya/	76,366	12,156	12,632	870	Neor lights, ceiling panels made from posters, magnetic poetry . . . you name it.
Cape Central High School	Cape Girardeau, MO	school	http://www.cape.k12.mo.us/CHS/default.htm	n/a	1,440	16,000	10,500	Overall excellent example of a high school library space and services.
Cape Central Middle School	Cape Girardeau, MO	school	http://www.cape.k12.mo.us/centralmidschool/myweb18/	n/a	1,400	16,000	n/a	A fur middle school example.
Carl Junction Junior High School	Carl Junction, MO	school	http://www.cj.k12.mo.us/jh/	n/a	494	n/a	n/a	Check out their eclectic lamp collection. They are proud to say their style is "classic tacky."
Carnegie Library of Pittsburgh	Pittsburgh, PA	public	http://www.carnegielibrary.org/teens/	458,597	2,000	750	385	Space, technology, and more.
Central Rappahannock Regional Library	Fredericksburg, VA	public	http://teenspoint.org/	255,800	n/a	n/a	n/a	One of Miranda Doyle's top six teen websites.
Cerritos Library	Cerritos, CA	public	http://www.ci.cerritos.ca.us/library/photos/young_adults.html	55,000	4,500–5,000	12,325	4,000	Rennovated in 2002. Art Deco style.
Chicago Ridge Public Library	Chicago Ridge, IL	public	http://www.chicagoridge.lib.il.us/teen_cafe_read/teen_cafe_read.html	13,750	1,500	1,000	400	A model library from the first edition.
Chino Hills Public Library	Chino Hills, CA	public	http://www.chlibrary.com/	66,787	11,304	6,420	900	See their teen magazine *4-Head*, a literary magazine written and produced by Chino Hills teens.
City of Mountain View Public Library	Mountain View, CA	public	http://www.ci.mtnview.ca.us/city_hall/library/teen_zone/default.asp	72,000	4,800	11,922	1,900	Active teen involvement and customer service oriented.
Cleveland Heights–University Heights Public Library, Lee Road Library	Cleveland Heights, OH	public	http://www.yazine.net/	61,194	1,976	9,287	3,675	Space opened in September 2006. It was a teen/library staff/architect collaborative. They also offer a program a day for teens.
Columbus Public Library	Columbus, GA	public	http://www.thecolumbuslibrary.org/teens.html	200,000	n/a	n/a	1,250	Colcrful, technology-oriented space.

Library	Location (City, State)	Type (public, school, other)	Website	Estimated Population Served by Library / Library System	Estimated Teen / Student Population Served	Estimated Teen Vols.	Estimated Teen Area (Sq. Ft.)	Notes
Contra Costa County, Hercules Public Library	Hercules, CA	public	http://nt-evanced.ccclib.org/evanced/lib/eventcalendar.asp?EventType=ALL&Lib=98df=calendar	24,776	n/a	n/a	3,100	Includes a teen homework center and a study room for all ages. It is acoustically insulated from the rest of the library. Designed by HGA Architects and Will Bruder Architects.
Coppell Middle School West	Coppell, TX	school	http://www.coppellisd.com/1520209261111549390/site/default.asp?	n/a	879	15,000	5,000	They have a teen advisory board and offer a program called "Friday Night Flicks."
Corfu Free Library	Corfu, NY	public	http://www.nioga.org/cor.html	756	n/a	n/a	75	Implemented "Changing Spaces" themed summer program to transform small teen area.
Corte Madera Regional Library	Corte Madera, CA	public	http://www.co.marin.ca.us/depts/LB/main/corte/index.cfm	16,832	n/a	1,338	120	Small teen "nook."
Crete Public Library	Crete, NE	public	http://www.crete-ne.gov/index.asp?NID=41	6,028	n/a	n/a	n/a	Small space example.
DC Everest Sr High School	Schofield, WI	school	http://www.dce.k12.wi.us/srhigh/	n/a	4,894	n/a	n/a	Small 10 x 11' café space at entrance of school library.
Denver Public Library	Denver, Co	public	http://teens.denverlibrary.org/#	592,092	50,371	50,717	n/a	Leader in virtual teen space with their Evolver website.
Deschutes Public Library, Bend Library	Bend, OR	public	http://www.dpls.lib.or.us/Page.asp?NavID=42	75,290	7,500	7,100	750	Small, portable space.
Deschutes Public Library, Redmond Library	Redmond, OR	public	http://www.dpls.lib.or.us/Page.asp?NavID=42	23,500	n/a	n/a	n/a	Teen-designed space called Teen Beat opened in April 2007. Collaboration between multiple staff, community members, and teens.
Dexter High School	Dexter, MO	school	http://dexter.k12.mo.us/index.php?library	n/a	590	n/a	n/a	Included student requests in their design.
Dorchester County Library	St. George, SC	public	http://www.dcl.lib.sc.us/young_adults.htm	107,004	n/a	n/a	n/a	Online teen newsletter.

Library	Location (City, State)	Type (public, school, other)	Website	Estimated Population Served by Library / Library System	Estimated Teen / Student Population Served	Estimated Teen Vols.	Estimated Teen Area (Sq. Ft.)	Notes
East Brunswick Public Library	East Brunswick, NJ	public	http://www.ebpl.org/teens/index.cfm	46,756	8,000	12,072	1,500	Space designed by Kimberly Bolan and DEMCO Library Interiors, and the teens of East Brunswick. Opened in September 2007 with active teen involvement and creative programming.
East Meadow Public Library	East Meadow, NY	public	http://www.eastmeadow.info/teens.html	52,000	5,100	n/a	n/a	Teen area opened in 2008. Teen advisory board wrote letters to local politicians and businesses asking for help in obtaining funds to furnish the new room.
Evanston Public Library	Evanston, IL	public	http://www.epl.org and http://eplteen.wordpress.com/	74,239	9,000	8,500	2,100	Active teen involvement and teen/library staff/architect collaboration from the very beginning. Teens were trained to be tour guides when the space opened. Good use of technology and creative programming. Space designed by Architecture Is Fun (Peter Exley) and Nagle Hartray Danker Kagan McKay Penney Architects Ltd.
Evansville Vanderburgh Public Library, Central Library	Evansville, IN	public	http://www.evpl.org/teens/	171,922	8,186	8,373	2,138	Welcoming service and flexible space. The Teen Zone opened in September 2004. Many student-led programs.
Farmington Public Library	Farmington, NM	public	http://www.infoway.org/TeenZone/index.asp and http://www.blendedzine.com/onlinepub/01-jan-2008/	113,081	6,000	16,244	901 (w/o teen computer area)	Terrific teen space as well as teen-centered programming such as their *Blended* zine project. Also featured in Kimberly Bolan's *School Library Journal* article from November 2006.
Farnsworth Public Library	Oconto, WI	public	http://www.nflls.lib.wi.us/oco/teens.htm	10,500	700	2,005	764	Created a fantastic teen space with no budget and active teen involvement. The Teen Book Nook opened in March 2007. See sample TAB agendas and Taboo News.
Flintridge Prep School	La Canada Flintridge, CA	school	http://www.flintridgeprep.org/home/default.aspx	n/a	500	n/a	n/a	Student involvement.
Forsyth County Public Library, Central Library	Winston-Salem, NC	public	http://www.forsyth.cc/library/generation_teen.aspx	188,758	29,597	18,206	1,500	Opened in fall 2005, Teen Central is not attached to any other department and has completely separate traffic flow.

Library	Location (City, State)	Type (public, school, other)	Website	Estimated Population Served by Library / Library System	Estimated Teen / Student Population Served	Estimated Teen Vols.	Estimated Teen Area (Sq. Ft.)	Notes
Fremont Public Library District	Mundelein, IL	public	http://www.fremontlibrary.org/index.php?option=com_content&task=view&id=90&Itemid=150 and http://www.nsls.info/articles/detail.aspx?articleID=116	29,620	n/a	n/a	n/a	The Teen Zone is dedicated to teens in grades 7–12. The librarian published the online article "The Public Library: A Third Place for Teens." Good website and online resources.
George School	Newtown, PA	school	http://www.georgeschool.org/	n/a	527	20,000	8,000	Open-minded services, practices, and approaches to technology. Mutual respect is emphasized throughout the school.
Gering Public Library	Gering, NE	public	http://www.geringlibrary.org/	7,751	n/a	1,448	110	Small space example.
Gloucester Lyceum and Sawyer Free Library	Gloucester, MA	public	http://www.sawyerfreelibrary.org//SFL%20Teen%20Zone/entrance.htm	30,817	2,168	11,738	1,488 (Sawyer)	Small space example.
Grand County Library	Moab, UT	public	http://www.moablibrary.org/	9,500	694	2,611	600	Small area turned into a vibrant teen space.
Greece Athena High School	Rochester, NY	school	http://www.greece.k12.ny.us/ath/library/	n/a	1,417	n/a	n/a	One of Miranda Doyle's top six teen websites.
Gretna Public Library	Gretna, NE	public	http://www.gretnapubliclibrary.org/teens/index.html	2,339	1,040	946	165	Small space example.
Guilderland Public Library	Guilderland, NY	public	http://www.uhls.org/guil/teen/teenpage.php	33,475	3,500	10,000	200+	Creative open-space solution. Teen participation and creative services.
Hamilton Public Library	Hamilton, ON, Canada	public	http://www.myhamilton.ca/myhamilton/LibraryServices/Teens/	n/a	n/a	n/a	n/a	Great teen website, blog, and a slew of technology.
Harford County Public Library	Belcamp, MD	public	http://www.hcplonline.info/teens/teenzone.html	234,715	26,055	21,790	435 (Abingdon); 195 (Jarretsville); 80 (other branches)	Multiple branch examples.

Library	Location (City, State)	Type (public, school, other)	Website	Estimated Population Served by Library / Library System	Estimated Teen / Student Population Served	Estimated Teen Vols.	Estimated Teen Area (Sq. Ft.)	Notes
Hennepin County Library, Minneapolis, Minneapolis Central	Minnetonka, MN, and Minneapolis, MN	public	http://www.hclib.org/teens and http://www.mplib.org/teens.asp	350,000 (Minneapolis)	20,000 (Minneapolis)	15,000 (Minneapolis)	2,000 (Teen Central)	Teen Central is located in Minneapolis Central. Creative shelving and merchandising, technology, a graffiti room, and more. http://www.hclib.org/teens is one of Miranda Doyle's top six teen websites.
Houston Area Library System	Houston, TX	public	http://www.hals.lib.tx.us/cust123/	n/a	n/a	n/a	n/a	Great web-based customer service training modules, including basic practices and skills overview, overcoming barriers in difficult situations, cultural diversity, basic skills (frontline public services), working with teens, Web and e-mail, telephone, and challenging situations.
Hudson Library and Historical Society	Hudson, OH	public	http://www.hudson.lib.oh.us/hudson%20website/YA/ya.htm	23,054	n/a	n/a	n/a	Progressive and colorful design, services, and more. Teen space designed by Meehan & Associates.
Independence Public Library	Independence, IA	public	http://www.indylibrary.org/	6,000	1,877	1,197	925	Currently building a new library that will have a teen space—something their town has never had. There will be sections for hanging out, talking, reading magazines, studying, and listening and viewing. Teens helped design the area.
Jackson Middle School	Jackson, MO	school	http://www.jacksonr2schools.com/	n/a	708	n/a	n/a	Excellent service, promotions, collections, and more.
Jacksonville Public Library, Pablo Creek and West Regional Branches	Jacksonville, FL	public	http://jpl.coj.net/teens/	861,150	n/a	n/a	910 (Pablo Creek); 1,220 (West Regional)	Multiple branch examples. DesignGroup served as the library planner, interior designer, and provided furniture, fixtures, and equipment.
Jerome Public Library	Jerome, ID	public	http://www.jerome.lili.org/node/69	8011	1,201	1,275	630	Remodel completed in May 2006. Strong teen collaboration and service model. Good ideas for inexpensive revamps. Teen advocacy grant program. Keep an eye on them—they have many ideas yet to come.

Library	Location (City, State)	Type (public, school, other)	Website	Estimated Population Served by Library / Library System	Estimated Teen / Student Population Served	Estimated Teen Vols.	Estimated Teen Area (Sq. Ft.)	Notes
Jurong Regional Library	Singapore	public	http://www.nlb.gov.sg/	3,608,500	n/a	n/a	n/a	This library has an entire floor dedicated to teens, and the space was not only designed by but is also managed by teenagers. It includes performing space and an extensive teen-friendly collection in multiple languages.
Kalamazoo Public Library	Kalamazoo, MI	public	http://www.kpl.gov/teen/default.aspx	119,517	n/a	n/a	n/a	Good programming, technology and service practices.
Kent District Library, Cascade Branch	Grand Rapids, MI	public	http://www.kdl.org/teens	32,017	4,131	7,887	1,340	Opened in spring 2006 with funds donated by a local family. Kent District has created the DESIGN method to implement design trends at all locations. They have an interactive website and online program registration.
Kent District Library, East Grand Rapids Branch	East Grand Rapids, MI	public	http://www.kdl.org/teens	10,373	n/a	n/a	n/a	Includes two study rooms, a teen art gallery curated by teen advisory board members, lots of natural light, and a variety of furniture and shelving.
King County Library System	Issaquah, WA	public	http://www.kcls.org/teens/ and http://www.kcls.org/lakehills/	109,569	12,552	n/a	n/a	Their Lake Hills Library utilized interesting marketing techniques. The entire library system offers dynamic program information via the Web with online registration options.
Lawrence High School Library	Lawrence, KS	school	http://library.lhs.usd497.org/home.html	n/a	1,342	24,232	n/a	Good marketing efforts.
Lawrence Public Library	Lawrence, KS	public	http://www.lawrence.lib.ks.us/	81,854	12,914	6,800	600	Model site from first edition.
Lee County Middle School	Leesburg, GA	school	http://www.lee.k12.ga.us/schools/lcms/lee.htm	n/a	1,450	19,023	4,642	Starting a teen advisory board in 2008 for their school library.
Lee's Summit West High School	Lee's Summit, MO	school	http://lswhs.leesummit.k12.mo.us/medialsw/	n/a	1,297	n/a	n/a	

Library	Location (City, State)	Type (public, school, other)	Website	Estimated Population Served by Library / Library System	Estimated Teen / Student Population Served	Estimated Teen Vols.	Estimated Teen Area (Sq. Ft.)	Notes
Leominster Public Library	Leominster, MA	public	http://www.leominsterlibrary.org/teens.htm	41,303	2,655	10,759	1,300	Model site from the first edition. Their new facility opened in 2007. All-around good ideas from participation to collection to programming and promotion.
Lesterville R-4 School Library	Lesterville, MO	school	http://www.lesterville.k12.mo.us/	n/a	200	4,270	5,872	Creative outdoor reading courtyard.
Lewis Cass Technical High School	Detroit, MI	school	http://schools.detroit.k12.mi.us/sites/cass/index.htm	n/a	2,129	n/a	n/a	Creative shelving and display.
Livonia Public Library, Carl Sandburg Branch Library	Livonia, MI	public	http://livonia.lib.mi.us/teen/index.php	100,545	13,732	4,252	170	Small space example.
London Public Library, Central Branch Library	London, ON, Canada	public	http://www.londonpubliclibrary.ca/teens/ and http://www.myspace.com/teenannex	373,008	36,067	6,112	3,800	Launched in January 2007, the Central Branch Library's Teen Annex was a pilot project that was part of an LSDF grant. Its success has led to expansion of teen services to create a Teen Annex in the other 15 branches.
Longview Public Library	Longview, WA	public	http://www.longviewlibrary.org/Teens.html	35,570	n/a	n/a	n/a	Funding example.
Los Angeles Public Library	Los Angeles, CA	public	http://www.lapl.org/ya/	3,957,875	300,000	30,000	4,000	Model site from first edition.
Louisville Public Library	Louisville, CO	public	http://www.ci.louisville.co.us/library/teens.asp	18,417	2500	5,500	1,616	The Loft is a colorful, uniquely shaped space that forms a mini-library within a library. Square footage includes a teen services room, a listening room, and a homework center.
Marion Public Library	Marion, NY	public	http://www.marionnypubliclibrary.blogspot.com/	4,901	500–700	500 (teen fiction only)	99	Small space example.
McMillan Memorial Library	Wisconsin Rapids, WI	public	http://www.mcmillanlibrary.org/index.shtml	37,433	4,000	3,661	500 (teen collection) and 5,000 (multipurpose space)	The Commons area is designed to be a community center for all ages. In the mornings, it is frequented by retirees. After school, it is well used by junior high school students socializing and using the Internet. In the evenings, many of the tables are used for homework and small meetings.

Library	Location (City, State)	Type (public, school, other)	Website	Estimated Population Served by Library / Library System	Estimated Teen / Student Population Served	Estimated Teen Vols.	Estimated Teen Area (Sq. Ft.)	Notes
Melton Public Library	French Lick, IN	public	http://www.melton.lib.in.us/teens.html	5,710	748	3,159	970	Active teen involvement. Teens have the power to police their own space.
Miller Lakeland Public Library	Lakeland, GA	public	http://www.sgrl.org/pages/miller.html	2,743	n/a	n/a	n/a	
Missouri River Regional Library	Jefferson City, MO	public	http://www.mrrl.org/teens/index.asp	86,794	8,294	6,328	400	Was awarded a Teen Spaces Development Grant and finished the space in December 2007.
Mitchell Library	Glasgow, Scotland	public	http://www.glasgow.gov.uk/en/Residents/Library_Services/The_Mitchell/	608,794	n/a	n/a	n/a	Winner of Delegates Choice 2007 award. Example of the changing face of libraries. Progressive design and policies.
Morley Library	Painesville, OH	public	http://www.morleylibrary.org/teens.htm	51,784	n/a	n/a	n/a	Colorful space designed by Meehan Architects.
Moses Greeley Parker Memorial Library	Dracut, MA	public	http://www.dracutlibrary.org/ya.htm	29,000	2,500–4,000	2,000	4,000	Interesting furniture, great color, lots of natural light, and more.
Mount Laurel Library	Mount Laurel, NJ	public	http://www.mtlaurel.lib.nj.us/teen/teens3.html	40,221	n/a	n/a	n/a	Selected as the first statewide demonstration site for Trading Spaces. Use visual merchandising techniques. The project wasn't solely focused on teen services, but it is a good overall marketing and merchandising example.
Mountain View Public Library	Mountain View, MO	public	http://150.199.190.199/	2,430	250	500	400	Small space example.
Multnomah County Library	Portland, OR	public	http://www.multcolib.org/teens/ and http://www.multcolib.org/teens/lounges.html	701,545	47,129	59,491	n/a	Teen Lounges and Homework Centers at a variety of branches.
New Trier Township High School	Northfield and Winnetka, IL	school	http://www.newtrier.k12.il.us/library/	n/a	4,044	n/a	n/a	One of Miranda Doyle's top six teen websites.
Newark Public Library	Newark, NY	public	http://www.newark.pls-net.org/TeenPage.htm	9,682	1,200	6,400	1,003	Active teen involvement on many levels. Successful long-range planning, progressive policies, and adult-youth collaborations.

Library	Location (City, State)	Type (public, school, other)	Website	Estimated Population Served by Library / Library System	Estimated Teen / Student Population Served	Estimated Teen Vols.	Estimated Teen Area (Sq. Ft.)	Notes
Noble Library	Noble, OK	public	http://www.pioneer.lib.ok.us/home	318,255	n/a	n/a	n/a	Highsmith library design.
Norfolk Public Library	Norfolk, VA	public	http://www.npl.lib.va.us/teens2/index_teens.html	234,100	n/a	n/a	n/a	Redesigned on a dime with help from a volunteer architect. The renovation increased teen library use and involved teen input. It was profiled in the April 2002 issue of *American Libraries*.
North Platte Public Library	North Platte, NE	public	http://www.ci.north-platte.ne.us/library/	35,900	2,000	4,748	94	Model site from the first edition.
Oak Park Public Library	Oak Park, IL	public	http://www.oppl.org/teensite/index.htm	52,524	n/a	n/a	n/a	Innovative, funky seating and shelving. Another branch has an after-hours teen coffeehouse complete with poetry slam.
Ocean County Library	Toms River, NJ	public	http://www.flickr.com/photos/tags/oceancountylibraryto msrivernjlibraryteen/	509,638	n/a	n/a	4,000+	Overall great space. Everything is on wheels in their Teen Zone.
Oprah Winfrey Leadership Academy for Girls	Henley-on-Klip in Meyerton, South Africa	school	http://www.oprah.com/presents/2007/academy/acade my_main.jhtml	n/a	152 (with potential for 450)	n/a	n/a	Inspirational boarding school for grades 7–12. For more details, see the website and the "Live and Learn" in *O at Home* magazine (Summer 2007).
Orange County Library System	Orlando, FL	public	http://www.ocls.info/Children/Teen/default.asp and http://www.myspace.com/ocls	1,000,000+	80,000	6,610	3,000	Great well-rounded model, from teen involvement, to space design, to technology, to collection and programming, to staffing, customer service, and policies and practices.
Otis Library	Norwich, CT	public	http://www.otislibrarynorwich.org/	37,040	4,775	4,850	n/a	A traditional library setting but their teen space is set up to be a comfortable hangout.
Ovid-Elsie Information Center	Ovid-Elsie, MI	school	http://www.oe.k12.mi.us/infocenter.htm	n/a	570	n/a	n/a	Started with a $1,000 budget. Includes 30 TVs, computers, café, radio station, and distance learning classrooms.

212

Library	Location (City, State)	Type (public, school, other)	Website	Estimated Population Served by Library / Library System	Estimated Teen / Student Population Served	Estimated Teen Vols.	Estimated Teen Area (Sq. Ft.)	Notes
Oxford Public Library	Oxford, MI	public	http://www.teenuplink.com/	16,025	1,439	8,359	1,200	Excellent collaboration between teens, staff, administrators, board, and architect. Space designed by Pnechansky Architects. Great statistics, too.
Palm Harbor Library	Palm Harbor, FL	public	http://www.palmharborlibrary.org/	62,000	4,000	3,800	700	Director wrote a $20,000 grant to renovate room and develop the collection. Great mural. Looking at expanding the facility, with goal of tripling the space.
Palos Verdes Library District	Palos Verdes, CA	public	http://www.pvld.mobi/teens/	67,286	n/a	7,200	1,500	The Annex is a retail space between a barber shop and a golf shop in a shopping center next door to the library. Terrific overall model.
Park Ridge Public Library	Park Ridge, IL	public	http://www.parkridgelibrary.org/ya/yaindexorange.html	37,775	4,100	5,390	840	Targeted at middle school students. There is a separate collection for high school students. Carol Abrams of Abrams Design Consultants was the designer.
Passages Academy School Library at Bridges	Bronx, NY	juvenile detention center	http://passagesacademy.org/home.html	1,000	1,000	n/a	n/a	Renovated in April 2004. Teens met twice a week with a mentor to brainstorm ideas for the space. There is a combined emphasis on security and teen needs.
Pattonville High School	Maryland Heights, MO	school	http://phs.psdr3.org/	n/a	2,000	28,000	13	Good use of color to liven up an otherwise typical space.
Peabody Institute Library at Danvers	Danvers, MA	public	http://www.danverslibrary.org/youngadult/ya2.html and http://yaink.wordpress.com	25,212	3,292	3,302	285	Good marketing, promotional, and outreach ideas as well as creative use of space for a small library.
Peabody Institute Library at Peabody	Peabody, MA	public	http://www.peabodylibrary.org/youth/index.html	48,129	5,734	5,167	2,460	Two separate rooms dedicated to teens are located on two different floors. Both were redesigned in 2007. The original young adult room houses the collection. The other is our young adult drop-in space, which is open four afternoons a week.
Phoenix Public Library	Phoenix, AZ	public	http://www.phoenixpubliclibrary.org/blaze	1,321,045	196,896	11,315	5,000	Model from the first edition. Still a great space. Excellent overall example, especially for a service model for programming and adult-teen collaboration and interaction.
Pickering Public Libraries	Pickering, ON, Canada	public	http://www.picnet.org/teens	94,400	11,250	n/a	n/a	Creative programming and services.

Library	Location (City, State)	Type (public, school, other)	Website	Estimated Population Served by Library / Library System	Estimated Teen / Student Population Served	Estimated Teen Vols.	Estimated Teen Area (Sq. Ft.)	Notes
Pikes Peak Library District, East Library	Colorado Springs, CO	public	http://www.ppld.org/Teens/index.asp	593,000	75,000	25,857	2,278	Active teen involvement. Great overall services and ideas. Opened in September 2007, the Teen Center at the East Library is planned to be the first of many teen centers in this district.
Plymouth District Library	Plymouth, MI	public	http://plymouthlibrary.org/ya.htm	37,000	3,500	11,468	1,940	Opened in summer 2007. Circulation grew 13 percent the first six months of 2008 compared to the same months in 2007. Paperback circulation increased 68 percent since being interfiled with hardcover fiction from the previous spinner racks.
Plymouth Whitemarsh High School	Plymouth Meeting, PA	school	http://www.colonialsd.org/pwhs/cwp/view.asp?a=810&Q=423475&pwhsNav=|8866|	n/a	1,560	27,000	8,227	Stylish, bookstore-like design.
Port Chester Public Library	Port Chester, NY	public	http://www.portchesterlibrary.org/	36,469	3,492	4,454	112	Received a $1,500 grant in May 2007 to revamp their small space. Good teen-adult collaboration.
Port Jefferson Free Library	Port Jefferson, NY	public	http://pjfl.suffolk.lib.ny.us/docs/YACAFE.HTML and http://www.myspace.com/pjya	13,515	1,584	3,447	620	Finished in August 2007, this is an excellent overall example located across the street from the main library.
Prince William Public Library System	Prince William, VA	public	http://www.pwcgov.org/library/teens/index.htm	421,664	n/a	n/a	n/a	Successful online teen summer reading program.
Public Library of Charlotte and Mecklenburg County, ImaginON	Charlotte, NC	public	http://www.libraryloft.org and http://eye4youalliance.youthtech.info	768789	n/a	10,549	4,000	Excellent online resources and technology services. Very active teen participation. PLCMC incorporates music, art, technology, and even a video production studio into regular library services. Eye4You Alliance Island started as a partnership with the Alliance Library System and PLCMC in Charlotte.
Queens Borough Public Library, Far Rockaway Library	Queens, NY	public	http://www.qbpl.org/index.aspx?page_id=45	222,9379 (Queens); 58,206 (Far Rockaway)	4,971	n/a	3,200	First: teen-only library in Queens. Includes 40 computers, 70 magazine titles, programming, and homework assistance. Designed by Kimberly Bolan and DLI.
Ramsey County Library, Maplewood Library	Maplewood, MN	public	http://www.ramsey.lib.mn.us/	n/a	n/a	n/a	n/a	New space opened in 2007.

Library	Location (City, State)	Type (public, school, other)	Website	Estimated Population Served by Library / Library System	Estimated Teen / Student Population Served	Estimated Teen Vols.	Estimated Teen Area (Sq. Ft.)	Notes
Ramsey County Library, Mounds View Library	Arden Hills, MN	public	http://www.ramsey.lib.mn.us/	20,000	2,380	5,139	180	Example of how teen services can be a priority without spending a lot of money.
Reuben Hoar Library	Littleton, MA	public	http://www.littletonma.org/content/53/115/1046/1058/default.aspx	8,851	750	2,922	459	Good collaboration of teens, staff, and the community. Good low-budget project.
Roaring Spring Community Library	Roaring Spring, PA	public	http://www.roaringspringlibrary.org/	6,242	955	1,422	289	Active teen advisory board.
Roberto Clemente Intermediate School #116	Bronx, NY	school	http://schools.nyc.gov/SchoolPortals/09/X166/default.htm	n/a	929	15,000	10,000	Serves grades 5–8. Features special areas for reading, playing games, and a staging area for poetry readings or presentations. Booths are available for students to plan and discuss projects, etc.
Rockhampton Regional Council (formerly Livingstone Shire Council)	Queensland, Australia	public	http://www.livingstone.qld.gov.au/library/ and http://paradigmlibrary.blogspot.com/2007/10/verbyl-youth-worker-blog.html	20,000	3,000	1,300	230 (70 sq. meters)	VerbYL combines library services with a teen hangout. This fairly small space includes a computer room, a plasma screen TV, and an extensive range of library resources including books, CDs, and magazines. Includes a number of comfy chairs, a game room for playing XBox, PlayStation, etc., as well as a "backyard" which is used as a spill-out area for activities (in good weather). See their blog for more details.
Rosemary Garfoot Public Library	Cross Plains, WI	public	http://www.scls.lib.wi.us/csp/	5,147	510	2,885	720	Deb Haeffner Building and Design Consultant. The first "green" library in their state, this is a sophisticated, teen-inspired space.
San Diego County Library	San Diego, CA	public	http://dbpcosdcsgt.co.san-diego.ca.us/screens/TEENS/index.html	1,049,868	81,729	78,537	n/a	Altruistic summer reading project.
San Jose Public Library, Almaden Library and Community Center	San Jose, CA	public	http://www.sjlibrary.org/gateways/teens/index.htm	974,000	77,406	139,868	n/a	2006 project. Joint-use facility co-managed by the library and the Department of Parks Recreation and Neighborhood Services. Field Paoli architects.
San Jose Public Library, Dr. Roberto Cruz–Alum Rock Branch	San Jose, CA	public	http://www.sjlibrary.org/gateways/teens/index.htm	974,000	77,406	139,868	1,064	Brand new branch opened in 2005. Colyer Freeman Group LLP Architects and Franco Associates Architects.

Library	Location (City, State)	Type (public, school, other)	Website	Estimated Population Served by Library / Library System	Estimated Teen / Student Population Served	Estimated Teen Vols.	Estimated Teen Area (Sq. Ft.)	Notes
San Jose Public Library, Hillview Branch	San Jose, CA	public	http://www.sjlibrary.org/gateways/teens/index.htm	974,000	77,406	139,868	967	2007 project. AEDIS Architecture and Planning.
San Jose Public Library, Rose Garden Branch	San Jose, CA	public	http://www.sjlibrary.org/gateways/teens/index.htm	974,000	77,406	139,868	503	2006 project. Banducci Associates Architects.
San Jose Public Library, Tully Community	San Jose, CA	public	http://www.sjlibrary.org/gateways/teens/index.htm	974,000	77,406	139,868	511	Brand new branch (2005). Anderson Brule Architects.
San Juan Island Library District	Friday Harbor, WA	public	http://www.sjlib.org/atl/technology.html	7,525	n/a	n/a	n/a	Internally loans laptops to teens.
Santa Monica Public Library	Santa Monica, CA	public	http://www.smplteens.org	87,800	6,410	5,300	1,116+	Teen-assisted space design and website. Moore, Ruble and Yudell (MRY) Architects and Planners.
Schaumburg Township Public District Library	Schaumburg, IL	public	http://www.stdl.org/teenpage.asp and http://www.stdl.org/teencenter.asp	129,839	11,000	1,900	750	Mocel site from first edition. Good ideas for service, programming, and teen participation.
Schuyler Public Library	Schuyler, NE	public	http://www.ci.schuyler.ne.us/library.asp	5,371	n/a	n/a	n/a	Small space, small budget.
Scottsdale Public Library	Scottsdale, AZ	public	http://library.ci.scottsdale.az.us/teens/teens.cfm and http://www.youtube.com/watch?v=dO75IxInH6o&feature=related	221,000	13,836	6,500	4,000	Knowasis: Thunderbirds Charities Teen Learning Center opened in February 2006. Created over a five-year" period with assistance from teens. Features include 16 flat-screen computers, homework help and group study rooms, college and career collections, 52" plasma TV, current music CD and listening stations, anime and manga collections, teen magazines, and snack vending and cafe area.
Seward Memorial Library	Seward, NE	public	http://www.sewardlibrary.org/teens/lah.html	6,900	500	1,350	300	Small library with progressive ideas.

Library	Location (City, State)	Type (public, school, other)	Website	Estimated Population Served by Library / Library System	Estimated Teen / Student Population Served	Estimated Teen Vols.	Estimated Teen Area (Sq. Ft.)	Notes
Sighthill Library	Edinburgh, Scotland	public	http://www.edinburgh.gov.uk/internet/leisure/libraries/your_nearest_library/CEC_sighthill_library	449,746	n/a	n/a	n/a	Winner of the Delegates Choice 2007 award. Undertook an in-depth consultation period, particularly with teenagers. This is very much a community-focused library in a very deprived area of the city.
Southeastern Massachusetts Library System	Lakeville, MA	public	http://www.myowncafe.org	n/a	n/a	n/a	n/a	One of Miranda Doyle's top six teen websites.
Southfield Public Library	Southfield, MI	public	http://www.sfldlib.org/pages/teens/teens.asp	78,000	6,883	8,320	1,140	Well-rounded space and services called Club Q&A.
Spartanburg County Public Library	Spartanburg, SC	public	http://www.infodepot.org/zTeen/SCPLteen.asp	264,230	n/a	n/a	n/a	Colorful space with restaurant-style booths, comfortable seating, and more.
Springfield Township High School Library	Erdenheim, PA	school	http://www.sdst.org/shs/library/	n/a	875	n/a	9,300	One of Miranda Doyle's top six teen websites.
Springfield-Green County Library, Republic Branch	Republic, MO	public	http://thelibrary.org/teens/	12,000	n/a	n/a	n/a	Opened in September 2007, this space had enormous community support. The space was made available through the Missouri State Library grant program, held in conjunction with workshops provided by Kim Bolan in 2006.
St. Charles Public Library	St. Charles, IL	public	http://www.st-charles.lib.il.us/teens/index.htm	47,855	n/a	n/a	n/a	Space for high school students where they can study together, work on group projects, relax and read, or just socialize with friends. Also have the Net.Gallery, a comfortable WiFi-enabled space.
St. Louis County Library	St. Louis, MO	public	http://www.slcl.org/teens/	870,000	90,000	36,620	n/a	Laptops at the Cliff Cave and Tesson Ferry locations can be used anywhere in the space.
St. Louis Public Library, Baden, Buder, Kingshighway, Schlafly, and Walnut Park Branches	St. Louis, MO	public	http://www.slpl.org and http://mytracs.slpl.org	353,837	52,637	17,784	180 (Baden); 400 (Buder); 200 (Kingshighway); 405 (Schlafly); 70 (Walnut Park)	Multibranch teen spaces funded by an LSTA grant. Also great ideas for marketing, promotion, and technology. They designed a wiki for teens by teens called MyTRACS.

Library	Location (City, State)	Type (public, school, other)	Website	Estimated Population Served by Library / Library System	Estimated Teen / Student Population Served	Estimated Teen Vols.	Estimated Teen Area (Sq. Ft.)	Notes
St. Thomas Public Library	St. Thomas, ON, Canada	public	http://www.st-thomas.library.on.ca/	36,100	n/a	n/a	n/a	Fun furniture and interesting shelving in this Teen Lounge.
State Library of Victoria	Melbourne, Australia	public	http://www.insideadog.com.au/about/index.html and http://www.slv.vic.gov.au/about/centreforyouthliterature/youthlit.html	n/a	n/a	n/a	n/a	Program ideas, including "Inside a Dog" blog for young adult literature.
Syosset Public Library	Syosset, NY	public	http://www.nassaulibrary.org/syosset/teenspace/	22,000	4,000	6,800	560	Separate room on the third floor of the library dedicated to teens. Relaxed rules and a welcoming atmosphere.
Taylor Community Library	Taylor, PA	public	http://www.lclshome.org/taylor/index.php	6,475	726	2,172	1,400	Opened in spring 2006. Active teen participation, relaxed rules, and developing programs. Use volunteers to staff space.
Teaneck High School	Teaneck, NJ	school	http://www.teaneckschools.org/index.php?id=26&id2=135	n/a	1,460	n/a	n/a	Interesting shelving and display.
Tekamah Carnegie Public Library	Tekamah, NE	public	http://www.tekamah.net/library.htm	1,892	n/a	n/a	143	Small library example. Dynamic planning, youth participation, and funding.
Thousand Oaks Library, Grant R. Brimhall Branch	Thousand Oaks, CA	public	http://www.toaks.org/library/	127,112	n/a	n/a	n/a	Translucent seating, windows everywhere, industrial-style interior.
Tinley Park Public Library	Tinley Park, IL	public	http://theloftonline.blogspot.com/	65,000	7,000	9,841	n/a	New construction opened in 2004.
Toronto Public Library	Toronto, ON, Canada	public	http://www.torontopubliclibrary.ca/	2,503,281	n/a	n/a	n/a	Successful youth advisory group and customer-friendly policies. Message: the library as a place for everyone.
Union County Public Library	Lake Butler, FL	public	http://www.newriver.lib.fl.us/UCPL_JRFofL.htm	15,000	2,000	2,000	500	Mocel site from first edition and model for Junior Friends of the Library group.
Vancouver Public Library	Vancouver, BC, Canada	public	http://www.vpl.ca/	584,601	n/a	n/a	n/a	Relaxed eating and drinking rules. Sleepovers offered for small groups of teens.
Washington District Library	Washington, IL	public	http://washington.lib.il.us/	18,500	n/a	n/a	1,008	New teen area opened in Fall 2007. Also using a grant to create a writing lab adjacent to their teen area.
Waukesha Public Library	Waukesha, WI	public	http://www.waukesha.lib.wi.us/tz/index.shtml	97,099	6,797	9,868	1,245	Completed in December 2005, this dynamic teen area presents an overall excellent model. Frye Gillan Molinaro architects.

Library	Location (City, State)	Type (public, school, other)	Website	Estimated Population Served by Library / Library System	Estimated Teen / Student Population Served	Estimated Teen Vols.	Estimated Teen Area (Sq. Ft.)	Notes
Waupaca Public Library	Waupaca, WI	public	http://www.waupacalibrary.org/teen/default.asp	20,000	900	3,000	1,000	Fantastic space. Teen involvement, technology, and progressive services. They also have a preteen space located outside the teen area.
Westerville Public Library	Westerville, OH	public	http://www.westervilleteens.org/	87,353	n/a	n/a	2,500	DesignGroup served as the architect of record, library planner, interior designer, and provided furniture, fixtures, equipment, and signage. Project date: 2006.
Whitman County Library	Colfax, WA	public	http://www.whitco.lib.wa.us/kara/kids%20and%20teens/teen%20zone.htm	15,960	n/a	2,731	300	Small library example with funky colors, bikes hanging on the walls, and comfortable furniture.
William H. Taft Educational Campus	Bronx, NY	school	http://www.insideschools.org/fs/school_profile.php?id=995	n/a	127	n/a	n/a	Transformed the library into a warm and inviting space for the students. Goal: to improve literacy rates.
William K. Sanford Town Library	Loudonville, NY	public	http://www.colonie.org/library/ys/index.htm	81,000	8,000	6,588	n/a	Teens involved in planning programs and raising money. Progressive polices and open-minded staff, plus great low-budget ideas.
Wilmington Memorial Library	Wilmington, MA	public	http://www.wilmlibrary.org/teens/index.html	22,556	2,300	5,037	450	Good teen input, youth-adult collaboration, and more.
Wolcott Civic Free Library	Wolcott, NY	public	http://www.wolcott.pls-net.org/	1,712	311	600	250	Small space example.

Index

All libraries included in the index also appear in appendix E. Page numbers in italic indicate templates or worksheets. Page numbers followed by *f* indicate figures or photographs.

You may also be interested in

Technology Made Simple: Implementing and maintaining effective technology services is a perennial challenge for libraries, and it can be overwhelming. Often without a technology expert, and with limited resources, you must address customers' growing appetite for electronic information amid constant technological changes. Not a techie? Not a problem. A librarian and technical expert join forces in this thorough and easy-to-understand primer. Expansive and practical, it offers detailed how-tos, nine reproducible forms, and inspiring stories from libraries that have demystified the technology implementation process.

Checklist of Library Building Design Considerations, 5th ed.: Planning construction of a new library facility or renovation of an existing one can be a daunting task. In this new fifth edition, veteran library administrator and construction consultant William Sannwald guides librarians and other members of a building design team through the stages of the design process. Updated materials include a new chapter on sustainable design, including issues of site selection, air quality, and energy and water efficiency; new sections on wireless networking, information commons, and media production and presentation labs; a new section on disaster planning; and much more!

Quick and Popular Reads for Teens: For more than ten years YALSA has produced two annual lists, Popular Paperbacks for Young Adults and Quick Picks for Reluctant Readers, consisting of recommended reading targeted at young adults who are not avid readers. *Quick and Popular Reads for Teens* compiles bibliographic information about the books honored by these two selected lists. Make choosing titles for teens fun, quick, and easy with this one of a kind resource!

Designing a School Library Media Center for the Future, 2nd ed.: Designing a school library media center may be a once-in-a-lifetime opportunity, so take advantage! In this hands-on guidebook, school library construction and media specialists Rolf Erikson and Carolyn Markuson share their experiences of working on more than 100 media center building projects around the country, using conceptual plans from actual school libraries. With thirty new illustrations and floor plans and an updated glossary of technical terms, readers will be knowledgeable and organized when discussing plans with contractors and vendors. Using the guidance here, you'll avoid the classic building and renovation hazards and build a library media center for the future!

For more information, please visit www.alastore.ala.org.